THE
ULTIMATE
BOOK OF
FAMOUS PEOPLE

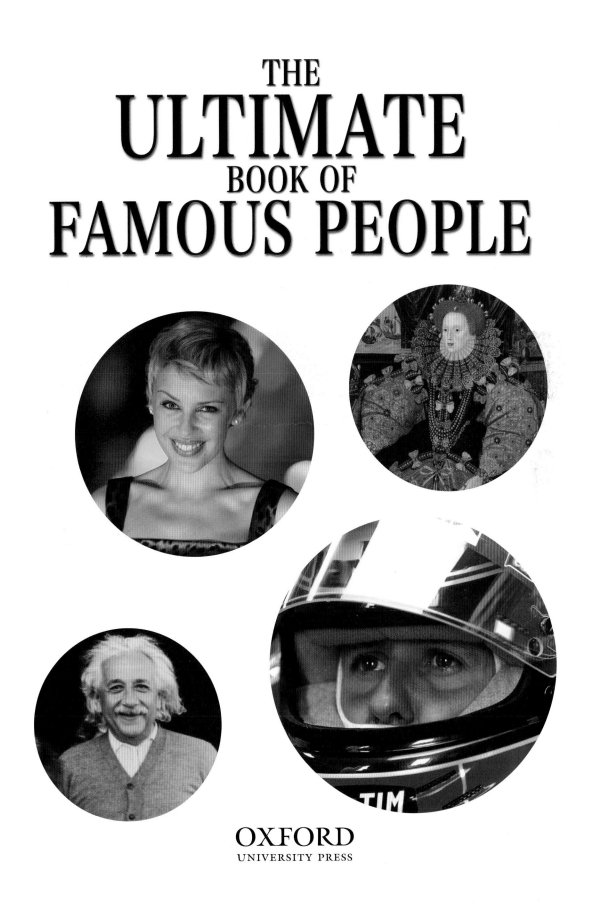

OXFORD
UNIVERSITY PRESS

THE
ULTIMATE
BOOK OF
FAMOUS PEOPLE

OXFORD
UNIVERSITY PRESS

OXFORD
UNIVERSITY PRESS

Great Clarendon Street, Oxford OX2 6DP

Oxford University Press is a department of the University of Oxford.
It furthers the University's objective of excellence in research, scholarship,
and education by publishing worldwide in

Oxford   New York

Auckland   Cape Town   Dar es Salaam   Hong Kong   Karachi
Kuala Lumpur   Madrid   Melbourne   Mexico City   Nairobi
New Delhi   Shanghai   Taipei   Toronto

With offices in

Argentina   Austria   Brazil   Chile   Czech Republic   France   Greece
Guatemala   Hungary   Italy   Japan   Poland   Portugal   Singapore
South Korea   Switzerland   Thailand   Turkey   Ukraine   Vietnam

Oxford is a registered trade mark of Oxford University Press
in the UK and in certain other countries

© Oxford University Press 2008

Database right Oxford University Press (maker)

British Library Cataloguing in Publication Data

Data available

ISBN: 978-0-19-913525-7

2 4 6 8 10 9 7 5 3

Printed in China.

Paper used in the production of this book is a natural,
recyclable product made from wood grown in sustainable forests.
The manufacturing process conforms to the environmental
regulations of the country of origin.

Contents

Introduction

This book is about the great and the good – and a few of the not-so-good: people from all over the world and from different eras, who have made their mark on history.

Who to put in and who to leave out

If you and a friend made separate lists of the ten most famous people who have ever lived, you would probably find that you only agreed on two or three names. Imagine the difficulty if your list were to include 800 people!

We assembled a team of nearly 50 consultants, all of them experts in areas as diverse as popular music and ancient history, sport and politics, and asked for their informed opinions on who should be included. We also consulted Oxford University Press offices around the world so that we could draw on their expertise to give the book an international perspective.

A particular challenge we faced was to compare the achievements of people doing different things or living at different times. For example, is the former US president Ronald Reagan more famous – or more important – than the athlete Carl Lewis? And does the fact that Carl Lewis could run the 100 metres faster than Jesse Owens make him a 'better' athlete – even though Owens was the winner of four gold medals at the Berlin Olympics of 1936?

There are no right or wrong answers to such questions, and that is why you will find a wide variety of people from all periods of history within these pages. Politicians, writers, and scientists are all included, as well as the stars of sport and film. Because the list is limited to around 800 entries, there are bound to be well-known men and women who do not appear; at the same time, there are plenty of people you may not have heard of. But that's part of the fun: in this book you can find out about Louis XIV the great king of France, and then learn all about the artist Picasso.

The 800 entries are arranged in themes so you can trace the history of a particular subject, such as scientists or rulers and leaders, all over the world. Each one starts with a short headpiece giving, at a glance, the person's name, a brief description of why they are famous, and their birth and (where appropriate) death dates. The abbreviation *c.* (short for *circa*, a Latin word meaning 'about') before a date means that it is only approximate. The main article then tells you more about the person's life: their inspirations, their achievements, their failures, or their good or evil deeds.

The entries are lavishly illustrated with hundreds of carefully selected pictures. These show not only what some of these famous people looked like but also some of their inventions, their paintings, their designs, and so on. Maps showing former empires and famous journeys have been specially created so you can trace an explorer's travels or see the extent of a ruler's empire.

At the end of some of the articles you will find a 'see also' link listing one or more names. This guides you to other people in the book who are linked in some way to the entry you are reading.

Fascinating stories and fantastic achievements – turn the pages and discover some of the people who have really made the world go round!

Index

After the main section of around 800 entries you will find the alphabetical index. This directory lists all the people in the book alphabetically so you can find someone easily if you are looking for a particular person. It also gives an instant record of their dates so you can see when someone lived and died.

Royalty

Constantine I ('the Great')

Roman emperor from 306 to 337
Born c.274   Died 337 aged about 63

By the time Flavius Valerius Constantinus, or Constantine, came to power in 306, the vast Roman Empire had been split into two parts: an eastern empire and a western empire. Constantine was proclaimed emperor of the west. For the next few years he fought many battles to defeat the emperor of the east and to win control over the whole empire. It was a long struggle but by 324 he had succeeded. He was then known throughout the huge empire as Constantine the Great.

   He set about building a new capital at Byzantium, completed in 330 and called Constantinopolis, 'City of Constantine'. Although he was not brought up as a Christian, Constantine did not persecute Christians as earlier emperors had done. In 313 he issued an edict (order) allowing Christianity to be a recognized religion in the empire for the first time.

Charlemagne

Holy Roman Emperor from 800 to 814
Born 742   Died 814 aged 72

As the eldest son of Pepin, king of the Franks, Charlemagne was born into a very powerful family. Charles, as he was then called, became king of the Franks in 771. He wanted to enlarge his kingdom and spread Christianity among the people whom he had conquered. During his long reign he organized military campaigns, and extended the kingdom into an empire that stretched across what is now northern Germany. His conquests earned him the name of Charlemagne ('Charles the Great') and he was crowned Holy Roman Emperor on Christmas Day in 800. He built magnificent palaces, which became centres of learning and art, and famous musicians and scholars were invited to spend time at them.

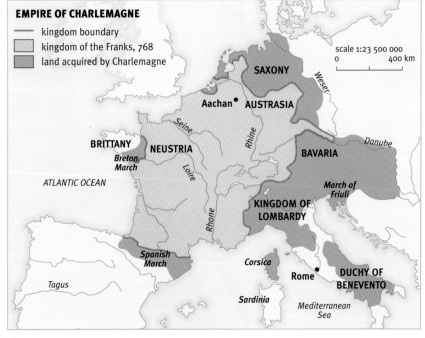

After Charlemagne's death, the great empire he had created fell apart.

Boudicca (d.61 CE)

The Iceni tribe was one of the few tribes in Roman Britain that were allowed to govern themselves. However, when the king of the Iceni died in 59 CE, the Romans decided to bring the area under full Roman rule. Boudicca gathered an army to fight the Romans. At first the rebellion went well, but then the Roman governor of Britain brought a great force and destroyed the rebel army. Boudicca poisoned herself to avoid capture.

Macbeth (c.1005–c.1057)

Macbeth was commander of the forces of Duncan I, king of Scotland. He seized the throne after he had killed Duncan in battle in 1040. Macbeth's reign was prosperous until he was defeated in 1054 by Duncan's son Malcolm III and Siward, Earl of Northumberland. However, Macbeth remained king until he was killed in 1057. Lulach, Macbeth's stepson, then reigned for a few months before Malcolm succeeded him.

King John (1167–1216)

John was king of England from 1199 to 1216. He went too far in attacking his enemies and his supporters began to lose faith in him. They let the French king invade Normandy. John tried to raise money in England to pay for the ensuing fight until finally his subjects refused to pay any more. In 1215 they made a great list of their rights called Magna Carta ('Great Charter'), and John had to agree to respect it.

Alfred

English king of Wessex from 871 to 899
Born 849   Died 899 aged 50

Alfred lived at a time when Britain was made up of many kingdoms. His kingdom of Wessex extended from present-day Devon to Hampshire. Like his brothers, Alfred was brought up to hunt and fight, but he was also interested in studying.

Danish invaders, who already occupied other parts of England, tried many times to take Wessex. Alfred led battles against them and even tried to pay them off. With a new army he finally beat them back and established a proper 'English' kingdom in southern England.

⬆ The man shown here is believed to be King Alfred.

Alfred, who became known as 'Alfred the Great', was as famous for his peacetime work as his wartime exploits. He founded the first English navy and a number of new towns called burhs. He issued a new code of laws and encouraged religious life by re-founding many of the monasteries that had been destroyed. He also encouraged the use of the Anglo-Saxon language, and during his reign the *Anglo-Saxon Chronicles* were begun.

Canute

King of England, Denmark, and Norway in the early 11th century
Born c.994   Died 1035 aged about 41

Canute was the son of Swein I, the king of Denmark. He came with his father on his invasion of England in 1013. Swein's Danish army had conquered the whole of England by the time he died, and Canute was declared king in February 1014. His reign in England nearly came to an early end, as the English king Ethelred (who had fled to Normandy when Swein invaded) returned. Canute went back to Denmark, but returned with an invasion force in 1015. By the end of the next year he really was the king of all England. He became king of Denmark in 1018 and king of Norway in 1030.

William I

King of England from 1066 to 1087
Born c.1027   Died 1087 aged about 60

William was born in Falaise, France. When he was about eight years old, his father died, leaving no other children. William grew up to be tough, determined, and a brave fighter. After a difficult struggle he gained control of Normandy. Meanwhile the king of England, Edward the Confessor, had promised the English crown to William, his cousin. But Harold of Wessex also wanted to be king.

When Edward died in 1066, Harold proclaimed himself king. William built a great invasion fleet and crossed the English Channel. The two armies met at the battle of Hastings, where Harold was killed. William went on to conquer the rest of England and became known as William the Conqueror. He gave land to his barons and erected royal castles. The barons also built castles and took control of lands, but they stayed loyal to William. In 1086 he organized a great survey that culminated in the *Domesday Book*.

⬆ The Bayeux Tapestry in France tells the story of the Norman Conquest of England.

Frederick I ('Barbarossa')

Holy Roman Emperor from 1155 to 1190
Born c.1123   Died 1190 aged about 67

Frederick was the son of the Duke of Swabia in south-west Germany, and nephew of Emperor Conrad III. When Conrad died in 1152, the German princes elected Frederick to be king. He was crowned emperor in Rome by Pope Adrian IV. The Italians called him 'Barbarossa', meaning 'red beard'.

Frederick made many attempts to increase his power in Italy but he was eventually forced to give in to Pope Alexander III – who did not approve of him – in 1177 after a long struggle. However, Frederick still managed to assert his power in Germany. Once this was assured he left the empire in the hands of his son, and went to fight in the Crusades in the Holy Land. He won two victories against the Muslims but was later drowned while crossing a river.

❷ This bronze and gold head of Frederick I dates from 1160.

Robert I

King of Scotland from 1306 to 1329
Born 1274   Died 1329 aged 54

Robert 'the Bruce' came from an aristocratic Scottish family. He was very ambitious, and grew up wanting to become king of Scotland. To gain the Scottish throne, Bruce stabbed his main rival in a quarrel, and a month later he was crowned Robert I.

At first things went badly for the new king. England was at war with Scotland, and wanted to have control over its neighbour. Many of Robert's family and supporters were captured and savagely treated by the English king, Edward I. Robert was forced to go into hiding and almost lost heart. There is a story that while he was sheltering in a cave, he saw a spider struggling again and again to climb up to her web and not giving up. The spider's example inspired him to keep on fighting against the English.

Finally, in 1314, he defeated Edward II's army in the fierce Battle of Bannockburn. He died of leprosy in 1329, a great hero.

Richard I

King of England from 1189 to 1199
Born 1157   Died 1199 aged 41

Richard was the third son of King Henry II and Eleanor of Aquitaine. In 1173 his mother persuaded him to rebel, with two of his brothers, against King Henry. The revolt failed, but 16 years later Richard forced his ageing father to make him heir to all the king's lands in England and France, leaving nothing for John, who was Richard's younger brother.

Once in power, Richard went on the Third Crusade to the Holy Land with the other kings and nobles of Europe. They failed to capture Jerusalem, but Richard defeated Saladin, the Muslim leader, at Arsuf. On the way back to England, Richard was taken prisoner by one of his enemies, the Duke of Austria. His government in England had to pay a huge ransom for his release.

Although he was king for ten years, Richard spent a total of only five months of his reign in England; the last five years of his reign were devoted to fighting the king of France. He died of blood poisoning, caused by an arrow in his shoulder, while besieging a town in the French kingdom of Aquitaine.

⨠ See also Saladin p. 60

Edward III

King of England from 1327 to 1377
Born 1312   Died 1377 aged 64

When Edward was 14, his mother and her lover Roger Mortimer murdered his father, Edward II, and crowned Edward. Three years later, Edward had Mortimer killed.

In 1339 Edward invaded France, starting a war that continued for 100 years. Under Edward and his son, nicknamed the 'Black Prince', the English won many battles. The greatest was at Crécy in 1346.

By 1370, most of the fighting companions of Edward's youth were dead, as was his wife. And in France, a strong king was taking back the lands that Edward had won. Edward lost his reputation as a knight, and died a broken man.

⬆ Part of a French manuscript showing a scene from the Battle of Crécy, won by Edward III.

Llywelyn the Great (c.1172–1240)

Llywelyn was heir to the kingdom of Gwynedd (Snowdonia) in north Wales, but he spent his childhood in exile. By 1200 he had become master of most of northern Wales and Llywelyn forced Welsh rulers to recognize his leadership. In 1218, two years after King John's death, the English acknowledged Llywelyn. He spent a lifetime encouraging the Welsh to think of themselves as a united people.

Kublai Khan (1215–1294)

Kublai Khan was a grandson of Genghis Khan. When he grew up and became leader of the Mongols he completed his grandfather's conquest of China and established his capital at Khanbalik (now Beijing). His rule was harsh and he enforced obedience. He appointed many foreigners, including the Venetian explorer Marco Polo, to work for him. It is through Polo's praise that Kublai Khan became known in Europe.

Tamerlane

Central Asian conqueror
Born c.1336   Died 1405 aged about 69

Timur, later known as 'Tamerlane' or 'Tamburlaine' in the West, was the great-grandson of a minister of Genghis Khan. His ambition was to rebuild the Asian empire of that great conqueror.

When he was about 20, Timur began to claim power over the other tribes in the area around Samarkand (now in Uzbekistan). By 1369, he had brutally defeated all his rivals. He then moved further afield. For the next 35 years he raided and conquered the regions from the Black Sea to the Indus. In 1404 he staged an immense celebration of his victories, displaying his captured treasures. His next great expedition was to be against China. He set out in 1405, but died on the way of a fever. He was buried in Samarkand.

Timur was lame in his right leg, and so the Persians called him 'Timur lenk', meaning 'Timur the lame', which became 'Tamerlane'.

» See also Genghis Khan p. 60

⬆ Tamerlane's burial place.

Henry V

King of England from 1413 to 1422
Born 1387   Died 1422 aged 35

Henry's father, Henry Bolingbroke, was at one time a trusted adviser to King Richard II. But when Richard banished Bolingbroke, the young Henry was left in the king's care. The next year (1399) Henry's father came back, seized the English throne from Richard, ruled as Henry IV, and declared young Henry to be heir to the kingdom of England.

Henry V became king on his father's death in 1413. King Charles VI of France did not take the new English king seriously, and Henry vowed to make him regret this. He made careful preparations for war and invaded France in 1415. Within two months Henry had destroyed the French army at Agincourt. Henry kept up the military pressure for the next five years, until the French king had to agree to let Henry marry his daughter, and so become heir to the French throne.

Henry was now the most powerful ruler in Europe, and he even started making plans to go on Crusade to the Holy Land. But seven years of fighting had exhausted him. During another long French siege he caught fever and died, leaving a nine-month-old baby as his successor.

Richard III

King of England from 1483 to 1485
Born 1452   Died 1485 aged 32

The son of the Duke of York, Richard lived in the shadow of his elder brother, who became King Edward IV in 1461, while Richard was created Duke of Gloucester. In the continuing feud for the English throne between the houses of York and Lancaster, Richard helped his brother defeat Lancastrian challenges. This struggle, which lasted for 30 years, became known as the Wars of the Roses because of the red rose badge worn by the Lancastrians and the white of the Yorkists.

When Edward died in 1483, Richard did away with the nobles who might become his enemies and imprisoned his brother's two sons, who were the rightful heirs to the throne, in the Tower of London (the two boys later disappeared), and had himself proclaimed king – all within three months.

Until this time Richard had been a popular and trusted man in England, but now he began to lose support. When England was invaded by Henry Tudor, a Lancastrian, Richard was deserted by many of his followers. He was killed on the battlefield at Bosworth and his crown was found on a thorn bush.

> *I shall despair. There is*
> *no creature loves me;*
> *And if I die, no soul*
> *will pity me.*
> FROM *RICHARD III*
> BY WILLIAM SHAKESPEARE

⬆ The Battle of Agincourt, at which Henry V defeated the French army.

Ferdinand and Isabella

Rulers of Castile and Aragon in Spain
Ferdinand Born 1452   Died 1516 aged 63
Isabella Born 1451   Died 1504 aged 53

When Ferdinand and Isabella were born, the Spanish peninsula contained five kingdoms. Three of them were small kingdoms: Portugal; Navarre (in the north-east); and Granada (in the south), which was inhabited by Muslims. The other two were Castile and Aragon. Isabella was the daughter of the king of Castile; Ferdinand was a son of the king of Aragon. In 1469 they married. As a result, they later became the joint rulers of the two kingdoms.

Ferdinand and Isabella wanted to make their kingdom the richest in the world, and they acquired new income by several means – for example by forcing nobles to return land that had once belonged to previous rulers. They also demolished the castles of any nobles who opposed their rule. In 1492 they conquered Granada and expelled the Muslims. In 1503 they conquered the kingdom of Naples in Italy, and in 1512 Ferdinand conquered Navarre.

Ferdinand and Isabella made Spain an important part of Europe. They supported the explorer Christopher Columbus, who discovered America for Spain. However, their reign also marked the start of the Spanish Inquisition, directed by Tomás da Torquemada.

See also Christopher Columbus p. 89, Tomás da Torquemada p. 235

Montezuma II

Emperor of the Aztecs for 18 years
Born c.1480   Died 1520 aged about 40

The Aztecs controlled most of Mexico and parts of Central America for over 100 years before they were conquered by the Spanish. Aztec emperors usually ruled with the help of a group of nobles to advise them.

Montezuma II became emperor in 1502. He was greatly feared. He gave great power to his own family and the nobility. During his reign, his army conquered many cities, and he brought lands ruled by the Aztecs firmly under his control. Then, in 1519 the Spanish, led by Hernán Cortés, entered the Aztec capital of Tenochtitlán. Montezuma was killed during one of the battles.

See also Hernán Cortés p. 83

This mask represents one of the most important Aztec gods, Tezcatlipoca.

Henry VIII

King of England and Wales from 1509 to 1547
Born 1491   Died 1547 aged 55

When Henry VIII came to the throne in 1509 he was tall, handsome, and good at hunting and jousting. He was religious, well-educated, and musical. He was devoted to his new wife Catherine of Aragon, and he soon found an energetic and loyal minister in Thomas Wolsey.

But Henry grew tired of Catherine, who had given him a daughter, Mary, but no son. He wanted to marry a woman of the court, Anne Boleyn. Wolsey failed to persuade the pope to give the king a divorce, and so he was dismissed from the post of minister.

Henry found a more ruthless solution – he broke with the Catholic Church. He married Anne Boleyn and became Supreme Head of the English Church.

In his old age Henry was a terrifying figure. He was so overweight that a machine had to haul him upstairs, but to many of his people he was a great king.

Henry VIII married six times and his wives suffered various fates. They were Catherine of Aragon (divorced), Anne Boleyn (beheaded), Jane Seymour (died), Anne of Cleves (divorced), Catherine Howard (beheaded), and Catherine Parr (survived). His three children were Mary I, Elizabeth I, and Edward VI.

See also Elizabeth I p. 16

Suleiman I

Muslim ruler of the Ottoman empire
from 1520 to 1566
Born c.1494   Died 1566 aged about 71

Suleiman was the only son of
Sultan Selim I. Under Suleiman's
rule, the Ottoman empire
prospered and expanded to its
greatest extent. His first military
success came when he conquered
Belgrade in 1521. The following
year he conquered the island of
Rhodes, and then in 1526 he
defeated the Hungarian armies
in a battle at Mohács.

Suleiman gathered around him
many statesmen, lawyers, architects,
and poets. The Ottomans gave
Suleiman the name Kanuni, which
means 'Lawgiver'. In Europe,
though, his opponents called
him 'Suleiman the Magnificent'.

In his later life, Suleiman's
reign was troubled by arguments
between his three sons. Suleiman
was still involved in military
matters when he died in Hungary.

⬇ This map shows Suleiman's empire at its
greatest extent.

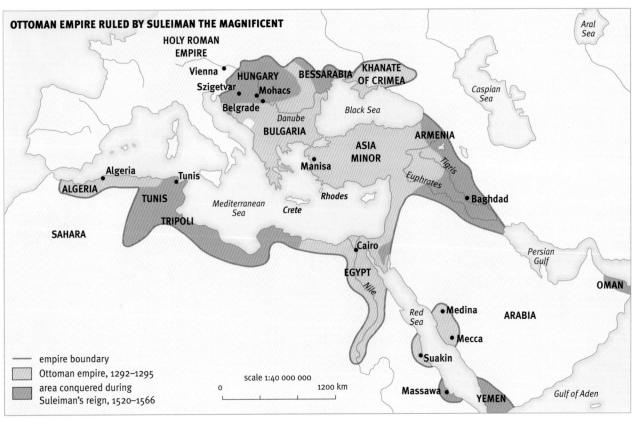

OTTOMAN EMPIRE RULED BY SULEIMAN THE MAGNIFICENT

Aral Sea
HOLY ROMAN
EMPIRE
Vienna
HUNGARY   BESSARABIA   KHANATE
Szigetvar   OF CRIMEA
Mohacs
Belgrade   Caspian
Danube   Sea
BULGARIA
Black Sea
ASIA   ARMENIA
MINOR
Manisa   Tigris
Algeria   Euphrates
Tunis   Rhodes
ALGERIA   Mediterranean Crete   Baghdad
TUNIS   Sea
TRIPOLI
SAHARA
Persian
Gulf
Cairo
OMAN
EGYPT
Nile
Medina
Red   ARABIA
Sea
Mecca
empire boundary   Suakin
Ottoman empire, 1292–1295   scale 1:40 000 000
area conquered during   0   1200 km   Massawa
Suleiman's reign, 1520–1566   YEMEN   Gulf of Aden

Charles V

Habsburg emperor who ruled over
vast territories
Born 1500   Died 1558 aged 58

Charles V, a devout Catholic,
ruled over the largest collection of
European lands since the time of
Charlemagne. He inherited the
throne of Spain in 1516, and three
years later became ruler of Austria
and the Netherlands, and was
elected Holy Roman Emperor. His
Spanish subjects also conquered a
vast new empire for him in Central
and South America. His advisers
wanted him to be 'God's standard-
bearer', uniting all the Christian
nations under his rule.

Although Charles worked hard,
he was not an inspiring leader of
men; he always seemed to need
more time, or money, to deal with
the problems in his many scattered
territories. By 1555 his long wars
with France had led to no definite
result, and he had failed to stop
the Protestant ideas of Martin
Luther from spreading in
Germany, although he did
manage to blunt the continued
Ottoman attack on Christian
Europe. He retired in 1556.

Philip II

King of Spain from 1556 to 1598
Born 1527   Died 1598 aged 71

Philip II of Spain was the richest and mightiest ruler in Christian Europe. His empire included parts of Italy, the Netherlands, and vast stretches of South and Central America, as well as Spain and Portugal. As his reign went on he spent more and more time in his monastery-cum-palace, the Escorial, near Madrid.

Philip was a devout Roman Catholic at a time when religious wars were ravaging Europe. He involved his peoples in many of these wars, but he rarely let his religious aims get in the way of more worldly ones. For example, when he sent the Spanish Armada to attack England in 1588, it was for military and not religious reasons. His reign was part of the so-called 'Golden Age' of Spain. However, Philip spent so much money on his wars that the era of power and prosperity was almost over by the time he died. Philip's second wife was Mary I of England.

⟫ See also Elizabeth I p. 16

Ivan the Terrible

Tsar of Russia from 1547 to 1584
Born 1530   Died 1584 aged 53

Ivan became Grand Prince of Moscow when he was only three years old. At 16 he had himself crowned 'tsar and grand prince of all Russia'. His rule marked a turning point for Russia in foreign affairs. In 1552 he defeated the Mongol-Tartars at Kazan, ending their 300 years of domination. The eastern road across Siberia to the Pacific was now open. Russia also tried to expand its borders towards the Baltic Sea, but, even after 20 years of war, Ivan failed to keep the land he had gained.

Ivan lived up to his name 'the Terrible': in an orgy of terror in 1581 he killed not only his enemies but also his friends, and even his own son. After his son's death he became quite insane and his mad howls could be heard ringing through the Kremlin. He died in a sudden fit in 1584.

⬆ By the age of 16, Ivan the Terrible was ruler of Russia.

William the Silent

Founder of the Republic of Holland
Born 1533   Died 1584 aged 51

William was born in the region now known as the Netherlands. He owned an immense amount of land and held the title of Prince of Orange. The Spanish king, Philip II, who ruled the Netherlands at the time, appointed William to be the governor of the regions of Holland, Zeeland, and Utrecht in 1555. But from about 1561 William, along with a number of other great lords, began to openly oppose Spanish rule in their country. Although the opposition was first about foreign control, it soon became a question of religion. The Spanish were devout Catholics but in the Netherlands the Protestant Christian religion, which had started in Germany earlier that century, was dominant. By 1566 there was open rebellion against Spanish rule.

Eventually William became the leader of the national group fighting against the Spaniards, and trying to unite the country under one independent banner. Although this did not last, William continued his fight against the Spaniards, who were so frustrated by his determination that they offered a reward for his assassination. In 1584 William was shot by a fanatical Catholic who is believed to have been a Spanish agent.

William was known as 'the Silent' because he could be relied upon to keep secrets.

⟫ See also Philip II p. 15

Elizabeth I

Queen of England from 1558 to 1603
Born 1533   Died 1603 aged 69

There was not much rejoicing when Elizabeth was born. Her father, Henry VIII, had wanted a son. When she was two, her mother, Anne Boleyn, was executed. Later, she was in great danger during her Catholic sister Mary's reign because she was a Protestant. The 25-year-old woman who became queen was cautious, clever and quick-witted.

Elizabeth could be very stubborn. She refused to change the Church of England set-up in 1559, though at first neither Catholics nor Protestants were satisfied. She also often put off difficult decisions. Although Mary, Queen of Scots was a great danger to her, she took

17 years to agree to her execution. Even then Elizabeth pretended she had been tricked into agreeing to it. She avoided war with Philip II of Spain for as long as possible. However, when the Spanish Armada set out to invade England, she was an inspiring war leader.

Queen Elizabeth I cleverly controlled her powerful courtiers by being charming, witty, or angry. Everyone expected her to marry, and she promised Parliament she would marry as soon as it was convenient – but it never seemed to be convenient.

> " *I have already joined myself in marriage to a husband, namely the kingdom of England.*
> ELIZABETH I TO PARLIAMENT "

⬆ Elizabeth I was known as 'Good Queen Bess', and was a popular queen.

Mary, Queen of Scots

Queen of Scotland from 1542 to 1567
Born 1542   Died 1587 aged 44

Mary was the daughter of King James V of Scotland. He died just a week after she was born, so Mary became queen of Scotland when she was only a few days old. Her French mother ruled the country, with a group of Scottish advisors, while Mary was a child.

Mary was born at a time of conflict between Scotland and England, and was brought up in the French court for safety. There she married the son of the French king. Her young husband died soon after they were married.

In 1558 the English throne passed to Elizabeth I, a Protestant, but many Catholics viewed Elizabeth as illegitimate and thought Mary had a better claim to the throne. She returned to Scotland in 1561, but her ambitions lay in England.

At first Mary managed to remain a Catholic queen without offending the powerful Scottish Protestants. However, she was accused of being involved in several scandals, including a plot to murder her second husband, the Earl of Darnley, and in 1567 she was forced to abdicate (give up the throne). She sought safety in England, but Elizabeth feared her and kept her in captivity for 19 years. Eventually Mary was found guilty of involvement in a Catholic plot to kill Elizabeth, and she was beheaded in 1587.

» See also Elizabeth I p. 16

Akbar

Emperor of the Mughal empire in India
Born 1542   Died 1605 aged 63

Akbar ruled the Mughal empire in northern India at the same time as Elizabeth I was queen of England. By the end of his reign, his lands covered an area as big as Europe.

Akbar was only 14 when he became emperor, and he had to fight hard to build up his power. Sometimes he was ruthless. When he destroyed a rebel fort at Chitor, he built his enemies' heads into the walls of a tower. But Akbar preferred peace, and won most of his lands through treaties and marriages. The Mughal emperors were Muslims, but the majority of Akbar's subjects were Hindus. To show that he respected their beliefs, he married a Hindu princess.

Akbar loved hunting with cheetahs, riding fierce camels and war elephants, and playing polo. He enjoyed painting, and also made tapestries and carpets. He had splendid palaces and he built the magnificent city of Fatehpur Sikri near Agra. It is still there today, almost unchanged.

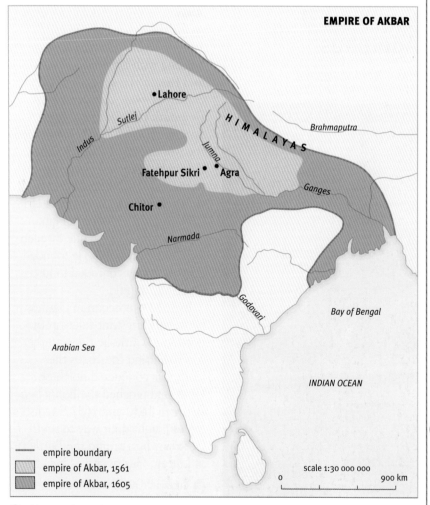

EMPIRE OF AKBAR

Lahore
Sutlej
Indus
H I M A L A Y A S
Brahmaputra
Jumna
Fatehpur Sikri • Agra
Ganges
Chitor •
Narmada
Godavari
Bay of Bengal
Arabian Sea
INDIAN OCEAN

— empire boundary
empire of Akbar, 1561
empire of Akbar, 1605

scale 1:30 000 000
0   900 km

🔼 This map shows the extent of Akbar's Mughal empire in northern India.

Tokugawa Ieyasu

Japanese ruler
Born 1542   Died 1616 aged 74

Tokugawa Ieyasu was born during a time when there were endless civil wars in Japan. Growing up surrounded by spies, he quickly learned to be tough and cunning. As a young warrior he supported the shogun (warlord) Oda Nobunaga, who fought successfully to bring large areas of Japan under his control.

After Nobunaga's assassination Ieyasu married the sister of Hideyoshi, a very powerful lord who controlled a lot of land. Ieyasu promised that if Hideyoshi died he would help his baby son, Hideyori, inherit all Hideyoshi's lands. However, Ieyasu broke his word and when Hideyoshi died, Ieyasu smashed Hideyori's supporters at the great Battle of Sekijahara in 1600. He then took over his opponents' lands and was appointed shogun in 1603. He abdicated two years later but still controlled affairs.

Ieyasu founded Edo (now Tokyo), which became Japan's biggest city. His family ruled for more than 250 years, bringing economic strength and improved educational standards to the country. After his death a fabulous shrine was built to honour him at Nikko.

> *Think of being uncomfortable as normal and you will never be bothered by it.*
> TOKUGAWA IEYASU

Henry IV

King of France from 1589 to 1610
Born 1553   Died 1610 aged 56

Henry of Navarre was born into a French noble family in the mid-sixteenth century. At this time the people of France were bitterly divided in matters of religion. In the Middle Ages all French people had been Catholic Christians, but from the 1530s, after the Reformation began in Europe, many had become Protestant Christians, or 'Huguenots'. From the 1560s Catholics and Huguenots fought each other.

Henry was brought up as a Huguenot and later fought in wars against the Catholics, who were led by the king of France, Henry III. In 1572 Henry married the king's sister in an effort to bring peace, but less than a week after the wedding thousands of Huguenots were killed in the St Bartholomew's Day Massacre.

In 1584, the king's brother died and Henry became heir to the throne. He was crowned in 1589. Catholics, however, would not accept Henry because he was a Huguenot. Another war broke out, but the Huguenots could not defeat the Catholics.

Wanting peace for France, Henry became a Catholic in 1593 and the fighting finally stopped in 1598. At the same time, Henry established political rights and some religious freedom for the Huguenots, and before long France began to prosper again. Henry died in 1610 when a Catholic fanatic stabbed him to death.

Shah Jahan

Indian Mogul leader
Born 1592   Died 1666 aged 74

In the sixteenth century, India was largely made up of independent states, each with its own ruler. One of the most important was the Mogul empire. Shah Jahan became ruler of this empire in 1627. During his reign, Mogul power extended and the capital at Delhi was rebuilt. In fact, Shah Jahan was always interested in architecture and many great buildings were erected during his time as emperor, the most famous being the Taj Mahal. This was built at Agra as a tomb for his favourite wife. Twenty thousand men worked on the Taj Mahal, producing a beautiful, white marble domed building.

Shah Jahan became ill in 1657, and this caused a war between his four sons. Eventually Aurangzeb, the third son, killed his rivals, imprisoned his father, and seized the throne. When Shah Jahan died he was buried at the Taj Mahal.

Gustavus II Adolphus

King of Sweden from 1611 to 1632
Born 1594   Died 1632 aged 37

When Gustavus Adolphus came to the throne at the age of 16, Sweden was in danger: it was fighting with Denmark, Poland, and Russia. To save his kingdom, Gustavus made a treaty with Denmark (1613) and stopped fighting Poland. But he continued the war against Russia, to stop Russia from taking Sweden's land to the east of the Baltic Sea. Russia finally made peace in 1617.

During the rest of his reign, Gustavus strove to make Sweden even more powerful. He founded schools and encouraged industry, especially mining.

In 1618 war began in Germany between Protestant rulers in the north and Catholic rulers in the south. During the 1620s the Catholics conquered northern lands and reached the Baltic Sea. Between 1630 and 1632 Swedish forces fought their way to south Germany but, during the Battle of Lützen, Gustavus was killed.

← Gustavus II Adolphus strove to make Sweden the most powerful nation in northern Europe.

Charles I

King of England and Scotland from
1625 to 1649
Born 1600   Died 1649 aged 48

Charles I was not born to be a king. He was backward and shy, and his brilliant elder brother, Henry, overshadowed him. But Henry died suddenly in 1612 and Charles became heir to the throne.

Charles was artistic, and his court was civilized and elegant. He was also very religious and wanted to make Church of England services more dignified and beautiful. However, Puritans and other critical people were afraid his strong-minded Catholic wife, Henrietta Maria, had too much influence and England would become Catholic again.

As king he ruled without Parliament from 1629 until 1640, and tried to force his Scottish subjects to accept English church services. When this led to a war he could not afford, he promised to share some of his power with Parliament. But many people in Parliament did not trust him and England slid into civil war.

Although he was defeated, Charles did not believe he should give up his power, and he broke promises to his enemies. He tried to start another war in alliance with the Scots, which eventually led to his trial and execution – he was the only English king to be publicly beheaded.

⬆ A painting depicting the execution of Charles I.

Atahualpa (c.1502–1533)

Atahualpa and his brother Huascar were the sons and heirs of the great Inca emperor Huayna-Capac. After the emperor's death in 1525, civil war broke out with the two brothers on opposite sides. Huascar was captured and killed, and Atahualpa became emperor. He had complete power over his people, but he was expected to be fair and generous, and to follow the ancient traditions of the Incas. Atahualpa was captured by a small Spanish army in 1532. Despite paying a ransom of gold and silver, he was executed the next year and the Spanish, led by Francisco Pizarro, conquered the Inca people.

James I (1566–1625)

James became king of Scotland when he was only a baby, and was brought up strictly by Scottish nobles. James was a highly intelligent man, but he was also lazy and extravagant. He was criticized for having favourites. When James became the first Stuart king of England he hoped for an easier life. But in 1605 a group of Catholics nearly blew him and Parliament up in the Gunpowder Plot. The Puritans were also dissatisfied, as he did not change the Church of England as they demanded. However, in his reign a fine new English translation of the Bible was made, now called the 'King James Bible'.

Charles II (1630–1685)

Charles II spent years in exile after his father Charles I was executed. When he regained his crown in 1660, he knew that he must rule with Parliament and support the Church of England. Although he was probably a Catholic, he kept quiet and went along with Parliament's laws, which punished people for not attending Church of England services. Charles's court was frivolous and worldly. He was easily bored by affairs of state and enjoyed the theatre and horse-racing. He had many mistresses, including the actress Nell Gwynn. However, he was also a patron of the arts and sciences.

Louis XIV

King of France from 1643 to 1715
Born 1638 Died 1715 aged 76

Louis XIV became king of France at the age of four on the death of his father. His mother, Anne of Austria, at first ruled for him, helped by her powerful chief adviser, Cardinal Mazarin. After Mazarin died, Louis was determined to rule alone. As he said himself, 'L'état, c'est moi' ('I am the State'). He became known as the Sun King because he chose the Sun as his royal badge.

Although he brought some improvements to France, there were darker sides to his reign. He fought expensive and unsuccessful wars, and made enemies of many other Europeans rulers at the time, who didn't like his greedy plans to expand his territories.

At home he was cruel to the Huguenots (French Protestants), telling them that they had to become Roman Catholics. Two hundred thousand of them refused to convert to the old religion, and left the country.

Louis had a magnificent palace built in Versailles and he enjoyed a lavish lifestyle at court. However, the life of luxury that he and his court enjoyed angered those who were struggling to survive. After ruling for 72 years, he died a lonely figure, no longer respected by his people.

William III

King of England, Scotland, and Ireland from 1689 to 1702
Born 1650 Died 1702 aged 51

William of Orange was born in the Netherlands, the son of Prince William II and Mary Henrietta, a daughter of Charles I of England. He was the Protestant ruler of the Dutch people. He was married to his cousin Mary, the eldest daughter of the Catholic king of England, James II.

William had one great aim: to stop the powerful Louis XIV of France from swallowing up more land in Europe. When, in 1688, William was invited by some leading English politicians to save England from the Catholic James II, he agreed, thinking that if he became the king of England he would be helped in his fight against the French. The plan met with virtually no resistance and in 1689 Parliament jointly offered him and Mary the crown of England, Scotland, and Ireland. This became known as the 'Glorious Revolution' because no blood was shed in the overthrow of the king.

Although he was a good diplomat, William was never a popular king, and the Catholic Irish people still supported James. William finally defeated James in Ireland at the Battle of the Boyne in 1690. Many Irish Protestants still call themselves 'Orangemen' because of William's victory.

William was devastated when Mary died in 1694, but he ruled the country on his own for the next eight years.

Peter the Great

Tsar of Russia from 1682 to 1725
Born 1672 Died 1725 aged 52

Peter came to the throne as joint tsar with his half-brother Ivan at the age of ten. After Ivan's death in 1696, Peter became sole ruler. He spent two years in western Europe studying various industries, and brought back to Russia teachers of all the arts and crafts that his country most needed.

Peter was also a soldier tsar. His greatest victory was against the Swedes at Poltava in 1709 during the 21-year 'Northern War'. His victories enabled him to build a new capital city for Russia, St Petersburg. Peter had a son, Alexei, by his first wife Eudoxia, but Alexei plotted against Peter and was put to death in 1718. Peter's second wife, Catherine, became empress when he died in 1725.

This shows Peter the Great as a ship's carpenter. Carpentry was a hobby at which he became skilled.

Frederick II ('the Great')

King of Prussia from 1740 to 1786
Born 1712   Died 1786 aged 74

Born in Berlin, Frederick II was son and heir to Frederick William I, the king of Prussia. Prussia's lands included territories around Berlin and further to the east. Frederick was an unhappy child. His father spent much of his time with the army. Frederick hated army life; he preferred books and music.

When Frederick became king he conquered Silesia, a rich territory ruled by Austria. Austria twice tried to take it back, but failed. In 1772 Prussia joined Russia and Austria in seizing parts of Poland. Frederick obtained the land between the two main parts of Prussia: Frederick had made Prussia a leading power in Europe.

> " My people and I have come to an agreement which satisfies us both. They are to say what they please, and I am to do what I please.
> FREDERICK II "

Maria Theresa

Empress of Austria-Hungary from 1740 to 1780
Born 1717   Died 1780 aged 63

Maria Theresa was the eldest daughter of Charles VI, who was the head of the Habsburg family that ruled Austria, Hungary, and other lands. Normally only a male could become ruler of the Habsburg lands, but Charles's only son died and he declared that Maria Theresa should inherit the family lands.

When her father died in 1740, foreign rulers would not accept Maria Theresa as ruler, and they tried to invade some of her territories. Frederick II of Prussia seized an area of her land called Silesia. Between 1757 and 1763 Maria Theresa's forces fought the Prussians, but they were unable to recapture their land.

Maria Theresa introduced many reforms to help the poorer people, and built up agriculture and industry, increasing the wealth of the empire.

A portrait of Empress Maria Theresa.

Louis XVI (1754–1793)

A weak man, Louis XVI often relied on the advice of his wife, Marie Antoinette. He was not much liked by either his nobles or the people. When the French Revolution started in 1789, Louis was kept under guard. He tried to escape in 1791 but was recognized and brought back. In 1792 Louis was found guilty of treason for having dealings with enemies of the Revolution, and in 1793 he was beheaded by guillotine.

Marie Antoinette (1755–1793)

Marie Antoinette was the 11th daughter of Francis I of Austria and Maria Theresa. In 1770 she married the future King Louis XVI of France. When the Revolution broke out, Marie Antoinette tried to persuade Louis to seek refuge with his army away from Paris, but he refused. In 1792 the monarchy was overthrown. Marie Antoinette was accused of betraying France to the Austrians and was guillotined in October 1793.

Charles X (1757–1836)

Charles of France enjoyed an extravagant lifestyle during his youth, and was not interested in affairs of state. He fled abroad during the Revolution, but when the monarchy was restored he came back and inherited the throne in 1824. His politics were not very well-liked though, as he introduced a lot of laws, like a class system, that the people had tried to overthrow during the Revolution. He was forced to abdicate in 1830.

Charles Edward Stuart

Last serious Stuart contender for the British throne
Born 1720   Died 1788 aged 67

Charles Edward Stuart is usually known as Bonnie Prince Charlie. His grandfather was King James II, who was expelled when the English people favoured the Protestant King William of Orange and his wife Queen Mary. But, like his grandfather, Charles was a Roman Catholic, and dreamed of going to Britain one day to claim the crown for himself. He believed he was the rightful heir to the British throne rather than the Hanoverian king, George II.

Having lived in exile in Italy, Charles landed on the west coast of Scotland in 1745. He took with him only 12 men – not much of a fighting force – but the Scottish Highlanders quickly rose to support the handsome prince. Four days later Charles found himself with more than 2000 supporters. Charles soundly beat an English army at Prestonpans, near Edinburgh. Charles and his army marched into England as far as Derby, but many of the Highlanders deserted on the march south so Charles retreated again to Scotland.

In 1746 his tattered army was beaten at Culloden Moor. For five months Charles was on the run, eventually escaping to France before finally settling in Italy. He turned to drink and did not do much with the rest of his life.

Catherine the Great

Ruler of Russia from 1762 to 1796
Born 1729   Died 1796 aged 67

Catherine came to Russia from Stettin, Prussia (now in Poland) at the age of 14. The following year she married Peter the Great's grandson, Peter III. After 17 years of marriage, Peter became tsar in 1762 but was quickly replaced by Catherine and put to death.

Catherine at once set about reforming Russia and turning it into a strong power. She took a great interest in education and also did a lot to improve the care of the sick. During her rule Russia expanded eastwards towards the Pacific Ocean, westwards to take over much of Poland, and southwards to the coast of the Crimea and the Black Sea.

While the landowning nobles lived well, most Russian people were serfs and badly treated. Catherine, who needed the support of the nobles, gave them even more powers over their serfs. This led to a serfs' revolt in 1773–1775, which was brutally put down. Later the French Revolution increased Catherine's fear of revolt, and she began to rule with a rod of iron.

🔍 An enamel and copper portrait of Catherine the Great.

George III

King of Great Britain from 1760 to 1820
Born 1738   Died 1820 aged 81

George was known as one of the most expert botanists in Europe. Unfortunately, when he succeeded his grandfather George II, he was not such a success as king. This was partly because he interfered rather awkwardly in the country's politics and lost many friends.

When the American colonies objected to the taxes the British made them pay, George was firmly against giving in to them. This led to the American Revolution in 1775, and George became even more unpopular when the British were driven out of America in 1781 after a long and bitter conflict.

George was a loving but jealous father. When his sons broke away from him he was so upset he suffered periods of mental illness. Doctors now suspect he was really suffering from porphyria, a disease that has symptoms of madness. From 1811, his son – later George IV – ruled as Prince Regent.

Napoleon I

Emperor of France from 1804 to 1814
and again in 1815
Born 1769   Died 1821 aged 51

Napoleon Bonaparte was only ten when he entered military school. After graduating, he was rapidly promoted and soon commanded an entire army and conquered northern Italy for France. Next he invaded Egypt in 1798, but his fleet was defeated by Nelson at the battle of the Nile. By this time, the French Revolution had been going on for ten years. However, the Directory, which was in charge, was in a mess so Napoleon returned to Paris because he believed France needed firm government. In November 1799, after a coup d'état (overthrow of a government), he became the new leader of France. Over the next five years, Napoleon worked hard and made many changes to improve ordinary people's lives. At the same time, his armies were successful abroad. In 1804 he became emperor, and by 1807 his was the largest empire in Europe since the days of Rome.

But then things began to go wrong. The Spanish, with British help, drove the French out of Spain. Then, in 1812, Napoleon made his worst mistake by invading Russia. The Russians steadily retreated,

drawing Napoleon's army deeper into Russia and further from its supplies. Napoleon reached Moscow, but still the Russians refused to make peace, and Napoleon realized that he had to retreat. His army was now caught by the bitter Russian winter, and his frozen, starving men died in their thousands.

By now many French people were disillusioned with Napoleon's rule. After his defeat at the Battle of Leipzig and the invasion of France in 1814, Napoleon was banished to the Mediterranean island of Elba.

In 1815 he escaped and landed in France. The soldiers who were sent to stop him welcomed him as emperor instead and he returned to Paris. But after his defeat at the Battle of Waterloo, Napoleon was again exiled, this time to the island of St Helena in the south Atlantic. He died six years later.

» See also **Horatio Nelson p. 62**

● *Napoleon Crossing the Alps*
by Jacques-Louis David.

Mongkut

King of Siam from 1851 to 1868
Born 1804   Died 1868 aged 64

As a young man Mongkut became a Buddhist monk. Meetings with American and French missionaries made him intensely interested in western languages and science. After becoming king in 1851 (when he became known as Rama IV) he encouraged trade between Siam (now Thailand) and western countries. Although he was unable to make many changes to Siam's traditional way of life, he ensured that his sons learned as much as possible about western culture so that they could begin to introduce great reforms.

Napoleon III

Emperor of France from 1852 to 1870
Born 1808   Died 1873 aged 64

After Napoleon Bonaparte was banished, the French king, Louis Philippe, returned. Louis Napoleon, Bonaparte's nephew, wanted to be ruler, though. In 1836 and 1840, he tried to start rebellions against the king. These failed and he was exiled to America. He later escaped from prison and went to England.

In 1848, Louis Philippe was expelled from France. Louis Napoleon was elected president, and then became Emperor Napoleon III in 1852. His style of rule was undemocratic but he brought improvements such as industrial development to France.

In 1870 France declared war on Prussia but was heavily defeated. Louis Napoleon was thrown out of France, and died three years later.

Queen Victoria

Queen of the United Kingdom from 1837 to 1901
Born 1819   Died 1901 aged 81

As a child, Victoria was lively and strong-willed. She could be moody, and had firm likes and dislikes, but she was sensible too. She was very interested in new inventions: she enjoyed travelling on some of the early railways, and photography fascinated her.

In spite of the fact that she was only 18 when she became queen, Victoria clearly had a thorough understanding of the British political system. Although the real ruling was done by Parliament, she succeeded in exerting some influence. At 21 she married her German cousin, Prince Albert. The queen was devoted to her 'dearest Albert', and they had nine children together. When Albert died suddenly of typhoid in 1861, Victoria refused to appear in public for some years. It was the prime minister Benjamin Disraeli, whose flattering ways she liked, who finally managed to coax her into public life again.

During Victoria's 63-year reign the British empire grew to a vast size. Her popularity now at its height, her Golden and Diamond Jubilees (marking 50 and 60 years on the throne) were causes for huge celebrations.

» See also Benjamin Disraeli p. 31

⬆ Queen Victoria was a strong figurehead for Britain's success as a global power.

Victor Emmanuel II

First king of Italy from 1861 to 1878
Born 1820   Died 1878 aged 58

Victor Emmanuel II became king of Sardinia-Piedmont, an Italian state, in 1849. He appointed Camillo Cavour as prime minister in 1852. Their vision of a united Italy, free from foreign rule, resulted in many battles. They enlisted the help of Giuseppe Garibaldi to help defeat the Austrians in northern Italy. In 1861 Victor Emmanuel became the first king of a united Italy. Only the Vatican, a small state ruled by the pope, stayed independent, and remains so to this day. In 1870 he made Rome his capital.

» See also **Giuseppe Garibaldi p. 64**

Cetshwayo

Last great Zulu king
Born c.1826   Died 1884 aged about 58

Cetshwayo fought as a warrior against white settlers at the age of 12 and in 1873 became king. At first the British in South Africa supported Cetshwayo, but in 1878 they invaded Zululand. The Zulus won an early victory but were defeated in 1879. Cetshwayo was captured and Zululand was divided amongst 13 chiefs. Cetshwayo visited London to plead his case and the British restored him as ruler of central Zululand in 1883. However, he was soon expelled by his subjects and was forced to flee the country.

Nicholas II

Tsar of Russia from 1894 to 1917
Born 1868   Died 1918 aged 50

The tragedy of Russia's last tsar was that he was a weak man who tried too hard to be a strong one. At first Nicholas II made all the big decisions about running the country himself, without a representative government. But this proved to be a disaster because he was ignorant of the country's real problems.

Russia's disastrous defeat by Japan in 1904–1905 was one of the main causes of the revolution that took place in Russia in 1905. Nicholas was forced to allow a Duma (parliament) to be elected. A period of relative prosperity followed and Nicholas won popular support for the war against Germany (1914). However, he then took personal command of the armies, leaving the government to the tsarina Alexandra and the priest Rasputin. (Rasputin was a rogue who seemed to have enormous influence over Alexandra after he had helped to treat the crown prince, who suffered from a rare blood disease.) Mismanagement of Russia's part in World War I and government chaos resulted in Nicholas giving up the throne in February 1917. He was imprisoned with his family until they were murdered in July 1918 near Ekaterinburg by the Communist revolutionaries.

» See also **Rasputin p. 235**

Tsar Nicholas II and his family, in a picture taken not long before they were murdered in 1918.

Haile Selassie

Emperor of Ethiopia from 1930 to 1974
Born 1892   Died 1975 aged 83

Haile Selassie became king of Ethiopia in 1928 and emperor in 1930. Before that he was known as Prince Ras Tafari.

In 1935 Italy invaded Ethiopia and Haile Selassie was forced to seek exile in Britain until the British helped him drive the Italians out in 1941. Once he was restored to the throne, he initiated a slow programme of economic and social reforms in an effort to modernize Ethiopia. However, he seemed to lose touch with the problems of the country, and his extravagant lifestyle made him unpopular. In 1974 he was overthrown by an army revolt and he died the following year.

Emperor Hirohito

Emperor of Japan from 1926 to 1989
Born 1901   Died 1989 aged 87

Hirohito was the eldest son of Crown Prince Yoshihito of Japan. Hirohito visited Europe in 1921, the first crown prince of Japan to travel abroad. When he returned, his father retired because of mental illness and Hirohito became prince regent, ruling in his place.

He became emperor on his father's death in 1926 and although his reign was foreseen as being one of *Showa* ('bright peace'), Japan soon became involved in war. First Japan invaded China and then joined World War II on the side of Germany and Italy. Hirohito did not want to go to war against powerful America, but he could not stop his military leaders from attacking Pearl Harbor, an American naval base in Hawaii. As soon as this attack took place, America declared war on Japan. Only at the end of the war did Hirohito overrule his generals. Speaking on the radio for the first time, he announced Japan's surrender in 1945.

After the war he stayed on as emperor, but real power was given to the people and their elected politicians. Japan became friendly with its old enemies in the West, but even after his death many could not forgive Hirohito for the things his armies had done during World War II.

🔽 Japanese emperor Hirohito salutes as he rides past his troops after inspecting them.

Elizabeth II

Queen of the United Kingdom and
Northern Ireland from 1952
Born 1926

Queen Elizabeth II is the 42nd ruler of England since William the Conqueror. Until she was ten years old she did not expect to be queen. It was only when her uncle, King Edward VIII, abdicated in 1936 that her father became King George VI and Elizabeth became heir to the throne. As a child she called herself 'Lilibet', a name that her family still uses today.

Just before the outbreak of war in 1939, Elizabeth met a young sailor at the Royal Naval College. He was Prince Philip of Greece and was a distant relation. They were married in Westminster Abbey when she was 21. They have four children: Charles, Anne, Andrew, and Edward.

When her father died suddenly in 1952, Elizabeth was already well-equipped to become queen. She had been taught much about the history of the United Kingdom and Commonwealth, and had travelled all over Britain.

As queen, she undertakes more than 400 public engagements a year and has visited nearly every Commonwealth country at least once. In 1967 she introduced the 'walkabout', so that she could meet more of the general public.

> " *I declare before you all that my whole life, whether it be long or short, shall be devoted to your service…*
> ELIZABETH II "

Sultan of Brunei

Head of the state of Brunei from 1967
Born 1946

Sultan Sir Muda Hassanal Bolkiah Mu'izuddin Waddaulah succeeded his father as Sultan (ruler) of Brunei in 1967. Brunei

⬆ The flag of Brunei.

had been under British control for nearly 80 years. It gained independence in 1984, and the Sultan became prime minister as well as ruler of the state. Brunei is an Islamic country, and the Sultan is regarded as the leader of its large Muslim community. Brunei is a country that has become wealthy because of its petroleum industry, and it is now an advanced nation. It has a high level of employment and well-developed systems of healthcare and education so its people are well looked after.

Diana, Princess of Wales

Born 1961   Died 1997 aged 36

In 1981 Diana married Charles, Prince of Wales, the heir to the British throne. They had two sons, William and Harry. Diana's beauty, elegance and kindness won her many fans, and she became a great supporter of charities and good causes. Diana and Charles separated in 1992 and later divorced. Diana withdrew from public life for a while, but later took up her charity work once more, notably campaigning to ban landmines. On 31 August 1997 Diana was tragically killed in a car crash in Paris, France, at the age of 36.

⬆ Princess Diana was able to talk easily and naturally with all kinds of people, especially small children.

Political Leaders

Niccolò Machiavelli

Italian political writer
Born 1469   Died 1527 aged 58

Niccolò Machiavelli was born near Florence in Italy. Little is known about his life until 1498, when he was appointed to an important post in the government of Florence. For most of the 15th century, Florence had been dominated by the Medici family. However, by 1494 the Medicis had been driven out. Machiavelli went to work for the new government. Between 1500 and 1508 he visited the courts of many foreign European rulers, including that of Cesare Borgia, a ruthless prince in central Italy.

In 1512 the Medici family fought back against being overthrown. They returned to Florence and expelled their enemies, including Machiavelli. He went home to the family farm, but he really wanted to return to work. He wrote several books about politics to try to please the Medici family and regain his position in government. In 1520 they gave him a minor post, but in 1527 they were again driven out of Florence. Machiavelli also lost his job and died soon afterwards.

> ❝ A wise ruler ought never to keep faith when doing so would be against his interests. ❞
> NICCOLÒ MACHIAVELLI

Armand Jean Richelieu

French cardinal and politician
Born 1585   Died 1642 aged 57

Armand Jean Richelieu became a bishop when he was only 22. He later came to the notice of Marie de Medici, then acting as regent for her son, Louis XIII. Through her influence Richelieu won a place at the French court and in 1622 was made a cardinal.

When he was 39 Richelieu became chief (prime) minister and together with Louis XIII, who was now king, he virtually ruled the country. One of his major aims was to restore the monarchy to its former absolute power. To do this he tried to curb the ambitious nobles. Richelieu's foreign policy was directed at restoring French influence and power in Europe, especially against Austria and Spain, which were controlled by the Habsburg dynasty.

By the time of his death in 1642, Richelieu had restored the power of the French monarchy, given order and unity to the country, and won for France a leading position in European affairs. However, his excessive taxation, his refusal to operate any form of democratic government, and his crushing of the power of the French nobility meant that he created many enemies for himself, and there were several attacks on his life.

⬆ Cardinal Richelieu was the most powerful man in France during the reign of Louis XIII.

Benjamin Franklin

American statesman and scientist
Born 1706   Died 1790 aged 84

Benjamin Franklin set up his own publishing business, and by the age of 23 was printing all the money for Pennsylvania. In 1757 he was appointed as representative of Pennsylvania in London. He spoke in Parliament against the British government's tax policies towards the American colonies. After helping Thomas Jefferson write the Declaration of Independence in 1776, he persuaded France to support the American colonists in the American Revolution.

🔾 This painting shows George Washington (standing left) during the American Revolution.

🔾 Benjamin Franklin proved that lightning was just a giant electrical spark.

George Washington

First president of the United States of America
Born 1732   Died 1799 aged 67

At 14 George Washington helped to survey some frontier land. A year later he had his own surveying business, and in 1752 he inherited his brother's land.

Britain and France were then rivals, both trying to control North America. Washington fought against the French for five years, and his exploits made him well known in Virginia.

After the war, Washington settled down to be a farmer. However, he gradually came to believe that the American colonists had to fight for freedom from Britain. In 1775 he was made commander-in-chief of the colonists' army in the American Revolution (War of Independence).

Washington's perseverance and grit kept the rebels going. They won the war and in 1789 he was unanimously chosen to be the first president of the United States. He accepted the job. He was re-elected in 1792, but he refused to serve a third term.

Thomas Wolsey (c.1474–1530)

Wolsey was made chancellor in 1515 by Henry VIII. He also became Archbishop of York, and later a cardinal. In 1529 the king wanted the pope to give him a divorce from Catherine of Aragon. Wolsey tried his best to get it, but the pope refused. Wolsey was sent away to York, but would not stop meddling in politics. Henry summoned him to London to accuse him of treason, but Wolsey died on the way.

Robert Walpole (1676–1745)

Robert Walpole was the first prime minister of Britain. He became a member of parliament in 1701. In 1721 he became first lord of the treasury and chancellor of the exchequer and so was the king's chief minister. His policy of avoiding foreign wars and so keeping taxes down helped him keep power; so did his tactic of giving well-paid jobs to his own supporters. His enemies accused him of corruption, and in 1742 he was forced to resign.

John Adams (1735–1826)

John Adams was elected to the House of Representatives and earned himself a reputation for being outspoken and decisive. He helped to write – and signed – the Declaration of Independence. Later he went to France to negotiate treaties to end the American Revolution. From 1789 to 1797, he was America's first vice-president, and became its second president in 1797. His son, John Quincy Adams, was America's sixth president.

Thomas Jefferson

President of the United States of America from 1801 to 1809; author of the American Declaration of Independence
Born 1743   Died 1826 aged 83

Thomas Jefferson was born in Virginia, a colony that was still ruled by Britain. He became a successful lawyer before going into politics and being elected to the local government. He joined in many debates on the colonies' independence from Britain and he was so respected that he virtually wrote the famous Declaration of Independence himself. This declaration resulted in the American Revolutionary War.

Jefferson was elected governor of Virginia (1779–1781), and eventually became president of the United States in 1801.

Perhaps his greatest achievement was the purchase of Louisiana from Napoleon I of France. The area was explored by Merriweather Lewis and William Clark. However, Jefferson was probably most proud of his last great achievement – the foundation of the University of Virginia in 1819.

⟫ See also Lewis and Clark p. 84

◖ Thomas Jefferson, third president of the United States.

Maximilien Robespierre

Famous leader in the French Revolution
Born 1758   Died 1794 aged 36

In 1789 Maximilien Robespierre was elected to represent his province in the Estates-General (parliament). Unlike many other deputies, Robespierre saw himself as representing the poor as well as the rich.

The French Revolution started in 1789 and Robespierre made a name for himself through the power of his speeches. He pressed for the ideas of liberty, equality, and fraternity (brotherhood) for all citizens.

By 1793 there was civil war in the west, an invasion in the north-east, and people were starving. Robespierre and his supporters decided to get rid of the Revolution's enemies.

➡ Robespierre is remembered for the thousands of people he sent to the guillotine.

This was the time of 'the Terror', when anyone might be accused of treason, tried, and executed. Robespierre thought this was necessary, but as thousands were killed, many saw it as brutal tyranny. By summer 1794, people were sick of the Terror. His revolutionary colleagues rose against him and he was executed.

Robert Peel

British prime minister from 1834 to 1835 and from 1841 to 1846; founder of the first police force
Born 1788   Died 1850 aged 62

Robert Peel was a brilliant scholar at Oxford University. Thanks to his father's money and influence, he became a member of parliament when he was only 21, supporting the Tory (Conservative) Party. He held a number of government posts in Britain and Ireland before becoming home secretary, where he was in charge of law and order. He started the London Metropolitan Police force, and policemen were called 'bobbies' and 'peelers' after him.

Peel was briefly prime minister from 1834 to 1835. Then, as leader of the Conservative Party, he became prime minister again in 1841, staying in power until 1846. To help poorer people he reduced the taxes on goods, especially food, and brought back income tax instead. His party split, though, when he repealed the Corn Laws (which had kept the price of bread high by putting taxes on imported grain), and he resigned as prime minister.

James Madison (1751–1836)

In 1787 Madison represented Virginia at a conference to plan the organization of the government of the new United States. He helped to draft the American constitution and was elected to the House of Representatives. There he planned the Bill of Rights, which made the constitution fairer in operation. Madison became president in 1809. He took the United States into the war of 1812 with Britain, which America won.

James Monroe (1758–1831)

Monroe fought in several battles during the American Revolution, in which he showed great courage. Between 1782 and 1816 he served as governor of Virginia and secretary of state. In 1816, he was elected president. He is best remembered for the 'Monroe Doctrine', which said that European countries should not interfere in American countries that were former colonies. This policy was followed for almost a century.

William Pitt (1759–1806)

William Pitt the Younger became a member of parliament in 1781 at the age of 22. In 1783 he became the youngest-ever prime minister. His government worked hard to ensure Britain's economic recovery after the American Revolutionary War. He raised taxes to pay off Britain's debts. He secured the Union of Great Britain and Ireland in 1800 but he died two years into his second term as prime minister.

Benjamin Disraeli

Prime minister of Great Britain in 1868, and again from 1874 to 1880
Born 1804   Died 1881 aged 76

Benjamin Disraeli was Jewish by birth, and did not go to a well-known school. It was difficult for someone with his background to get to the top in Victorian Britain. As a young man, he dressed in flashy clothes, and wore his black hair in long ringlets. He wrote some successful novels, including *Coningsby* (1844) and *Sybil* (1846). However, although he became a member of parliament in 1837 and was chancellor of the exchequer several times, he did not have a long spell as prime minister until he was nearly 70!

Disraeli believed that the Conservative Party should improve the lives of ordinary people, especially when so many had the vote. In 1867, when he was chancellor of the exchequer, he introduced an important Reform Act that gave the vote to working men living in towns and cities. Between 1874 to 1880, when he was prime minister, he encouraged better housing for working people, and cleaner conditions in towns.

Disraeli wanted to see the British empire grow stronger than ever. He was supported in this by Queen Victoria, whom he charmed and flattered. In 1875 Britain took control of the newly built Suez Canal. This canal formed the shortest route to India – which was an important part of the British empire.

⬇ Benjamin Disraeli was a favourite of Queen Victoria.

Andrew Jackson (1767–1845)

Andrew Jackson was a soldier in the American Revolution. Later he caused a scandal by marrying his landlady's daughter before her divorce was final. Even so, his new family helped him to become a politician, a judge, and a major-general. In 1812 America declared war on Britain and Jackson's actions in the war made him a hero. He was elected as the seventh president of America in 1828, and again in 1832. He was the first president to represent the pioneers of the West, moving all Native American Indians to the west of the Mississippi River – a policy that caused them great suffering.

Daniel O'Connell (1775–1847)

Daniel O'Connell was one of the main campaigners for rights that the Catholic Irish people had lost when their country was united with Britain in 1801. His first campaign was to change the law forbidding Catholics to hold positions of power. He set up a Catholic Association, which even the poorest peasants were invited to join. The British Parliament passed a law for Catholic freedom in 1829 and he became an MP. O'Connell is remembered because he always stood for political campaigns, not violence, to win what he thought was right.

Charles Parnell (1846–1891)

Charles Parnell was a Protestant landowner in Ireland but he sympathized with the Catholic farmers and believed that the Irish should have their own government. In 1880 he became leader of the Home Rule Party. He was also president of the Land League, which backed farmers who refused to pay rents for the land. By 1885 demand for Home Rule could not be ignored and prime minister William Gladstone decided to grant it, although it did not come for another 35 years. Parnell led more campaigns for Home Rule up to 1890 but then the Home Rule Party voted against him as their leader; he died the following year.

Abraham Lincoln

American president from 1861 to 1865
Born 1809   Died 1865 aged 56

As a child, Abraham Lincoln hardly ever went to school, but he loved reading. Books were scarce and expensive then so he read the Bible and Aesop's Fables over and over again.

Lincoln tried various jobs before becoming a lawyer, a politician, and eventually a candidate for the presidency of the United States. During his campaign to be elected president, one of his main concerns was the split between Americans who thought slavery was wrong and those who thought it was right. In a speech in 1858, he said 'I believe this government cannot endure permanently half slave and half free'. Two years later he was elected president.

After the start of the American Civil War (1861–1865), Lincoln was criticized at first because the North did not win quickly. Then, on 1 January 1863, he introduced the Emancipation Proclamation, freeing all US slaves. (Southerners, of course, did not free their slaves until they had lost the war.)

In 1863, Lincoln made a speech after the terrible Battle of Gettysburg, saying that the soldiers had died so that 'government of the people, by the people, for the people, shall not perish from the Earth'. Later, Americans realized that Lincoln had summed up the spirit of democracy.

Lincoln had plans for healing the wounds caused by the war, but he was shot dead by a fanatical supporter of the southern states.

》 See also Ulysses S. Grant p. 34, Robert E. Lee p. 64

The statue of Abraham Lincoln at the Lincoln Memorial in Washington, D.C.

William Gladstone

English prime minister four times
between 1868 and 1894
Born 1809   Died 1898 aged 88

William Ewart Gladstone was
clever and deeply religious. He was
also energetic, working a 16-hour
day even when he was an old man.

Gladstone was 23 when he first
became a member of parliament,
and was prime minister for the
last time aged 84. He began as
a Conservative but later created
the Liberal Party. He believed
that people should have the
chance to help themselves. In
1870, when he was prime minister,
school education was provided
for every child under ten. In
1884 ordinary men – but not
women – in the countryside got
the vote.

Unlike his great rival Benjamin
Disraeli, Gladstone did not have
an easy relationship with Queen
Victoria. She was never
comfortable in his presence and
disapproved of his policies, which
she considered to be revolutionary.

Gladstone wanted above all to
bring peace to Ireland. He fought
hard to give Home Rule (the right
to run their own affairs) to the
Irish. Many people in the British
Parliament and in Ulster opposed
him. In 1894 poor health forced
him to resign as prime minister,
and he died four years later.

See also Benjamin Disraeli p. 31

> *No man ever became
> great or good except through
> many and great mistakes.*
> WILLIAM GLADSTONE

Camillo Cavour

Italian politician
Born 1810   Died 1861 aged 51

When Camillo Cavour was born,
the French ruled Italy. After the
defeat of the French emperor,
Napoleon, Italy was divided
between Austria (in the north),
the pope, and smaller kingdoms
and areas that were ruled by
dukes in the south.

Cavour, who came from a noble
family in Turin, became an officer
in the army. In 1847 he entered
politics and in the following year
sat in the parliament in the
Piedmont kingdom.

Cavour wanted to see all of
Italy united and freed from foreign
rule. He became prime minister of
Piedmont in 1852. By the time of
his death in 1861 he had his wish
– Italy was free of foreign rule and
united under one king, Victor
Emmanuel II.

See also Victor Emmanuel II p. 25,
Giuseppe Garibaldi p. 64

John A. Macdonald

First prime minister of Canada, from
1867 to 1873 and from 1878 to 1891
Born 1815   Died 1891 aged 76

John Alexander Macdonald
emigrated with his family from
Scotland to Kingston, Upper
Canada (now Ontario) when
he was five years old. When
he was ten he was sent to a
boarding school. At the age
of 15 he began to work in a
law office and before he turned
21 he opened his own office and
became a successful lawyer.
Macdonald's personal life was
not always happy. His first son,
John Alexander, died when just
a baby. His first wife, Isabel,
spent most of her life sick in
bed. A daughter from his second
marriage was disabled.

Macdonald was first elected to
government in 1844. In 1865 he
and a former rival, George Brown,
began persuading others to unite
Britain's six North American
colonies to form a single country.
He chaired the London conference
of 1866 to create the Dominion of

↑ John A. Macdonald – the first prime
minister of Canada.

Canada and he was chosen to
be Canada's first prime minister.

During his years as prime
minister, Canada expanded
territorially with the new provinces
of Manitoba, British Columbia,
and Prince Edward Island, and
also experienced economic growth.
He encouraged the building of a
railway across the country and the
development of industry.

Otto von Bismarck

Prussian leader who helped create
a united Germany
Born 1815   Died 1898 aged 83

Otto von Bismarck came from
a noble family in Prussia, one of
many German-speaking states.
After serving in the army, he was
elected to the Prussian Parliament.
He dreamed of uniting Germany
under Prussian leadership.

In 1862 King Wilhelm of Prussia
made Bismarck prime minister.
Bismarck then started to pursue
an aggressive policy against
neighbouring countries. After
capturing Danish territory with
Austrian help, Prussian armies
fought and defeated Austria in the
Seven Weeks' War of 1866. More
success came in 1871 when Prussia
defeated France and expanded
Prussian borders.

These victories persuaded other
German states to join a German
Reich (empire) with King Wilhelm
as kaiser (emperor) and Bismarck
as chancellor. In 1879 Bismarck
made an alliance with the Austro-
Hungarian empire. However, his
career ended after Wilhelm died.
His successor, Wilhelm II, was
jealous of Bismarck's power and
dismissed him in 1890.

⊕ Bismarck's Prussian army bombards
Strasbourg during the Franco-Prussian War.

Ulysses S. Grant

Commander of the Union armies in the
American Civil War; American president
from 1869 to 1877
Born 1822   Died 1885 aged 63

After 11 years in the army Ulysses
Simpson Grant resigned and tried
farming. He failed, and so took a
job in his father's leather goods
business. When the American
Civil War broke out in 1861 he
volunteered for the Union army
of the northern states. Within four
months his expertise and skill as
a commander had earned him
promotion to brigadier-general.
A series of victories, including
Vicksburg and Gettysburg in 1863,
led President Abraham Lincoln to
appoint Grant commander-in-chief
of all the Union armies. Grant's
drive and ruthlessness forced the
Confederates of the southern
states to surrender in April 1865.

Three years later, in 1868,
Grant won the American
presidential election for the
Republicans with the slogan
'Let us have peace'. Even though
scandals and bribes rocked his
government, he managed to win
re-election in 1872.

Grant refused to run for a third
term and retired in 1877. He
invested his considerable savings
in a firm that went bankrupt in
1884, leaving him with heavy
debts. To make money he wrote
his memoirs. It was a race against
time, for he knew he was dying
of cancer. Almost as soon as he
finished the work he died, but the
book earned his family $450,000.

» See also Abraham Lincoln p. 32,
Robert E. Lee p. 64

Paul Kruger

President of the first South African Republic from 1883 to 1904
Born 1825   Died 1904 aged 78

Paul Kruger's parents were Boer farmers in southern Africa. The Boers were descendants of Dutch settlers who did not like British power in southern Africa. In 1835 Kruger's family, along with many other Boers, travelled north to form their own independent country. They settled in territory they called the Transvaal.

In 1877 Britain decided that it should rule the Transvaal. Kruger, by this time a respected politician, led the opposition to this and became a general in a rebel army against British troops. In 1883 the Transvaal regained its independence from Britain and Kruger was elected as its first president. He was re-elected three times.

However, more trouble was to come. When gold was first discovered, prospectors from all over the world rushed out to South Africa. The new settlers were not popular with the Boers, and Kruger did his best to exclude them from the Transvaal, banning them from full citizenship until they had been in the country for at least seven years. The British government objected to this, and the second Boer War followed. After the Boers were defeated, Kruger went to Europe and eventually died in Switzerland.

➤ A sketch of Paul Kruger from a 1900 edition of the magazine *Vanity Fair*.

Ito Hirobumi

Japanese statesman who served four times as prime minister
Born 1841   Died 1909 aged 68

Ito Hirobumi was the son of a peasant. He became an attendant in a samurai (warrior) family and at the age of 14 was adopted by the family. He later took part in the revolution that overthrew the rule of the Tokugawa shogun (warlord) in favour of the emperor. He spent the rest of his life working for the newly formed government, which wanted to reform the country and take on some western ideas. Ito helped to organize a new tax system and travelled abroad in order to study European constitutional models before writing the Japanese constitution, which set up a Diet (parliament). He served four times as prime minister, the first time in 1885 and the last in 1900.

In 1904–1905 Japan defeated Russia in a war over which country should control Korea. Ito was sent to govern Korea for the Japanese. He wanted to work with the Koreans but he was assassinated by a Korean nationalist.

⟫ See also Tokugawa Ieyasu p. 17

Ramsay MacDonald (1866–1937)

Ramsay MacDonald became the first Labour prime minister in 1924. He won a second term in 1929. In 1931 he recommended a cut in unemployment benefits to help solve a financial crisis, but his cabinet rejected this idea. MacDonald formed a coalition government with the support of Conservatives and Liberals. The Labour Party expelled him, but he remained in office until 1935.

Jan Smuts (1870–1950)

Jan Smuts worked as a lawyer and fought against the British in the Boer War. In 1910 the Union of South Africa was created, but it remained part of the British empire. During World War I, Smuts became a member of the War Cabinet in London. He was prime minister of South Africa in 1919–1924 and in 1939–1948. He was defeated by Daniel Malan, who put forward 'apartheid' policies in South Africa.

William Lyon Mackenzie King (1874–1950)

King became leader of the Canadian Liberal Party in 1919 and was elected prime minister in 1921. His government introduced Canada's first old-age pension. He returned to power in 1935 and led his nation through the war years. After the war he provided free training for returning soldiers and introduced family allowances and unemployment insurance.

Georges Clemenceau

French premier during World War I
Born 1841   Died 1929 aged 88

Clemenceau spent time in America as a young man because his republican ideals were not popular in France. On his return in 1870 he helped create the new French Republic and worked for many years as a journalist and politician, as deputy in the French Parliament from 1876 to 1893 and again from 1902 until 1920.

After serving as premier from 1906 to 1909, he returned to lead his country in 1917. After the war he helped to draw up the Treaty of Versailles with other Allied leaders. He stood for election as president in 1920, but he lost and retired.

Woodrow Wilson

President of the United States of America from 1913 to 1921
Born 1856   Died 1924 aged 67

Wilson was elected president of America in 1913. When World War I broke out in Europe in 1914, Wilson kept America out of it, but in 1917 German submarines began sinking American ships, so America declared war on Germany. Just before the end of the war, Wilson outlined 'Fourteen Points' for a peace settlement. He persuaded other countries to agree to most of these points, including the setting up of the League of Nations. Although America did not join the League, Wilson was awarded the 1920 Nobel Peace Prize for helping to found it.

Henri Philippe Pétain

French general and head of state from 1940 to 1944
Born 1856   Died 1951 aged 95

Henri Philippe Omer Pétain was a French soldier who became an army instructor before being made a general in 1914.

In World War I he became a national hero because he was responsible for organizing the halting of the German advance at the great battle of Verdun in 1916. In 1917 he was rewarded by being made French commander-in-chief.

Pétain served in a number of army posts before retiring from the military in 1931 to enter politics. He was made minister for war in 1934, and in this position he was responsible for the preparations leading up to World War II.

In 1940 he became prime minister of France. The country was having a difficult time stopping the Germans from invading, and Pétain signed a truce with Germany that surrendered three-fifths of France to German control. From 1940 to 1942 Pétain was head of a French government set up in the town of Vichy. This had no real power, and had even less when German forces completed their occupation.

At the end of World War II Pétain was arrested by the Allies and tried for treason because he had worked with the Germans. He was sentenced to death but this was altered to life imprisonment.

> " To write one's memoirs is to speak ill of everybody except oneself. "
> HENRI PHILIPPE PÉTAIN

J'AI ÉTÉ AVEC VOUS DANS LES JOURS GLORIEUX

JE RESTE AVEC VOUS DANS LES JOURS SOMBRES...

SERVIR

1918   1940

⬆ In this poster, Henri Pétain, the hero of World War I, tries to reassure the French people that, as prime minister, he will help them through the difficult times – namely World War II.

Theodore Roosevelt

President of the United States of America from 1901 to 1908
Born 1858 Died 1919 aged 60

Theodore Roosevelt was a weak child who suffered from asthma. He was always known as 'Teddy', and cartoonists likened him to a bear. Toy-makers began making stuffed animals that they called 'teddy bears'.

Roosevelt entered politics at the age of 23, but the death of his wife and his mother on the same day in 1884 shattered him, and he became a cattle-rancher in Dakota instead. In 1898 Roosevelt led a cavalry regiment, the Rough Riders, in Cuba during the Spanish-American War. Then he became vice-president of America in 1901. Six months later, when President McKinley was assassinated, Roosevelt became president.

As president, Roosevelt settled a damaging coal strike, and bought a strip of land to build the Panama Canal. Through his efforts, Panama became independent from Colombia.

After he was elected president in 1904, he helped to bring peace in a war between Russia and Japan and was awarded the Nobel Peace Prize in 1906.

When he retired, Roosevelt hunted big game in Africa and led an expedition to explore the River of Doubt in Brazil, now called the Roosevelt or Teodoro River.

>> See also Franklin D. Roosevelt p. 43

● Theodore Roosevelt is one of four US presidents whose faces are carved into Mount Rushmore in South Dakota, USA.

David Lloyd George

British prime minister from 1916 to 1922
Born 1863 Died 1945 aged 82

As a young Liberal member of parliament, David Lloyd George began to fight for a better life for poorer people. By 1908 he was appointed chancellor of the exchequer, and in 1911 he introduced new legislation making richer people pay more in taxes to help the sick and unemployed.

When World War I broke out in 1914, Britain at first did not do very well. Two years later the prime minister, Herbert Asquith, was pushed out and Lloyd George took his place. He set about winning the war, and struggled to make army generals change their old-fashioned ways. In 1918 victory came, and Lloyd George easily won the general election that followed. He began the task of helping to rebuild Europe, and helped set up the League of Nations to keep the peace. In 1922 he was forced to resign by his opponents, but he remained an important figure in British politics until the 1940s.

Clement Attlee (1883–1967)

While teaching at the London School of Economics, Attlee lived amongst poor people in the East End and was disturbed to see the problems they faced. In 1935 he became leader of the Labour Party. When he replaced Churchill as prime minister in 1945, he increased state benefits and pensions and, in 1948, created the National Health Service. Attlee's government also granted independence to Britain's Asian colonies.

Harry S. Truman (1884–1972)

Harry S. Truman became president in 1945, in World War II. Truman decided to drop atomic bombs on two cities in Japan, which killed almost a million people but ended the war. After that he turned to Europe and provided Marshall Aid to help rebuild countries ravaged by war. During his two terms of office, Truman helped to create the North Atlantic Treaty Organization (NATO) and led America into the Korean War in 1950.

Michael Collins (1890–1922)

Michael Collins took part in the failed Easter Rising of 1916 in Dublin, to try to win Irish independence. Later he became a Sinn Fein MP and led the IRA. When a truce was declared in 1921, Collins signed a treaty that made most of Ireland independent but which left Northern Ireland under British rule. In the civil war that followed Collins led the Irish government and its army, but was killed by his opponents in 1922.

Josip Tito (1892–1980)

In 1921 Josip Tito founded the Yugoslav Communist Party. The government declared it illegal, so in the 1920s and 1930s he was either in prison for his beliefs or working for Communist causes in other countries, which is where he first came to use the undercover name 'Tito'. He led a resistance force against the German occupation in World War II, and eventually drove them out. Tito became leader of a new Communist state in Yugoslavia in 1953. Although it was Communist, the government gave the people more freedom and let workers and farmers manage their own factories and farms. Tito was made president for life in 1974.

Hermann Goering (1893–1946)

Hermann Wilhelm Goering flew in World War I with the famous Richthofen squadron. He joined the Nazi movement in 1922, and became one of Adolf Hitler's close advisers. In 1928 he was elected to the German Reichstag (parliament) and became its president in 1932. He was made commander of the German air force in 1934 after Hitler had come to power, and began secretly to build up the Luftwaffe (air force). Goering fell out of favour when the Luftwaffe lost the Battle of Britain during World War II. He was sentenced to death for war crimes at the Nuremberg trials, but swallowed poison to avoid execution.

Jomo Kenyatta (c.1894–1978)

Kenyatta became president of the Kenya African Union in 1947. At this time many people of the Kikuyu tribe formed a secret group called 'Mau Mau', which tried to drive white farmers from Kikuyu lands. Although he denied it, Kenyatta was suspected by the British rulers of Kenya of leading Mau Mau. When Kenya became independent in 1963, Kenyatta became the first prime minister. In the following year he was made the first president of the Republic of Kenya, bringing some stability and prosperity to the country.

Mahatma Gandhi

Indian leader in the struggle for independence from British rule
Born 1869   Died 1948 aged 78

Mohandas Karamchand Gandhi was a shy, nervous boy, but when he was 18 he travelled alone to study in London. He returned to India in 1890 and struggled to make a living as a lawyer. In 1893 Gandhi accepted an offer to represent a firm of Indian merchants in a court case in South Africa. Soon after his arrival, he realized how many problems black people, Asians, and other non-whites faced, and he decided to stay on to help his fellow countrymen. During this time, Gandhi developed his strategy of non-violence. The idea was to oppose unjust laws by non-violent protest. He was sent to prison three times, but he showed no sign of anger or hatred.

When he first returned to India in 1915, Gandhi was not opposed to British rule. But after a massacre in 1919, when soldiers opened fire on a crowd of unarmed Indians, killing nearly 400

Gandhi pictured in 1931, just before meeting Prime Minister Ramsay MacDonald.

people and wounding over 1000, Gandhi changed his mind. Over the next 20 years, Gandhi led the Indian National Congress party in three major campaigns against British rule, but on each occasion he was arrested and sent to prison.

During these years Gandhi campaigned to improve the status of the untouchables, the lowest group in the Hindu social order. He also believed that people and nations should be self-sufficient. He set an example by devoting part of each day to spinning home-made cloth. In his eyes, industrialization, as in Europe and North America, usually led to exploitation, greed, and squalor.

Gandhi struggled in vain to overcome the growing gap between Hindus and Muslims, which led in 1947 to the creation of the separate Muslim state of Pakistan. When India and Pakistan became independent from Britain in 1947, there was an explosion of violence between the different communities. Gandhi appealed for peace. He was assassinated by a Hindu extremist in January 1948.

Although his real name was Mohandas Gandhi, he was known by millions of people as Mahatma, meaning 'Great Soul'.

Vladimir Lenin

Communist ruler of the new USSR
from 1917 to 1924
Born 1870   Died 1924 aged 53

When Lenin was 17, his elder brother was hanged for trying to kill the Russian tsar. This opened Lenin's eyes to the problems of his country: a weak tsar, a corrupt Church and nobility, and millions of poor and angry peasants and factory workers. Like many people, Lenin saw revolution and the Communist ideas of Karl Marx as the only solution, and he was sent first to prison and then into exile in Siberia for political activity.

In 1898 the Russian Social-Democratic Workers' Party was formed. Lenin helped to split the party in 1903, leading the Bolsheviks ('Majority') against the Mensheviks ('Minority').

From 1905 until 1917, Lenin lived in exile. He returned to Russia when the tsar was overthrown and a new government began to rule. Lenin wanted to put a Bolshevik government into power and this revolution led to him becoming the real ruler of Russia. In 1922 the old Russian empire became the Union of Soviet Socialist Republics (USSR). It lasted until 1991.

⟫ See also Karl Marx p. 80

Chaim Weizmann

Russian-born first president of Israel
Born 1874   Died 1952 aged 77

At school in Russia, Chaim Weizmann became interested in science. He was extremely able but laws against Jews made entry into university difficult, so he left Russia to finish his education. Manchester University offered him a job and he settled in England. During World War I he worked in a laboratory producing vital chemicals for explosives.

Weizmann believed passionately in Zion, an independent homeland for Jews in Palestine. Britain announced backing for the idea (the Balfour Declaration, issued in 1917) and Weizmann travelled the world seeking the support of other nations. He became leader of a political group known as the Zionists.

After World War II the British governed Palestine and some Jews began a campaign of terror against them. Weizmann condemned this action, and the Zionists dismissed him as their leader. In the end, however, Weizmann was needed to persuade the Americans to support a Jewish nation. In 1948 the nation was born and called Israel. Weizmann was elected its first president.

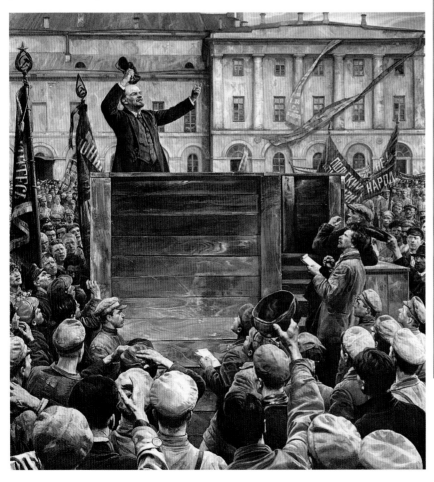

⦿ On the 100th anniversary of his birth, a third of the people in the world were living in countries run by Communist governments inspired by Lenin's first successful Communist revolution.

Winston Churchill

British statesman who led Britain during World War II
Born 1874   Died 1965 aged 90

Winston Churchill did not do well at school, but joined the army and had many adventures in Cuba, India, and the Sudan. In 1899 Churchill left the army and went to South Africa as a newspaper reporter during the Boer War.

In 1900 he was elected to Parliament as a Conservative, but in 1904 he fell out with his party and joined the Liberals. He held several government posts, including president of the board of trade (1908–1910), when he introduced labour exchanges (job centres), and the home secretary (1910–1911). Before and during World War I he was head of the Admiralty, and then resigned to command troops in France for a time. After serving again as a Liberal minister after the war he returned to the Conservative Party, and was chancellor of the exchequer from 1924 to 1929.

During the 1930s Churchill was not a government minister. He warned that there was a danger of another world war, but many people ignored him. When World War II came the prime minister, Neville Chamberlain, put Churchill in charge of the Admiralty again. When German armies were overrunning Europe in May 1940, King George VI asked him to be prime minister and lead a coalition government of all parties.

His courage and his speeches inspired the people to withstand air raids and military defeats, and carry on to victory. Churchill remained prime minister until the general election of 1945 brought Labour to power, just before the war ended. He was prime minister again from 1951 to 1955, and finally gave up politics in 1964.

🚫 Churchill poses for the camera after becoming prime minister.

Robert Menzies (1894–1978)

After working as a lawyer in Melbourne Menzies started a career in politics. Within a few years he was a member of the federal government and in 1939 became prime minister of Australia. He was forced to resign two years later, but returned in 1949. The United Australia Party had become the Liberal Party and Menzies remained its leader for 17 years. During his time in office Australia changed considerably.

Joseph Goebbels (1897–1945)

Paul Joseph Goebbels joined the newly formed Nazi Party in 1924. At first he edited the party newspaper and later was put in charge of Nazi propaganda. This enabled him to spread hatred against Jews and any other people who did not fit the Nazi idea of a perfect German. He remained at the centre of the Nazi government throughout World War II but eventually committed suicide, first killing his wife and six children.

Zhou Enlai (1898–1976)

Zhou Enlai helped to build up Chiang Kai-shek's Nationalist Party, until Chiang turned against the Communists in 1927. Zhou escaped and joined up with Mao Zedong. After the creation of the People's Republic of China in 1949, Zhou became its first prime minister. During Mao's Cultural Revolution he restrained extremists and helped restore order. He also played a major role in building good relations with America.

Muhammad Iqbal

Indian political leader and poet
Born 1877   Died 1938 aged 61

Muhammad Iqbal studied in Lahore, Cambridge, London, and Munich. He earned his living working as a university teacher and a lawyer, but his fame came through his poetry. He wrote about the past glory of Islam and the need for Muslims to try to revive it.

In his role as a political leader, Iqbal at first supported the struggle to free India from British rule. However, later he became convinced that Indian Muslims needed a separate country of their own, not just independence from Britain. In 1930 he spoke to the annual meeting of the Muslim League at Allahabad and called upon his fellow Muslims to set up such a state. He did not live to see his suggestion approved. The League finally decided to do this in 1940, two years after his death. The new country – Pakistan – came into being in 1947.

Iqbal had written his poetry in both Persian and in Urdu, and Urdu became the national language of Pakistan. Pakistanis consider Muhammad Iqbal to be the father of their country and they celebrate a special holiday – Iqbal Day – every year in his honour.

> " *If faith is lost, there is no security and there is no life for him who does not adhere to religion.*
> MUHAMMAD IQBAL "

Yoshida Shigeru

Japanese prime minister
Born 1878   Died 1967 aged 89

Yoshida Shigeru made his career as a statesman and politician. He served as Japan's ambassador to Scandinavia, Italy, and Britain. However, the military in Japan did not trust his international outlook and he did not serve during World War II. He was imprisoned in June 1945 for recommending that Japan should surrender, and then released three months later with the arrival of American Occupation troops. He served as foreign minister 1945–1946 and prime minister 1946–1947 and 1948–1954. Yoshida opposed Communism and favoured close links between Japan and America. Under his firm rule his country started on the road to recovery.

Leon Trotsky

One of the leaders of the Russian Revolution
Born 1879   Died 1940 aged 60

Lev Davidovich Bronstein was born of Jewish parents on a farm in the Ukraine, part of the Russian empire. He was expelled from university for political activities and was then banished to Siberia when he opposed the tsar's rule. He escaped from there and fled the country under his new name, Trotsky, which he took from one of his prison guards.

Trotsky returned to Russia in 1917 when the tsar had been overthrown. He joined Lenin's Bolshevik Party (later to become known as the Communist Party). He was one of the main organizers of the October Revolution, when the Bolsheviks seized power. He then took charge of foreign affairs and defence, and built a new army, the Red Army, which won the bitter Russian civil war of 1918–1921.

Trotsky was a brilliant linguist, writer, and speaker, but his bitter tongue made him many enemies in the Communist Party. After Lenin's death, he was deprived of power by Stalin. In 1927 he was expelled from the party and driven out of the USSR. He was murdered in Mexico on Stalin's orders.

>> See also **Vladimir Lenin p. 39**

 Leon Trotsky was one of the most important figures of the Russian Revolution.

Joseph Stalin

Dictator of the Soviet Union from the
1920s to 1953
Born 1879   Died 1953 aged 73

Joseph Vissarionovich
Dzhugashvili's parents wanted him
to be a priest, but he was expelled
from his Christian college for his
'disloyal ideas'. Later he joined the
Russian Social-Democratic
Workers' Party and became a full-
time revolutionary. He proved to
be tough, brave, and dedicated,
and was invited by Lenin to join
the Bolshevik Party leadership in
1912. It was then that he took the
name 'Stalin' ('man of steel').

In 1917, Stalin was a loyal
supporter of Lenin's seizure of
power during the Revolution,
and in 1922 he became
secretary of the Communist
Party (as the Bolsheviks were
now known). However, as
Lenin lay dying, he asked his
comrades to remove Stalin
from this important post
because 'he is too rude and
uncomradely'. But Lenin died
in 1924 before any action
could be taken.

In the years that followed,
Stalin helped to build a strong
nation through a series of
Five-Year Plans, intended to
industrialize and modernize
the Soviet Union. His greatest
achievement was to lead his
country, as 'Generalissimo', to
victory over the Nazis in World
War II. After this, Communist
influence spread through much of
Europe. But all this was done at
great human cost. Stalin arranged
for all his rivals to be killed until
he became dictator. Soviet people
lived in fear of arrest, torture, and
execution by the notorious secret
police (later called the KGB).
Millions of people were sent to
labour camps for opposing Stalin's
wishes, and in the countryside
millions more died of starvation
during the 1920s and 1930s.

It was only after his death
in 1953 that people felt free to
criticize Stalin. The leaders of
the Communist Party denounced
him in 1956, and in 1961 his body
was removed from its place of
honour in the Lenin Mausoleum
in Red Square.

◉ A cartoon depicting Stalin as
the captain of his country.

》 See also Vladimir Lenin p. 39

Kemal Atatürk

President of the new Republic of Turkey
from 1923 to 1938
Born 1881   Died 1938 aged 57

Mustafa Kemal was born in
Thessalonika, now part of Greece.
At military college in Istanbul,
then capital of the Ottoman
empire, he was so good at
mathematics that he was given
the name 'Kemal', which is Arabic
for 'perfection'.

As officer in the army, he
fought in World War I when
the Ottoman empire joined the
German side. As the war
ended in 1918, Kemal
joined a number of other
Turkish politicians
in calling for Turkey
to become an
independent nation
free of foreign control.

With his military skill,
the Turks defeated the
Greeks when Greece and
Turkey went to war in
1921. Shortly after that,
the Ottoman sultans were
deposed and in 1923 a
Turkish National
Assembly was elected with
Kemal as president of the
new republic. As president
he ruled as a virtual
dictator. His main policy
was the modernization
of Turkey. In 1934,
he introduced the idea
of surnames and took
the surname Atatürk ('father
of Turks').

◉ Kemal Atatürk shown dressed in
Turkish national costume.

Franklin D. Roosevelt

President of the United States of America four times, from 1933 to 1945
Born 1882   Died 1945 aged 63

Franklin Delano Roosevelt, a cousin of the former American president 'Teddy' Roosevelt, developed polio at the age of 40, and his legs were almost paralyzed.

In 1928 he was elected governor of New York State, and four years later became president of America. At this time, America was in the Depression and millions were unemployed. Roosevelt promised a 'New Deal', and launched a programme that enabled banks to reopen and created jobs. The success of this programme ensured his election as president again in 1936.

In 1940 Roosevelt was elected for a third term. He guided the country through the dark days of World War II and won a fourth election in 1944, but only six months later, and with war victory in sight, he suddenly died.

⬆ Roosevelt's New Deal programme of reform made him popular with working people.

Eamon De Valera

Irish statesman
Born 1882   Died 1975 aged 92

Eamon De Valera was born in America, but at the age of three he went to live in Ireland as his mother was Irish. He later joined the Volunteers who rebelled in 1916 against British rule. The rebels had to surrender and most of their leaders were shot.

De Valera was reprieved and later became leader of Sinn Féin ('Ourselves Alone'), which fought a guerrilla war against British rule from 1919 to 1921. Sinn Féin and the British then signed a treaty to set up an Irish Free State, but De Valera would not agree to it because Ireland was to be partitioned.

In 1926 he started a new party, Fianna Fáil ('Warriors of Ireland'). It won the 1932 general election, and De Valera was prime minister until 1948. He broke nearly all of Ireland's links with Britain, and in 1949 Ireland became a fully independent republic. Between 1951 and 1959 he was Taoiseach (prime minister) of the Republic, and between 1959 and 1973 he was president.

Joseph McCarthy (1908–1957)

US senator Joseph McCarthy found fame in 1950 by announcing he knew the names of 205 Communists in the US State Department. Although he provided no proof, many people in public life were accused of 'un-American activities'. In 1954 McCarthy accused US army officers of being Communist sympathizers. The hearings were shown on television and McCarthy was shown to the American public as a bully and a liar.

Lyndon B. Johnson (1908–1973)

Johnson was elected to the US House of Representatives in 1937 and to the Senate in 1949. He became president when John F. Kennedy was killed. When presidential elections were held the following year, he won by a massive majority. He improved healthcare for the elderly and civil rights for black Americans. However, he lost a lot of support for increasing American involvement in the Vietnam War.

Mohammed Anwar el Sadat (1918–1981)

As a young Egyptian army officer, Sadat helped overthrow King Farouk in 1952. In 1964 he became vice-president of Egypt and president in 1970. After the 1973 war between Israel and its Arab neighbours, Sadat felt Egypt was strong enough to make a peace deal with Israel. He and the Israeli prime minister, Menachem Begin, were awarded the Nobel Peace Prize in 1978.

Benito Mussolini

Dictator of Italy from 1926 to 1943
Born 1883   Died 1945 aged 61

Benito Mussolini was involved in politics from an early age and was often arrested for his activities. He began to believe that the only way to change society was through the use of violence.

After World War I, many people were scared that there would be a revolution in Italy, as there had been in the Soviet Union. In 1919 they gave Mussolini funds to set up the Fascist Party to oppose the Socialists and Communists. His Fascists attacked trade unionists, broke up strikes, and then 'marched' on Rome in 1922. The king asked Mussolini to be prime minister and Mussolini gradually took more power for himself. By 1926, il Duce ('the Leader'), as he was now known, had become a dictator.

In 1935, to increase Italy's power and his own glory, Mussolini invaded and conquered Ethiopia. His great friend in Europe was Hitler. They formed an alliance, which took Italy into World War II on Germany's side in 1940. However, Mussolini's armies suffered many defeats. By 1943

Mussolini had been overthrown and placed under arrest. German paratroops rescued him and put him back in power in northern Italy. The end, though, was not far away. When Italy was finally defeated, Mussolini was shot by his Italian enemies and his body was hung upside-down in the Piazza Loreto in Milan.

>> See also Adolf Hitler p. 45

◀ Italian dictator Benito Mussolini in a photograph taken in 1928.

David Ben-Gurion

Israel's first prime minister
Born 1886   Died 1973 aged 87

David Ben-Gurion emigrated from Poland to Palestine in 1906. At that time Palestine was part of the Turkish Ottoman empire, and Ben-Gurion was expelled as a trouble-maker by the Turks. He went to America and joined the Jewish Legion, which fought in the British army in Palestine in World War I.

After the war Palestine came under British rule. Ben-Gurion became general secretary of the Histadrut (the Confederation of Palestine Jewish Workers), and organized the defence of the Jewish settlers against hostile Arabs.

When European Jews were not allowed to enter Palestine, Ben-Gurion began campaigning for an independent Jewish state. In 1947 the United Nations decided that Palestine should be divided between Jews and Arabs, and in 1948 Ben-Gurion proclaimed Israel's independence. He became prime minister but retired in 1953. He was recalled in 1955 until 1963.

>> See also Chaim Weizmann p. 39, Menachem Begin p. 50

⬆ The flag of Israel.

Chiang Kai-shek

Ruler of China from 1928 to 1949
Born 1887   Died 1975 aged 87

Chiang Kai-shek trained as an army officer. In 1911 he took part in a rebellion intended to overthrow the dishonest rulers of the Chinese empire. China became a republic but was soon divided among the warlords who kept power with their private armies rather than being ruled by the people.

Chiang Kai-shek joined the Nationalist Party, which believed in improving life for the peasants and poor workers. He became commander of the Nationalist armies after the death of Sun Yat-sen, who had been one of the original organizers of the Nationalist Party. Chiang Kai-shek used the armies to put down the warlords, and became ruler of China in 1928. He used his armies to try to crush the trade unionists and Communists but was not successful. Mao Zedong became leader of the remaining Communists.

When Japan invaded China in 1937, both Nationalists and Communists fought the Japanese occupiers. In 1945, when the Japanese had surrendered, the Communists started a civil war against the Nationalists. In 1949 Chiang Kai-shek had to flee to the island of Taiwan, which became known as the Republic of China (or Nationalist China). Chiang Kai-shek was its president until he died.

>> See also Zhou Enlai p. 40, Mao Zedong p. 48

Adolf Hitler

Austrian-born dictator of Nazi Germany
Born 1889   Died 1945 aged 56

Hitler fought in the German army during World War I and was awarded the Iron Cross for bravery. When Germany lost the war, Hitler was so angry about the terms of the peace treaty that he turned to politics. He joined the National Socialist (Nazi) Party and soon became its leader. Many joined the Nazi Party, and in 1923 they tried to seize power in Munich. This attempt failed and Hitler went to prison. There he wrote *Mein Kampf* ('My Struggle', 1923), which set out his ideas: he believed Germany's problems were caused by Jews and Communists and that Germany needed a strong Führer (leader). He was invited by President Paul Hindenburg to become chancellor (chief minister) in 1933.

Hindenburg died in 1934 and Hitler became president, chancellor, and supreme commander of the armed forces. All opposition to his rule was crushed. Millions of people were sent to concentration camps, and Jews gradually lost all their rights. Hitler became an ally of Fascist Italy and in 1938 he invaded

> Hitler pictured at a rally in 1934, the year in which he succeeded Paul Hindenburg as head of state.

" *The broad mass of a nation … will more easily fall victim to a big lie than a small one.* "
ADOLF HITLER

Austria and in 1939 occupied Czechoslovakia and finally attacked Poland too. This started World War II. However, after almost six years, and having ordered the deaths of millions of Jews and others, he was defeated. He shot himself in Berlin.

>> See also Hermann Goering p. 38, Benito Mussolini p. 44

Pandit Jawaharlal Nehru

First prime minister of independent India from 1947 to 1964
Born 1889   Died 1964 aged 74

Nehru supported Mahatma Gandhi and became one of the most prominent leaders of the Indian nationalist movement. In 1920 he started working for the Indian National Congress, an organization that led India's struggle to gain freedom from British rule. However, he was often imprisoned for his opposition to British rule.

In 1946 he was again elected president of the Indian National Congress. He led the team that negotiated with the British the terms for India's independence. He became the first prime minister of independent India in 1947.

Nehru brought rapid economic development to his country. His government established large-scale industrial units and new hydroelectric projects to generate power to meet India's needs.

His reputation suffered a severe blow when China invaded India in 1962 and he died two years later.

» See also **Mahatma Gandhi p. 38**

> *The light has gone out of our lives and there is darkness everywhere.*
> NEHRU (SPEECH FOLLOWING GANDHI'S ASSASSINATION)

Dwight D. Eisenhower

American president from 1953 to 1961
Born 1890   Died 1969 aged 78

From his childhood everybody called Dwight Eisenhower 'Ike', and his cheerful grin made him friends everywhere. He became a soldier during World War I and by World War II, although he had never been in action, he had risen to the rank of brigadier-general. His organizing skills led to his promotion to command American forces in Europe in 1942.

Eisenhower held two more important army posts; he was chief of staff of the US army, and in 1951 he was invited to be supreme commander of the NATO forces in Europe.

In 1952 the Republican Party persuaded Eisenhower to run for president. He left the army to begin his campaign, and his supporters swept him to power in the election with the slogan 'I like Ike'.

Eisenhower served for two terms, winning a second election in 1956. During his presidency he brought the Korean War to an end and began the US space programme that would result America putting a man on the moon the year he died.

Ho Chi Minh

Founder of the Vietnamese Communist Party and president of North Vietnam
Born 1890   Died 1969 aged 79

Ho Chi Minh (meaning 'He who shines') was born in Vietnam when it was part of Indo-China, a colony ruled by France. He went to live just outside Vietnam so he could organize a Communist Party inside Indo-China without being arrested, founding the Indo-China Communist Party in 1930.

In 1941, during World War II, Japan entered Indo-China and Ho set up an underground movement, the Vietminh, to fight them. He hoped to take over when the Japanese left in 1945, but the French returned. Ho finally defeated them in 1954.

Ho became President of North Vietnam but was determined to reunite the country. In 1965 the United States began to bomb North Vietnam. The bombing made the people more loyal to Ho. Six years after his death, the Vietnams were united under the rule of the Communist Party.

↤ When the city of Saigon was captured in 1975, it was renamed Ho Chi Minh City in Ho's honour.

Charles de Gaulle

President of France from 1958 to 1969
Born 1890   Died 1970 aged 80

As a child, Charles de Gaulle enjoyed playing war games. Later he went to St Cyr Military Academy. When he left in 1912 his reports said that he was 'average in everything except height'. He was wounded and captured during World War I, and remained a soldier after the war. At the start of World War II he commanded a tank division. When France was invaded by the Germans in 1940, he escaped to England. From there he became the leader of all the French troops who had also escaped from occupied France. The Free French forces, with de Gaulle at their head, returned victorious to Paris in 1944 alongside the British and American troops.

De Gaulle was elected president of France in 1945, but resigned after only ten weeks. It was not until 1958 that he returned to power, when France was going through a political crisis. He survived a number of assassination attempts to become one of the most powerful presidents in French history. He insisted that France should be able to defend itself with its own nuclear weapons, and often argued with other leaders in Europe and the West.

When he was defeated in a referendum (national vote) in 1969, he retired to his home village, where he died the following year.

Francisco Franco

Spanish dictator from 1939 to 1975
Born 1892   Died 1975 aged 82

Francisco Franco was born into a navy family, but he decided to be a soldier. He became an officer at 18 and was gradually promoted until he was one of Spain's top generals. Then, in 1931, King Alfonso XIII left the country and Spain became a republic. Franco often criticized this republican government for the disorder in Spain.

In 1936 there was a military uprising against the republican government. Franco joined the rebels and soon became their leader. Civil war began between the two sides, and Franco was given military aid by Mussolini and Hitler. One million people died before Franco won the war in 1939. Franco then became caudillo (dictator) and ruled Spain without allowing any opposition or criticism for 36 years. Before he died, he named Juan Carlos to be king after his death.

🔼 Francisco Franco ruled as dictator for 36 years.

Mao Zedong

One of the founders of the People's
Republic of China in 1949
Born 1893   Died 1976 aged 82

Mao Zedong was one of the first to
join the new Chinese Communist
Party in 1921. This worked
alongside the Guomindang
(Nationalist Party), led by Chiang
Kai-shek, until 1927, when the
Nationalists had many Communists
killed. At first the Communists
fought off the Nationalists, but
in 1934 the attacks became too
strong. Mao then led the
Communists on the 'Long
March', nearly 10,000 kilometres
to a new base.

In 1937 the Japanese invaded
China. Chiang Kai-shek retreated
to the mountains, but Mao sent
the 'people's liberation army' to
help people in occupied villages.
When the Japanese finally left,
Mao received great support from
the people in the civil war against
Chiang Kai-shek.

By 1949 Mao had set up a
People's Republic and was leader
of a quarter of the world's people.
He encouraged peasants to
overthrow their landlords and
work together on collective farms.
Other peasants were told to open
factories or furnaces to make iron.
This was all part of Mao's plan for
a 'great leap forward' in industry.
However, many of the schemes did
not succeed because not enough
money was being spent on new
technology and education.

In 1959 Mao retired from
the post of chairman of the
Republic but re-emerged in 1966
to start the 'Cultural Revolution'.
This new movement was
intended to keep Chinese
Communism free from outside
influence and to ensure that Mao
and his ideas remained at the
forefront of life in China.

See also Deng Xiaoping p. 49

Chinese Communist leader
Mao Zedong.

Nikita Khrushchev

Soviet leader who denounced Stalin
Born 1894   Died 1971 aged 77

Nikita Sergeyevich Khrushchev
was a Russian metal-worker who
joined the Communist Party in
1918. He became a party worker
in Kiev and Moscow, and
eventually became first secretary
in 1935. He was made secretary
of the Ukraine region in 1938, but
resigned during World War II so
he could help organize resistance
in the Ukraine against the
invading German forces.

When the Russian leader
Joseph Stalin died in 1953 a
power struggle broke out amongst
the Communist leaders.
Khrushchev emerged as first
secretary of the Communist Party.
In an historic speech at the Party
Congress in 1956 he took the
bold step of denouncing Stalin.
People finally realized the bad
things Stalin had done, and
Khrushchev's power grew.

In 1958 he became prime
minister. Although he wanted
peace with America he almost
went to war with them over the
Cuban missile crisis in 1962.
Two years later he was replaced
by Brezhnev and Kosygin, who
initially shared power.

See also Joseph Stalin p. 42,
John F. Kennedy p. 51

> *Politicians are the same
> all over. They promise to
> build bridges even when
> there are no rivers.*
> NIKITA KHRUSHCHEV

Golda Meir

Prime minister of Israel 1969 to 1974
Born 1898 Died 1978 aged 80

Golda Meir was an active member in the Zionist movement, which fought for a homeland for Jews in Palestine. She held various government posts before being appointed foreign minister in 1956 – a position she held for nine years. In 1969 the prime minister died suddenly, and Meir was asked to take over until the elections. She was such a success that she was asked to carry on. She took a tough line with Israel's Arab enemies, while trying to reach a lasting peace. In 1973 the Yom Kippur War, the fourth conflict between Israel and the Arab countries, broke out. Although peace was soon negotiated, her government was severely criticized because of early defeats, and she resigned.

◉ Golda Meir was one of the world's first female prime ministers.

Deng Xiaoping

Chinese political leader
Born 1904 Died 1997 aged 92

Deng Xiaoping became a Communist in 1920 and by 1956 he was a leader in the Communist government, but he did not support Mao Zedong's extreme ideas. When Mao turned against those who disagreed with him, Deng lost all his power.

Mao died in 1976, and two years later Deng was the most powerful man in China. He used his power to improve standards of living. More food was grown, and factories began to produce goods such as clothing, sewing machines, bicycles, and television sets. Deng also ended the severe government censorship of television and newspapers. However, many people began to protest about the lack of democracy in China. Deng's Communist government felt threatened. In 1989 troops were ordered to put down a massive protest in Tiananmen Square, Beijing, and hundreds of demonstrators were killed.

⟫ See also Mao Zedong p. 48

Eva Perón (1919–1952)

Maria Eva Duarte was born near Buenos Aires in Argentina, and became an actress. She married Juan Perón in 1945. When he became president of Argentina in 1946, Eva (or 'Evita' as she was known) virtually ran the ministries of labour and of health. By 1947 she owned or had control over virtually every radio station in the country and had banned over 100 newspapers and magazines. She was a gifted speaker and campaigned hard for women's rights. She was blocked in her bid to become vice-president by military leaders and died from cancer shortly afterwards.

Pierre Trudeau (1919–2000)

Pierre Trudeau became involved in politics when he supported the workers during a miners' strike at Asbestos, Québec, in 1950. In 1965 he was elected to Parliament and he became prime minister in 1968. He insisted on the use of French and English as the two official languages of Canada. In 1982 he negotiated a new law which meant that Britain no longer had to give formal approval for changes to the Canadian constitution. The same law also gave Canadians a charter of rights and freedoms.

Lee Kuan Yew (b.1923)

Lee Kuan Yew founded the People's Action Party in Singapore in 1954. He became the first prime minister of independent Singapore in 1959 and helped to make the country one of the most prosperous in Asia, with excellent public housing, transport, health, and education services. He insisted on discipline and order, imposing strict laws against litter, long hair, and chewing-gum. Intolerant of criticism, he was quite prepared to lock up awkward journalists, strikers, and political opponents. Lee gave up office in 1990 but remained powerful behind the scenes.

Ronald Reagan

President of the United States of
America from 1981 to 1989
Born 1911   Died 2004 aged 93

Ronald Reagan came from a poor
family in Illinois. After working his
way through college, he became a
radio sports announcer. His good
looks and voice helped him get a
Hollywood contract in 1937, and
he made his first film that year.

His acting career was
interrupted when he joined the
air force in World War II. (He did
not see active service but made
training films instead.) Witty and
energetic, for several years after
the war he was president of the
Screen Actors Guild. He also
worked in television. He was so
good at making speeches that
many people told him he should
be a politician.

Reagan joined the Republican
Party in 1962 and was elected
governor of California in 1966.
He believed that government had
become too powerful, it cost too
much, and was hindering instead
of helping most Americans.
Having lost the Republican
presidential nomination in 1968
and 1976, he won it in
1980 and defeated
Jimmy Carter to
become president.
He was re-elected
for another term
in 1984.

● Ronald
Reagan began his
career as an actor,
and made more
than 50 films.

Reagan was not only the oldest,
but also one of the most popular
and conservative American
presidents. During his presidency,
military expenditure increased
enormously while less money was
spent on welfare benefits for the
poor. In 1987 a treaty was signed
with Mikhail Gorbachev of the
Soviet Union to eliminate all
ground-based, intermediate-range
nuclear missiles.

≫ See also **Mikhail Gorbachev p. 57**

Willy Brandt

German chancellor and statesman
Born 1913   Died 1992 aged 78

Brandt was elected to the German
Parliament in 1949, and became
mayor of West Berlin in 1957.
He led the city through the crisis
of 1961, when the Berlin Wall was
built. This experience made him
determined to improve relations
with the Communist east. His
chance came when he was elected
chancellor of West Germany in
1969. He created policies of
Ostpolitik, designed to reduce
tension between east and west.
For this he was awarded the Nobel
Peace Prize in 1971. Three years
later Brandt was forced to resign
when one of his assistants was
found to be a spy.

Menachem Begin

Polish-born prime minister of Israel
from 1977 to 1983
Born 1913   Died 1992 aged 79

Menachem Begin escaped the
Nazi invasion of Poland in 1939,
and enlisted in the Polish army.
He travelled to Palestine, where
he became the commander of a
guerilla group that fought against
the British army.

Begin was chosen to be leader of
the Herut (Freedom) party in 1948
and in 1970, he became co-leader
of the Likud (Unity) coalition.
After 30 years in opposition he
became prime minister in 1977.

Begin and Mohammed Anwar
el Sadat, shared the Nobel Peace
Prize in 1978 for their work in
trying to bring peace to the
troubled Middle East.

Richard Nixon

President of the United States of
America from 1969 to 1974
Born 1913   Died 1994 aged 81

When Dwight D. Eisenhower
became president in 1953, Nixon
was his vice-president and Nixon
himself won in 1968. At the time
US troops were involved in the
Vietnam War. Nixon realized that
the Communists could not be
defeated and began to withdraw.

During the 1972 election
campaign, some of Nixon's
supporters burgled the Watergate
Hotel, the headquarters of the
opposing Democratic Party. Nixon
denied all knowledge of the break-
in, but eventually he had to admit
he had helped to cover up the
facts. He resigned in 1974.

François Mitterand

President of France from 1981 to 1995
Born 1916   Died 1996 aged 79

François Mitterand was wounded
and captured by the Germans
during World War II. He
managed to escape and joined the
French resistance, fighting against
the German occupation. After the
war he entered politics and was
elected to the National Assembly.
During the 1950s he served as a
government minister in a number
of posts and then in 1971 became
leader of the Socialist Party.
He stood unsuccessfully for the
post of president of France on two
occasions before finally being
elected in 1981. Although he
encountered many problems
during his first seven years of
office, he was re-elected in 1988.

John F. Kennedy

President of the United States of
America from 1961 to 1963
Born 1917   Died 1963 aged 46

John Kennedy won his first
election as a Democratic member
of the House of Representatives
in 1946 and then became a
senator for Massachusetts in 1952.
In 1960 he was elected president.
Handsome and inspiring, in his
first speech he said, 'Ask not what
your country can do for you, but
what you can do for your country'.

He soon faced problems – he
helped Cuban refugees trying to
invade Communist Cuba. They
failed, making America look
foolish. Nevertheless, he did stop
the USSR from building nuclear
missile bases on Cuba in 1962.
He also sent troops to Vietnam,
which led to American
involvement in the Vietnam War.
At home, he proposed laws to give
black Americans equal rights,
although Congress did not pass
them. In November 1963 Kennedy
travelled to Dallas, Texas, to gather
support in the American South.
He was shot and killed by a sniper
while travelling in an open car.

⟫ See also Nikita Khrushchev p. 48

⬆ John F. Kennedy was the youngest man to be elected President of the United States.

Indira Gandhi

Prime minister of India from 1966 to
1977 and from 1980 to 1984
Born 1917   Died 1984 aged 66

Indira Priyadarshani was the
only child of Jawaharlal Nehru,
India's first prime minister.
She married a journalist, Feroze
Gandhi. Indira Gandhi followed
her father's interest in politics
and was elected president of the
Indian National Congress in
1959. She became minister for
information and broadcasting in
1964 and prime minister in 1966.

For several years she was
quite successful and popular.
However, opponents in the
Congress party thought she had
too much power. In 1975, she
declared a state of emergency.
Opponents of her policies were
even sent to prison. This made
her very unpopular and she lost
the general election of 1977.

She came back to power in
1980. Soon after she was faced
with unrest in the Punjab where
some Sikhs were demanding
their own state. A group of
armed Sikhs occupied the
Golden Temple, the holiest Sikh
shrine, in Amritsar. In 1984 Mrs
Gandhi's troops stormed the
Temple and many people were
killed. A few months later, Mrs
Gandhi was shot dead by one of
her Sikh bodyguards in revenge.

> *A nation's strength
> ultimately consists of what it
> can do on its own, and not in
> what it can borrow from others.*
> INDIRA GANDHI

Gamal Abdel Nasser

President of Egypt from 1956 to 1970
Born 1918   Died 1970 aged 52

As a boy, Gamal Abdel Nasser
joined demonstrations against the
British, who ruled Egypt at that
time with the help of the Egyptian
king, Farouk. Then, when Nasser
was in the army, he joined a secret
group who managed to overthrow
King Farouk in 1952 and get rid of
the remaining British troops. Two
years later Nasser became prime
minister and then, in 1956, he was
created president.

● Nasser addressing a huge crowd in Cairo
in 1961. When he died in 1970, he was
greatly mourned. He had helped to turn
Egypt into a politically powerful country.

In the same year Egypt was
invaded by troops from Britain,
France, and Israel after Nasser
took over the Suez Canal from its
foreign owners. Their action was
criticized by many nations and
they were soon forced to withdraw,
leaving Nasser with even more
power in Egypt.

Nasser tried to use this power to
unite the Arab countries, but their
divisions proved too deep and
lasting for peace to be agreed
between them. In 1967 Egypt was
defeated in the Six-Day War by
Israel. Nasser died of a heart
attack three years later.

Nelson Mandela

President of South Africa from 1994 to 1999
Born 1918

Nelson Mandela is related to the Xhosa royal family, but spent much of his childhood herding cattle. After going to university, he qualified as a lawyer.

Mandela helped form the Youth League of the African National Congress (ANC) in 1943. The Youth League stressed the need for the ANC to identify with the hardships and struggles of ordinary black people against racial discrimination. The ANC led peaceful mass protests against apartheid ('separate development'), the policy introduced by the National Party (NP) in 1948 to justify and strengthen white domination. Many protesters were imprisoned or killed. In 1960 the ANC was outlawed. In reply, Mandela and others established 'Umkhonto we Sizwe' (Spear of the Nation), a guerrilla army, in 1961.

In 1964, after months in hiding, Mandela was arrested and imprisoned for life. Offered a conditional release by the government, he refused to

↑ Nelson Mandela (centre) and F. W. de Klerk were awarded the Nobel Peace Prize in 1993 for their efforts to end apartheid.

compromise over the issue of apartheid. Eventually, as a result of internal and international pressure, Mandela was released in 1990 by President de Klerk. He led the ANC in negotiations, which resulted in the first democratic elections in South Africa. The ANC won, and Mandela became president. In his new role, Mandela has promoted reconciliation among all South Africans.

⟫ See also F. W. de Klerk p. 58

Yitzhak Rabin

Prime minister of Israel from 1974
to 1977 and from 1992 to 1995
Born 1922   Died 1995 aged 73

Yitzhak Rabin joined the Jewish
Defence Force during World War
II. He later played an important
part in Israel's victory over the
Arab troops in the Six-Day War
(June 1967). In 1973 Rabin became
a Labour member of parliament,
and a few months later prime
minister. From 1984 to 1986 he
was defence minister in a coalition
government, then became prime
minister again in 1992.

Rabin believed that Israel
should withdraw from the Arab
territories it had occupied since
the Six-Day War. He began
negotiations with Yasser Arafat,
head of the Palestine Liberation
Organization. This outraged many
Jewish people, and there were
violent clashes between Jews
and Palestinians. Rabin was
assassinated in October 1995.

Julius Nyerere

President of Tanzania from 1964 to 1985
Born 1922   Died 1999 aged 77

Julius Nyerere was born the son
of a chieftain at a village on
Lake Victoria, Tanganyika (now
Tanzania). After working as a
teacher, he helped to form the
Tanganyika African National
Union (TANU), which did very
well in Tanganyika's first elections
in 1958. Tanganyika became
independent in 1961 as a result
of TANU's success. Nyerere was
elected prime minister. He
resigned after a short time,
but became president
of the Republic of
Tanganyika in 1962.

Two years later
Tanganyika and
Zanzibar merged
to form the United
Republic of
Tanzania. Nyerere
became president. He
was re-elected at five-
yearly intervals, and was one of the
longest-serving leaders in Africa.
His views were listened to across
the world and Tanzania is one of
the most politically stable countries
in Africa.

➔ This is the first official
portrait of Julius Nyere,
made in 1963.

Robert Mugabe

First prime minister of independent
Zimbabwe
Born 1924

Robert Mugabe was born at a
Catholic mission north of
Salisbury, the capital of Southern
Rhodesia (now Zimbabwe).

At that time Rhodesia was a
colony ruled by Britain. Robert
Mugabe travelled around Africa in
the 1950s and saw people fighting
for independence from Britain. He
decided he wanted the same thing
for Rhodesia.

> « *It could never be a correct
> justification that, because
> the whites oppressed us
> yesterday, the blacks must
> oppress them today.* »
> ROBERT MUGABE

With others, he founded the
Zimbabwe African National Union
(ZANU) to fight for majority rule
by black people. ZANU was
banned and Mugabe was sent to
prison. On release he joined the
ZANU guerrilla fighters who were
attacking Rhodesian forces from
Mozambique. A ceasefire was
declared and free elections took
place in 1980. Mugabe became
prime minister and Rhodesia was
renamed Zimbabwe.

Many governments around the
world have condemned Mugabe's
leadership. In 2008 he was forced
to sign a power-sharing agreement,
with Morgan Tsvangiri, who
became the new prime minister.
Mugabe remains president.

Margaret Thatcher

British prime minister from 1979 to 1990
Born 1925

Margaret Thatcher was born Margaret Roberts. She studied chemistry at Oxford University and later became a barrister. Having been elected to Parliament in 1959, she gained her first cabinet post as minister of education in 1970. She replaced Edward Heath as Conservative Party leader in 1975.

In 1979 the Conservatives won the general election, and Margaret Thatcher became the first woman prime minister of Britain. She at once set about lowering taxes and reducing government control of businesses. Later, many state-owned businesses like British Telecom were sold to private owners.

In 1982 Thatcher reacted quickly when Argentina invaded the British colony of the Falkland Islands. A British task force recaptured the islands.

In 1987 she became the first prime minister in the twentieth century to be elected to a third consecutive term.

Thatcher's toughness in foreign affairs earned respect from many people throughout the world. By the end of 1990, though, her popularity had declined. She came under attack from colleagues in the Cabinet who thought that her style of government was too autocratic, or domineering, and she resigned.

➲ Thatcher was renowned for her tough style, and she tolerated little disagreement.

Fidel Castro

Leader of the Communist revolution in Cuba
Born 1927

Under the harsh rule of General Batista, many poor Cubans found themselves living in terrible conditions. Fidel Castro was one of a group of people who decided to overthrow the government. He gathered more and more support until finally, in 1959, Batista fled the country.

Castro immediately began to change the Cuban way of life. He organized the take-over of foreign-owned companies, but because many of these companies were American, the United States stopped all trade with Cuba.

Castro then turned to Communist countries, such as the Soviet Union and China, for help in fighting against America.

In 1962, the Soviet Union tried to build nuclear missile bases in Cuba, with Castro's permission. The missiles were removed after the United States had blockaded Cuba and put pressure on Russia, but this crisis had brought the world closer to nuclear war than it had ever been before.

Although Castro greatly improved conditions for poor people in Cuba, many other Cubans wanted more freedom, and fled to America.

Fidel handed power to his brother, Raul Castro, in 2006 owing to ill health.

Zulfikar Ali Bhutto

President and then prime minister of Pakistan from 1971 to 1977
Born 1928   Died 1979 aged 51

At the age of 30 Bhutto joined Ayub Khan's cabinet and within five years had become foreign minister of Pakistan. In 1967, he started his own party, the Pakistan People's Party, which came to power in 1971.

After the 1977 elections there were riots because some people thought Bhutto had rigged the vote. General Zia-ul-Haq overthrew Bhutto's government. Bhutto himself was arrested and charged with the murder of a political opponent. He was hanged in April 1979.

Pol Pot

Prime minister of Cambodia from 1975 to 1979, and leader of the Khmer Rouge
Born 1928   Died 1998 aged 73

In 1960 Communists in Cambodia founded their own party, later called the Khmer Rouge. Pol Pot organized people in the country to fight the government and in 1975 he became prime minister. He forced people from the city into the countryside and ordered that his enemies should be killed; more than two million people died and were buried in what became known as 'the killing fields'. In December 1979, the Vietnamese army invaded Cambodia and Pol Pot fled to Thailand.

Robert Hawke

Prime minister of Australia from 1983 to 1991
Born 1929

Hawke worked as a lawyer for the Australian Council of Trade Unions. Later he became its president and from 1970 until 1980 he was a skilful negotiator on behalf of trade unionists. In 1980 he was elected to Parliament and three years later became leader of the Labour Party. Within a month he was prime minister as the Labour Party swept to victory. He won four general elections between 1983 and 1990 before being replaced by Paul Keating. He retired from politics in 1992.

Yasser Arafat

Palestinian leader
Born 1929   Died 2004 aged 75

Yasser Arafat devoted his life to the struggle to create a homeland for the Palestinians who fled abroad when Israel fought for its independence from Britain in 1948. In the 1950s he joined various guerrilla groups, which organized raids against Israel. In 1969 he became leader of the Palestine Liberation Organization (PLO), recognized by Arab nations as the representative of all Palestinians.

After many years of attack and counter-attack, Arafat and the PLO reached an agreement with Israel in September 1993, in which the first steps were made towards a settlement between both sides.

⊙ Yasser Arafat, leader of the Palestine Liberation Organization, sought a Palestinian homeland free from Israeli rule.

Helmut Kohl

German chancellor from 1982 to 1998
Born 1930

Helmut Kohl became an active member of the German Christian Democratic Union (CDU) Party in 1947, and in 1959 he was elected to the local Parliament in West Germany. In 1982 he became chancellor (prime minister) of West Germany.

Kohl made strong links with the USA, and strengthened the ties between West Germany and the rest of the European Community. After World War II Germany was split into two parts, and Berlin was divided by a huge wall. When the Berlin Wall fell in 1989, Kohl helped bring East and West Germany together. When they merged in 1990 to become the Federal Republic of Germany, Kohl became chancellor.

Boris Yeltsin

Russian president who led his country
to democracy
Born 1931   Died 2007 aged 76

Boris Nikolayevich Yeltsin joined
the Communist Party in 1961.
By 1968 he was a full-time party
worker, and in 1976 was
appointed first secretary of the
Sverdlovsk District Central
Committee. Life in the Soviet
Union changed in the 1980s when
Mikhail Gorbachev became
general secretary of the Soviet
Communist Party. The many
changes he introduced were
welcomed by Yeltsin, who became
first secretary of the Moscow City
Party Committee in 1985.

However, Yeltsin soon clashed
with Gorbachev, who tried to stop
him running for president of
Russia in 1990. Yeltsin, no longer
a member of the Communist
Party, stood for election anyway
and won easily. This gave him
the authority to become a world
figure. When there was an
attempt to overthrow Gorbachev
in 1991, Yeltsin bravely led the
opposition to the coup. With the
break-up of the Soviet Union into
individual country states, Yeltsin
continued to lead Russia to
democracy. But economic
problems caused a lot of
discontent and Yeltsin made the
decision to dissolve the Russian
parliament in 1993 in order to
push through his economic
reforms. His Communist opponents
led an armed uprising against him
but Yeltsin put this down with the
help of his loyal troops.

See also Mikhail Gorbachev p. 57

Mikhail Gorbachev

Leader of the USSR from 1985 to 1991
Born 1931

Mikhail Gorbachev joined the
Communist Party in his second
year at university. At the age of
39 he became party leader of the
Stavropol region. In 1985 he
became general secretary of the
Communist Party and took over
the leadership of the USSR.

For the first time in 60 years, the
USSR had a relatively young and
reforming leader. He launched
three new policies: *perestroika*,
meaning 'restructuring', to make
the economy more efficient;
glasnost, to make the country
more open and honest; and
demokratizatsiya, to give people
initiative. His policies were
popular abroad: he withdrew
Soviet troops from Afghanistan
and he signed an agreement with
America to reduce the number of
short-range nuclear missiles.

But problems grew at home. The
nationalities (Latvians, Ukrainians,
Moldavians, and others) began to
demand more independence. His
reforms displeased the Party's
conservatives and they tried to
overthrow him in 1991. Even
though he survived that coup,
his power was much weakened.
When Russia and the other states
of the union formed a new
Commonwealth of Independent
States, Gorbachev resigned.

Mikhail Gorbachev, with the American president Ronald Reagan in 1985.

F. W. de Klerk

President of South Africa from 1989
to 1994; deputy president from 1994
Born 1936

Frederick Willem de Klerk became
president of South Africa in 1989.
He surprised the world in 1990
by releasing political prisoners,
including Nelson Mandela. De
Klerk also legalized outlawed
political parties such as Mandela's
African National Congress (ANC),
which eventually led to the end of
apartheid. De Klerk and Mandela
were awarded the Nobel Peace
Prize in 1993 for their part in this.

In 1994 the first election was
held in which all adult South
Africans could vote. It was won
easily by the ANC. De Klerk
became deputy president.

>> See also **Nelson Mandela p. 53**

Saddam Hussein

↑ Saddam Hussein with his two sons.

President of Iraq from 1979 to 2005
Born 1937   Died 2006 aged 69

Saddam Hussein came from a poor
peasant family. When he was 22
Hussein took part in a plot to kill
the prime minister of Iraq. After
living in exile in Egypt, he helped
overthrow the Iraqi government in
1968. Although he had never been
in the army, he appointed himself
general and president in 1979.

Hussein's war against Iran
(1980–1988) ended in stalemate
and his invasion of Kuwait
(1990–1991) ended in defeat.
Despite this, Hussein remained in
power. He was feared by his people
but also admired for standing up
to western powers such as
America. He was captured after
the invasion of Iraq in 2003, and
was executed in December 2006.

Lech Walesa

President of Poland from 1990 to 1995
Born 1943

Lech Walesa started work as an
electrician in the shipyards in
Gdansk. He soon became involved
in protests against the treatment
of workers, and in 1976 he was
sacked. In 1980 he created a new,
independent trade union called
Solidarity and ten million workers
joined. The Communist
government was alarmed,
Solidarity was banned and Walesa
detained. He was awarded the
Nobel Peace Prize in 1983.
Eventually the government gave
way and Solidarity became legal
in 1989. The trade union became
a political party and Walesa,
as its leader, won against the
Communists in the 1990 elections
and became president of Poland.

George W. Bush

President of the United States from 2001
to 2009
Born 1946

In 1988 George Walker Bush's
father, George senior, became
president of the USA. George
helped his father in his election
campaign. In 1994 George junior
decided to go into politics himself.
He ran for the post of governor of
Texas and won.

George successfully ran for
president in 2000. In January 2001
he became the 43rd President of the
United States. He was president
when the Twin Towers were
attacked on September 11th 2001.
The US invaded Afghanistan in
2001 and Iraq in 2003.

Barack Obama

President of the United States 2009
Born 1961

Barack Hussein Obama was born in Hawaii and raised by his mother and maternal grandparents. He grew up in Hawaii, Indonesia and Illinois. He majored in Political Science at Columbia University, New York City, and went on to study at Harvard Law School where he became editor of the *Harvard Law Review*. After graduating, Obama became a civil rights attorney before going into politics. He served in the Illinois Senate and US House of Representatives and was elected leader of the Democratic Party in 2008. Obama ran for the presidency and defeated the Republican candidate, John McCain, becoming the first African American president, and the 44th President of the United States. He is famous for his stirring speeches and is well-known for being an accomplished orator.

Vaclav Havel (b.1932)

The Russians invaded Czechoslovakia in 1968, and Havel was imprisoned for helping to create Charter 77, a declaration for human rights. In 1989 he was jailed again for inciting a rebellion against the government. Later he helped form Civic Forum, which led mass protests to demand freedom and democracy. Havel was elected president after the Communists resigned. He tried to preserve a united Czechoslovakia, but it was split into the Czech and Slovak Republics; Havel was president of the Czech Republic.

Mu'ammar al-Qaddafi (b.1942)

Qaddafi came to power in Libya in 1969 as the leader of an army revolt, and made himself president in 1977. He used Libya's oil wealth to improve living conditions in his country, and also to buy weapons for the armed forces. Qaddafi's government has been involved in a number of incidents with neighbouring countries.

Benazir Bhutto (1953 – 2007)

Benazir Bhutto was studying abroad when her father, Prime Minister of Pakistan, Zulfikar Ali, was executed. She returned to Pakistan and spent a total of six years either in prison or under house arrest.

She formed her own party and became prime minister in 1988. In 1990, the opposition forced her out of office. She campaigned to be re-elected and won but was dismissed in 1996. In 2007, she campaigned for re-election but died in an explosion.

Tony Blair (b.1953)

Tony Blair was a member of the Labour Party and elected to Parliament in 1983. In 1994 he became Labour Party leader and in 1997 became prime minister. The following year he signed a peace settlement in Northern Ireland, after nearly 30 years of violence in the province. In 2003 he took the country to war with Iraq. He resigned in 2007.

Military Leaders

Attila

Leader of the Huns against the
Roman empire
Born 406   Died 453 aged 46

Attila was born into the tribe
of the Huns, a race of warring
nomads who had moved from
the Asian steppes right up to
the borders of the Roman empire
in the West by the time he
was born.

When he became king of the
Huns in 434, Attila united his
scattered people in a campaign
against the Roman empire. For
the next 20 years the Huns under
Attila conquered and plundered
almost the whole of Europe.
Attila's greatest desire was to
destroy Rome, and the pope was
forced to pay him huge sums of
money to save the city.

While his followers lived in
luxury, Attila ate only meat out
of a wooden bowl. He was a short
man, with deep-set eyes and a
gaze that was hard and arrogant.
Although far from handsome, he
was married many times; legend
has it that he had as many as
300 wives. When Attila died,
the Huns cut their cheeks so that
they could mourn their leader
with tears of blood.

> " *A wise chieftain never*
> *depends on luck. Rather,*
> *he always trusts his future to*
> *hard work, stamina, tenacity*
> *and a positive attitude.* "
> ATTILA THE HUN

Saladin

Muslim soldier
Born 1137   Died 1193 aged 55

When he was 14, Saladin became
a soldier and fought against other
Muslims in Egypt. Before he could
attack the Christian crusaders, he
had to unite the different Muslim
kingdoms. This took him 15 years
to achieve. In 1187 he led the
Muslims against the Christians in
the Holy Land. Saladin destroyed
the Christian army at Hattin,
recaptured Jerusalem, and resisted
the new Christian attack led by
Richard the Lionheart (Richard I
of England).

Although he was a great
soldier, Saladin could also be
kind and gentle. He built schools,
mosques, and canals, and
encouraged scholars and
theologians. His people saw him
as a hero who revived memories
of the first Muslim conquests
under Muhammad.

» See also **Richard I p. 10**

Genghis Khan

Mongol emperor
Born 1162   Died 1227 aged 65

Genghis Khan was first called
Temujin. As soon as he was old
enough, he set about making
himself leader of all the Mongol
tribes. His methods were brutally
efficient: to make sure there was
no rebellion from defeated tribes,
he killed all the adult warriors and
made the children swear allegiance.

By 1206 he was recognized as
lord of all the Mongols. He took
the title 'Genghis Khan', which
means 'Ruler of All'. Now he led
his armies against the Chinese
empire. By the time of his death
his empire extended from the
shores of the Pacific to the
northern shores of the Black Sea.

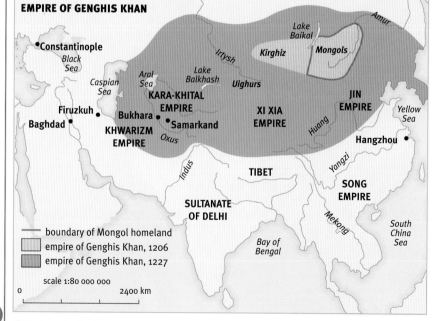

EMPIRE OF GENGHIS KHAN

— boundary of Mongol homeland
▢ empire of Genghis Khan, 1206
▢ empire of Genghis Khan, 1227

scale 1:80 000 000

0 ——— 2400 km

⬆ Before his death, Genghis Khan and his followers created the largest empire in history.

Joan of Arc

French peasant girl who led the French against the English
Born 1412   Died 1431 aged 18

Joan, the daughter of a peasant, grew up in north-east France. She was a devout and intelligent child and, unlike many children then, she could also read and write.

As Joan later remembered: 'I was in my thirteenth year when God sent voices to guide me. At first I was very frightened.' The voices kept returning and she stopped being afraid. She recognized them as St Michael, St Catherine, and St Margaret, the patron saints of France. They spoke about the sufferings of France since the English had invaded. The true heir to the French throne, Charles the dauphin, had not yet been crowned king. The saints told Joan to put on men's clothes to lead the fight against the English.

A portrait of Joan of Arc from 1420.

Joan managed to persuade Charles of her mission. He sent her with troops to Orléans, the last city in northern France still resisting the English. Within a week of her arrival in May 1429, the siege of Orléans ended. Two months later, the English had been defeated and Charles was crowned in Reims Cathedral.

Known as 'the maid of Orléans', Joan carried on the fight. However, after a year she was eventually captured by the Duke of Burgundy, an ally of the English. King Charles of France made no attempt to rescue her.

The English put Joan on trial as a witch and a heretic (a person who disagrees with the Church's teaching). They insisted that the Devil inspired her to wear men's clothes and to claim such power. Joan was found guilty and was burnt at the stake in Rouen in May 1431. Twenty-five years later, the French king proclaimed her innocent, and nearly 500 years after her death the pope declared her a saint.

See also Henry V p. 12

El Cid (c.1043–1099)

When the Spanish soldier El Cid lived, Spain was divided into many small kingdoms. Most of these were ruled by Muslim invaders from North Africa; a few were governed by Christian Spanish kings. El Cid collected an army of brave and loyal men around him. Sometimes they fought for a Christian lord, sometimes for a Muslim king. Although El Cid was bloodthirsty, he was a successful leader.

Owain Glyndwr (c.1354–c.1416)

Owain Glyndwr was a northern Welsh landowner who was angered by the way his countrymen were being crippled by English taxes. In 1400 Glyndwr proclaimed himself Prince of Wales and summoned his first independent Welsh Parliament at Machynlleth in 1404. Henry IV, the king of England, could do little to stop the revolt. In 1405 the tide turned against Glyndwr, but he still fought on as an outlaw.

Oliver Cromwell (1599–1658)

Cromwell was a Puritan, and believed that God had specially chosen him to do His will. Cromwell's chance came when the civil war began, and he commanded his own army. After Charles I was beheaded, Cromwell declared Britain a republic and became lord protector. He tried to rule with Parliament, though he also used his army to enforce what he thought was right. He was offered, but refused, the crown.

Horatio Nelson

Britain's greatest admiral
Born 1758   Died 1805 aged 47

Horatio Nelson joined the navy when he was 15, and at 21 was given command of his own ship.

Nelson made a name for himself as a skilled commander. His success began during Britain's war against the French in 1793. Despite being blinded in his right eye during a battle, Nelson was soon made an admiral. More injuries followed, including the loss of his right arm from below the elbow. But still he pursued the French, destroying their navy in 1798 at the Battle of the Nile.

Nelson is most famous for the Battle of Trafalgar in 1805. His 27 ships encountered 33 French and Spanish vessels. Nelson signalled to his fleet, 'England expects that every man will do his duty', and once again the French navy was beaten. However, during the fighting Nelson was shot by a French sniper and died on the deck of his ship, the *Victory*.

See also Napoleon I p. 23

Duke of Wellington

One of England's greatest generals, and prime minister from 1828 to 1830
Born 1769   Died 1852 aged 83

Arthur Wellesley was born in Dublin, Ireland. He joined the army at the age of 18 and served in India for eight years. But it was in Spain and Portugal that he won his great reputation (for which he was made Duke of Wellington), during the Peninsular War against Napoleon's French armies. In 1812 and in 1813 the English attacked, with support from the Portuguese and Spanish troops, driving the French out of Spain.

When Napoleon escaped from Elba, Wellington led the allied armies against him. At the Battle of Waterloo in 1815, Wellington's troops defeated the French again.

After Waterloo Wellington continued to serve his country, serving as prime minister from 1828 to 1830. For a time he was unpopular because he did not want to give the vote to more people, but by the end of his life most people admired him.

See also Napoleon I p. 23

Nelson explaining his plan of attack to his officers just before the Battle of Trafalgar.

Marquis de Lafayette (1757–1834)

Frenchman Marquis de Lafayette became a popular American hero when he joined the French fighting alongside American colonists against the British. He became the vice-president of the National Assembly in France and introduced a declaration of citizens' rights. Hated by king and court, he was forced to flee in 1792. He returned later and played a leading part in the revolution of 1830.

Mehemet Ali (1769–1849)

An Albanian by birth, Mehemet Ali entered the service of the sultan (king) of the Ottoman empire. In 1798 he was sent to Egypt to fight off French invaders, and in 1805 he used the strength of his troops to make himself 'Pasha' (ruler) of Egypt. He set up a modern army and navy, and improved agriculture and education. He is regarded by many as the founder of modern Egypt.

Crazy Horse (c.1849–1877)

Crazy Horse and his followers fought against the American government's policy of making Native Americans stay in areas called 'reservations' while white settlers moved west. However, the US army eventually proved to be too powerful for him, and he had to surrender at Camp Robinson in 1877. When Crazy Horse realized he was going to be locked up, he tried to fight his way out but was killed in the attempt.

José de San Martin

Argentinean soldier and statesman
Born 1778   Died 1850 aged 72

Although he was born in Argentina, José de San Martin lived in Spain from the age of six and was an officer in the Spanish army for 20 years. Then, in 1812, he was persuaded to switch sides and join the South American rebels who were fighting for independence from Spain. He raised an army in northern Argentina and then led them over the Andes to defeat the Spanish at Santiago, thus assuring the independence of Chile. He then landed his troops on the Peruvian coast and took control of the capital, Lima. He was given the title of protector of Peru in 1821. In the following year he met with Simón Bolívar and, after some initial disagreement, he left the liberation of the rest of Peru to Bolívar. San Martin sailed to Europe, where he lived for the rest of his life.

Simón Bolívar

Venezuelan general
Born 1783   Died 1830 aged 47

Eager to free his own country, Venezuela, from Spanish rule, Simón Bolívar joined a group of rebels. In 1810 they captured Caracas, the capital city, but the Spaniards fought back. Bolívar recaptured Caracas in 1813 and was given the title 'Liberator'.

In 1819 his forces defeated the Spaniards in Colombia. That same year he became president of Gran Columbia, a group of states.

Although Bolívar was respected, few agreed with his idea of uniting the whole of South America. When he died in 1830, Bolívar was hated by many for his dictatorial ways, but is also admired as South America's greatest liberator.

↑ In 1821 Bolívar's army liberated Venezuela.

Shaka the Zulu

First great chief of the Zulu nation in southern Africa
Born c.1787   Died 1828 aged about 41

Shaka was born the son of Senzangakona, a chieftain of the Zulu nation in southern Africa. His mother, Nandi, was an orphaned princess of the Langeni tribe. When he was a child, Shaka and his mother were banished from the Zulu villages by Senzangakona and were forced to go back to the Langeni. There they were treated very badly and were eventually banished once again by the tribe.

They found shelter with the Mtetwa tribe, and there Shaka became a warrior. After Senzangakona's death, Shaka returned to the Zulu as chieftain. He reorganized the Zulu army into regiments known as the *impi*, giving them more deadly *assegais* (stabbing spears), changing their battle tactics, and training them to march up to 80 kilometres a day. This harsh training made the Zulu the strongest nation in southern Africa at the time.

When Shaka became chief, there were fewer than 1500 Zulu; by 1824 he ruled over 50,000 people because, as he waged his battles, he incorporated defeated clans into the Zulu nation. He could, however, be a very cruel leader: when his mother died in 1827, he had 7000 Zulu put to death as a sign of his grief. Shaka was murdered in 1828 by his own half-brothers.

⟫ See also **Cetshwayo** p. 25

Robert E. Lee

Commander of the Confederate troops during the American Civil War
Born 1807   Died 1870 aged 63

Robert Edward Lee studied at the US military academy at West Point, before becoming an army officer. In the war between America and Mexico (1846–1848), his bravery made him famous.

Many years later, when the Civil War broke out, Lee decided to return to Virginia where he was born. In April 1861 he resigned from the US army and trained the Confederate army of the South. They won several major victories but were poorly equipped; they did not have enough guns and had little food.

At the Battle of Gettysburg in 1863 Lee's forces were out-numbered and defeated. For the next year and a half he was forced back on the defensive until his ragged and hungry army surrendered at Appomattox Courthouse in April 1865.

Lee spent the last five years of his life as president of Washington College in Virginia.

See also Abraham Lincoln p. 32, Ulysses S. Grant p. 34

Giuseppe Garibaldi

Italian guerrilla fighter who helped to unite Italy
Born 1807   Died 1882 aged 74

As a young man, Garibaldi worked as a sailor, becoming a sea captain in 1832. After taking part in an unsuccessful mutiny in 1834, he escaped to France and then to South America.

Well-known now as a brave but reckless fighter, Garibaldi led a group of Italians back to northern Italy in 1848, to help in the war against Austria. The next year he helped to defend Rome against the French, before being forced into exile in 1849. He returned to Italy in 1854, retiring to Caprera.

He came out of retirement to fight for Victor Emmanuel II, the king of Piedmont. In 1860 he led guerrilla volunteers in a successful revolt in Sicily, and then defeated the army of the king of Naples. Southern Italy became united under Victor Emmanuel.

See also Victor Emmanuel II p. 25

A wall painting showing Garibaldi and Victor Emmanuel II meeting in 1860.

Horatio Kitchener (1850–1916)

From 1900 to 1902 Kitchener led the British army in the Boer War. In 1914 war broke out in Europe. The prime minister made Kitchener secretary of state for war. Kitchener feared that the war would be long and gruelling, and Britain would need a bigger army. He modernized the British forces and soon recruited a million men. In summer 1916 he sailed for Russia, but his ship hit a mine and sank. Kitchener drowned.

Sun Yat-sen (1866–1925)

While studying as a doctor in Hong Kong, Sun Yat-sen joined a group of revolutionaries trying to overthrow the corrupt Manchu dynasty in China. In 1911, a revolution succeeded and Sun Yat-sen was made president, although in a part of south China only. He founded the People's National Party to carry out his 'Three Principles of the People' – a united China, democracy, and the modernization of industry to help the people.

Miguel Primo de Rivera (1870–1930)

Miguel Primo de Rivera was a military leader and later dictator of Spain. After serving in Cuba, the Philippines, and Morocco he returned to Spain and was made ruler after the existing government was overthrown. He ended the war with Morocco and tried to unite his country under the beliefs of 'Country, Religion and Monarchy'. His popularity waned, though, and he was forced to resign.

Sitting Bull

Sioux Indian chief
Born *c.*1834   Died 1890 aged about 56

Sitting Bull was a Sioux Indian chief. He is most famous for his part in the defeat of General Custer at the Battle of Little Bighorn in 1876. This battle came about because the Americans broke the Sioux resettlement treaty. After this battle, Sitting Bull and his followers were relentlessly pursued by the American army and were forced to escape to Canada. They returned to America in 1881 and Sitting Bull became famous once again, this time for his appearances in Buffalo Bill's Wild West shows. He finally settled on a reservation in South Dakota, where he continued to lead the Sioux in their refusal to sell their lands to white settlers. He was killed shortly after while 'resisting arrest' during an uprising there.

» See also **Buffalo Bill p. 232**

◑ Chief Sitting Bull.

George Armstrong Custer

American Civil War general
Born 1839   Died 1876 aged 36

After his training as an army officer, George Armstrong Custer fought in the American Civil War from 1861 to 1865. His commanding officer called him 'gallant' but 'reckless'. The newspapers called him the 'Boy General' because he was only 23 when he was promoted. His long, golden hair streaming, he raced his cavalry to victory after victory and became a legendary hero.

After the Civil War, Custer was sent to fight the Native Americans who still roamed the Great Plains. He often fought rashly and did not treat his men well, but the newspapers still praised him.

Then, in 1876, Custer and all 266 of his troops were killed at Little Bighorn, South Dakota, by a larger force of over 3000 Sioux Indians, led by Chief Sitting Bull.

➲ Custer's defeat at Little Bighorn became known as 'Custer's Last Stand'.

Douglas MacArthur

Commander of the United States army
during World War II
Born 1880   Died 1964 aged 84

Following in his father's footsteps, Douglas MacArthur joined the US army. He was an outstanding soldier. In 1930 he was appointed Chief of Staff, and from 1935 he organized American defences in the Philippines (a US territory).

In December 1941, more than two years after the beginning of World War II, Japanese armies landed in parts of South East Asia, including the Philippines. MacArthur and his forces resisted the invasion at first but were eventually forced out. MacArthur was transferred to Australia and for two years commanded Allied attacks against the Japanese. Finally, in the spring of 1945, American troops recaptured the Philippines.

MacArthur, who was now the commander of all US army forces in the Pacific, received the Japanese surrender in September 1945. He was then placed in command of the Allied occupation of Japan and took an active role in many reforms.

Five years later, North Korea invaded South Korea. The United Nations agreed to support the South and MacArthur was ordered to oppose the invasion. His forces pushed the North Koreans back, but were forced to retreat from an invading Chinese army. He eventually repelled the Chinese but then had ideas about attacking China itself. President Harry S. Truman would not agree to this plan and MacArthur was dismissed.

↩ General Douglas MacArthur, photographed in the Philippines in 1944.

Bernard Law Montgomery

English commander of Allied forces
during World War II
Born 1887   Died 1976 aged 89

Bernard Law Montgomery trained at the military academy at Sandhurst and fought in World War I. He stayed in the army after the war and by the time of the outbreak of war in Europe again in 1939, he commanded the 3rd Division of the British army. He took part in the invasion force to France and its evacuation from Dunkirk. In 1942 he took command of the 8th Army and it was under his leadership that the British won one of the most important battles of the war in the Middle East, at El Alamein.

Montgomery continued the offensive against the German army (led by Rommel) in North Africa. Then, in February 1943 Montgomery's forces came under the command of the American general, Dwight Eisenhower. They took part in the invasion of France in June 1944 and Montgomery received the German surrender at his headquarters on 3 May 1945. In the following year he was created Viscount Montgomery of Alamein, taking the title from his most famous victory.

> *Leadership is the capacity and will to rally men and women to a common purpose, and the character which inspires confidence.*
> BERNARD LAW MONTGOMERY »

Erwin Rommel

German field commander in North Africa
in World War II
Born 1891   Died 1944 aged 52

Erwin Rommel joined the German army in 1910 and won medals for gallantry in World War I. Remaining in the army after the war, he also wrote books about military tactics.

At the start of World War II he was put in charge of the guards at Hitler's headquarters, but in 1940 he moved to a Panzer tank division and headed the invasion of France in May. Then, when Italian forces collapsed in North Africa, Rommel was sent out as head of the Afrika Korps. He became known as the Desert Fox, and he fought a successful campaign in North Africa against the British Field Marshal Montgomery, until he was defeated at El Alamein in October 1942. Rommel then served in France as inspector of coastal defences.

He had gradually become unhappy with Hitler's leadership and so he gave his support to a plot to assassinate the Nazi dictator. In July 1944 the plot failed, however, and Rommel's involvement was discovered. Already badly injured by an Allied air attack on his car, he took poison to save his family from trial and execution.

⊗ See also **Adolf Hitler p. 45**

Che Guevara

Latin American revolutionary
Born 1928   Died 1967 aged 39

Ernesto Guevara de la Serna was born in Rosario, Argentina. He trained to be a doctor, but after going on a long journey through Latin America, the poverty he saw convinced him that there had to be a revolution to improve life for the poor. In 1956 he joined Fidel Castro's campaign to overthrow the Cuban dictator Batista.

Guevara fought as a guerrilla leader and then, when Castro won, he became a diplomat and a minister in the Cuban government. But Guevara wanted to spread the revolution to other poor countries. He travelled secretly in Africa and South America before he surfaced in Bolivia, where he was executed by the army. After his death Che Guevara became a romantic symbol of revolution and his face is known all over the world.

↑ General Erwin Rommel leading German troops in North Africa in 1941.

Religious Leaders

Jesus

Jewish prophet and teacher who became the founder of Christianity
Born *c.*4 BCE   Crucified *c.*28 or 29 CE aged about 32 or 33

Apart from the story of his birth in a stable in Bethlehem, not much is known about Jesus's childhood. At about the age of 30, he was baptized by his cousin, John the Baptist, and he began to preach, teaching people to love God and their neighbours.

Jesus's followers came to believe that he was the Messiah or Christ (a king that the Jewish people were waiting for to save them).

Jesus chose 12 men – the Apostles – to help preach his message.

Jewish religious leaders felt that Jesus was a threat to them. Realizing that his life might be in danger, Jesus made a special occasion of his last meal with the Apostles (known as the Last Supper). Later that night, Jesus was arrested. He was put on trial before the Roman governor, Pontius Pilate, and sentenced to death by crucifixion (being nailed to a wooden cross).

On the third day after Jesus's death, news spread that he had risen from the dead. Easter Sunday is the day when Jesus's resurrection is celebrated. Jesus's followers became known as Christians.

Gregory I

Italian religious leader, and the first monk to become pope
Born *c.*540   Died 604 aged about 64

Gregory came from a rich and noble Christian family. His great-great-grandfather had been pope, three of his aunts lived as nuns, and his father was an official in the government in Rome. Gregory himself was made chief magistrate of Rome. However, in 574 he gave up everything so that he could become a monk. He lived in the family house, which he turned into a monastery.

This peaceful life was frequently interrupted by official duties that he had to carry out for the pope. Then, in 590, Gregory himself was chosen by the people of Rome to become pope. Although he was sad to leave the quiet of his monastery, he vowed to serve God in this new capacity. He was very active in his papal duties and took them very seriously.

Gregory sent his monks out to preach the word of God all over Italy and also to Britain so that he could spread the word of God. He reformed the way in which the Church carried out its business and how its services were presented and sung. Through his writings and by the way he lived his own life, he changed the way Church leaders behaved. Gregory showed how it was possible to combine a monk's existence of reading and prayer with a pope's life of action and power.

⬅ This 13th-century painting shows the Last Judgement of Christ.

Muhammad

Islamic prophet
Born *c.*570   Died 632 aged about 62

Muhammad was brought up under the protection of his grandfather, Abdul Muttalib, and his uncle, Abu Talib. They came from the powerful Quraish tribe, who looked after the Kaaba, the central religious shrine in the city of Mecca in Arabia.

Muhammad used to pray alone in a cave on Mount Hira outside Mecca, and there he received his first revelations from God. Muhammad believed that he had to preach to the people of Mecca that there is only one God, Allah, and that they were wrong to worship idols (images). The people laughed at him and insulted him.

In 619 Muhammad's wife Khadija and Abu Talib died, and some of the Meccans plotted to kill Muhammad. In 622 he emigrated from Mecca to Medina with his followers. This move is called the *hijra* (migration). In Medina Muhammad led several campaigns and defeated the Meccans. In 630 Muhammad entered Mecca peacefully. The people there became Muslims and destroyed the idols. By the time of Muhammad's death most of the tribes in the Arabian peninsula had acknowledged his authority.

➲ The Dome of the Rock mosque in Jerusalem covers the sacred spot from which Muslims believe Muhammad ascended into Heaven.

Abu Bakr (c.573–634)

Abu Bakr lived in the town of Mecca and was one of the first to believe in the prophet Muhammad. When Muhammad fled, Abu Bakr went with him to Medina and became his chief adviser. When Muhammad died in 632, Abu Bakr was accepted as the 'successor of the Prophet of God', or Caliph of Islam. Abu Bakr extended the influence and rule of Islam by bringing the rest of Arabia under his control.

Desiderius Erasmus (c.1466–1536)

Desiderius Erasmus thought the wealthy Catholic Church of his day had forgotten the teachings of Jesus. He made a new, accurate Latin translation of the New Testament (1516). He also wrote a best-selling book poking fun at worldly, lazy monks, *The Praise of Folly* (1511). However, he never wanted to leave the Church, and disagreed strongly with the Protestant ideas of Martin Luther.

Ulrich Zwingli (1484–1531)

Zwingli was a Catholic priest, but around 1518, he decided that the Church needed to be more like that of Jesus's time, and supported the new Protestant Church. Zwingli moved to Zurich, where he tried to simplify church rituals – removing paintings and statues from churches, and closing down monasteries. The Zurich Church broke with the pope, but Zwingli was killed in a battle between Protestants and Catholics in 1531.

Mary Baker Eddy (1821–1910)

Mary Baker was a semi-invalid, but in 1862 her life was transformed by a healer-hypnotist, who believed that illness was an illusion. Mary claimed to have cured herself with the inspiration of the Bible, thus founding 'Christian Science'. Her ideas were set out in her book, *Science and Health* (1875), through a newspaper, the *Christian Science Monitor*, and with the help of her husband, Asa Eddy.

Ali

Arab ruler; the fourth Caliph of Islam
from 656 to 661
Born c.600   Died 661 aged about 61

Ali ibn Abi Talib was the cousin of the great prophet of Islam, Muhammad. Ali became a Muslim as a boy and married Muhammad's daughter Fatima. Pious, wise, and brave, in 656 Ali was chosen as the fourth Caliph – the leader of the Muslims and ruler of the expanding Arab empire. Al-Najaf, near Kufa in Iraq, became his capital and a great centre of learning.

A revolt against Ali's rule was led by Muawiyah, the governor of Syria and a member of the powerful Umayyad family. In 661 Ali was assassinated and his power was passed to the Umayyads, who ruled from Damascus. A group of Muslims, known as the 'Shiat Ali' (party of Ali), refused to accept Umayyad rule as they thought only descendants of Ali should be Caliphs. They became known in Muslim history as Shiites.

Martin Luther

German religious reformer
Born 1483   Died 1546 aged 62

Luther became a priest in 1507 and a teacher at the University of Wittenberg in Saxony. However, it was not long before an argument began between Luther and other churchmen. He said that people must study the Bible for themselves, and did not need to go to special church services. In 1520 he was expelled from the Catholic Church. The following year he was ordered to appear before a meeting of all the princes in Germany. Luther refused to give up his beliefs, even though he was in danger of being put to death.

Fortunately, the ruler of Saxony protected him and he was able to spend the rest of his life teaching and writing. By the time Luther died, his followers had formed a new Protestant Church, which was quite separate from the Catholics.

» See also John Calvin p. 71

⬆ The Golden Temple in Amritsar is the holiest of all Sikh temples.

Guru Nanak

First leader of the Sikhs
Born 1469   Died 1539 aged 70

Nanak was born a Hindu, but when he grew up he worked for a Muslim and learned about the Muslim religion too. When he was older he became a religious teacher, preaching a new faith that took ideas from both Hinduism and Islam. This new religion, called Sikhism, was based on one God and on the equality of all human beings.

Nanak believed that he had seen God and wrote about his experience in one of his early songs, now in the Sikh holy book, the Guru Granth Sahib. To reach unity with God he said people should meditate, pray, sing hymns, and follow the advice of a spiritual guide ('Guru').

Nanak travelled a great deal to teach people about God's path. Before he died, Nanak appointed his most trusted follower, Lehna, as his successor. Lehna was given the name Guru Angad.

⬆ Protestant reformer Martin Luther.

Ignatius Loyola

Spanish founder of the Society of Jesus
(also known as the Jesuits)
Born 1491   Died 1556 aged 65

Born in Spain, Ignatius Loyola
became a knight and fought in
battles. In 1521, however, he was
hit in the legs by a cannonball.
He was badly wounded and while
recovering, he read books about
Jesus that affected him deeply.

After this spiritual transformation
Loyola lived in a cave for a year,
thinking and praying. After
visiting Jerusalem in the Holy
Land, he returned to Spain to
study to be a priest.

Later Loyola went to Rome,
where he and his companions
decided to create a new 'order' of
religious men. Called the Society
of Jesus, its members ('Jesuits')
aimed to spread the ideas of
Christianity. In 1540 Pope Paul III
gave his approval for the Society.
Loyola became leader, and wrote
the Society's rules. He also
completed his famous book of

⬆ A portrait of Ignatius Loyola by Rubens.

prayers, *The Spiritual Exercises.*
By the time of Loyola's death there
were over 1000 Jesuits, working
in many countries.

John Knox

Scottish religious reformer who set
up the Protestant Church of Scotland
Born 1505   Died 1572 aged 67

John Knox was a devout Protestant.
He went to England as chaplain
to Edward VI, but fled to
Switzerland when Catholic Mary I
came to the throne. There he was
influenced by John Calvin.

In 1559 he returned to Scotland,
determined to set up a Protestant
Kirk (Church). His fiery preaching
helped to begin a rebellion, which
forced out the Catholics. He drew

up the 'Scottish Confession', a
statement of Protestant beliefs.

Knox made things very difficult
for the Catholic Mary, Queen of
Scots, and she lost her throne
in 1567, partly because of him.
Protestants in Scotland who
followed him were afterwards
called Presbyterians.

> " *The First Blast of the
> Trumpet Against the
> Monstrous Regiment
> of Women.*
> JOHN KNOX (TITLE OF ONE OF
> HIS PAMPHLETS) "

John Calvin

French-born Swiss Protestant reformer
Born 1509   Died 1564 aged 54

John Calvin was born and grew
up in France and nearly became a
Catholic priest. He was impressed
by Martin Luther's teachings, and
soon began to criticize the wealth
and power of the pope and the
Catholic Church.

It became too dangerous for him
to stay in Catholic France, and he
fled to the Protestant city of Basel
in Switzerland. In 1536 he wrote a
best-selling book, *The Institutes of
the Christian Religion.* Calvin said
Christians must use the Bible as
their guide, not the pope or the
Catholic Church. He taught that
people could never be good enough
to deserve to go to heaven, but
God chose some people specially
to be His 'elect'. He said that
Christians should in any case live
according to the teachings of Jesus.

In 1541 Calvin was asked to go
to Geneva to lead the Protestants.
There he organized schools and
a university. There were all kinds
of strict rules for everyday life;
dancing, theatre-going, and
card-playing were forbidden.
Shopkeepers were punished if they
charged too much. Unfaithful
husbands and wives were
executed, and a boy was beheaded
for striking his parents. People had
to wear plain clothes and avoid
bright colours, and women had to
cover their hair. Calvin became
the effective ruler of Geneva. By
the time he died, his religious ideas
were spreading across Europe.

≫ See also Martin Luther p. 70

George Fox

English founder of the Society of Friends
(the Quakers)
Born 1624   Died 1691 aged 66

George Fox grew up as a strong
Christian. However, he became
confused about the best way to
worship God, believing that there
was an 'inner light' in everyone
that helped them to understand
Christ's teachings. He thought
that people should meet together
to worship God quietly as equal
friends, without priests and
ceremonies. He began to win
followers, who became the 'Society
of Friends'.

Fox travelled around preaching.
He ignored the manners of the
time, speaking as an equal to
upper-class people, and never
taking his hat off to show respect.
This soon got him into trouble.
Once, when on trial, Fox told the
magistrate that he should quake
before the Lord: in response the
magistrate called him and his
followers 'Quakers'. He was
imprisoned eight times, but he
kept the Friends together in spite
of persecution.

 George Fox, seen here
in a painting from 1654,
believed in looking for the
good in everyone.

William Penn

English Quaker who founded the colony
of Pennsylvania
Born 1644   Died 1718 aged 73

William Penn was very religious
from an early age and eventually
converted to the Quaker faith, for
which he was later imprisoned.

On his release Penn met other
Quakers looking for a place where
they could follow their own beliefs.
In 1680 Penn asked King Charles
II for a gift of land in America.
The land was called Pennsylvania
('Penn's woods'). Penn sailed out
there with other Quakers. Once
established, he was so honest and
just in his dealings with the local
Native Americans that there was
very little trouble between them.

Gobind Singh

Tenth and last Sikh Guru
Born 1666   Died 1708 aged 41

Guru Gobind Singh was the son
of the ninth Guru, Tegh Bahadur.
In 1699 Guru Gobind Singh asked
for five Sikhs who were prepared
to give their lives for their faith.
These five went through a new
form of initiation into the order
of the Khalsa (the order of Sikhs
dedicated to following the Guru).
Many more followed them. The
men added Singh ('lion') to their
names and the women added
Kaur ('princess').

Guru Gobind Singh was killed
by a mystery assassin. As he lay
dying, he said that the Sikh holy
book was to succeed him rather
than another human being. The
book became known as the Guru
Granth Sahib.

John Wesley

Founder of the Methodist Church
Born 1703   Died 1791 aged 88

John Wesley was ordained as a priest in 1728. With his brother, Charles, he formed a group of men who tried to lead methodical lives, praying and reading the Bible. They were nicknamed 'methodists'.

In 1738 Wesley had an experience that changed his life. At a gospel meeting he felt his heart 'strangely warmed' and he knew that he was 'saved' by Jesus. From then on he committed himself to changing the lives of ordinary people through God's love. For 50 years he travelled all over England, holding services and preaching. Although Wesley wanted to remain loyal to the Church of England, a split came in 1784 when Wesley broke Church rules by ordaining a group of Methodist preachers.

➊ John Wesley holding a service during a storm while travelling to America.

Brigham Young

American leader of the Mormon community
Born 1801   Died 1877 aged 76

Brigham Young had very little education and started work as a house painter. In 1832 he became dissatisfied with the Methodist Church that he had been brought up in, and became a Mormon, a group that have split from other Christians because of disagreements about their beliefs.

In many parts of America, Mormons were disliked and driven from their lands. In 1847 Young became leader of the Mormons, and decided to find a new, peaceful home for them. He led 148 Mormon settlers to the Great Salt Lake of Utah and established what became Salt Lake City. By the time he died, 147,000 Mormons were living in Utah.

Brigham Young believed in polygamy, and had 27 wives and 56 children.

Ramakrishna

Indian holy man and religious teacher
Born 1836   Died 1886 aged 50

Gadadhar Chatterji was born into a poor Indian family in a small town near Calcutta in West Bengal. His only language was Bengali; he spoke no English or Sanskrit. His parents were religious people and are said to have had visions, and from a very early age Ramakrishna's only real interest was his own religious spiritual quest. His eldest brother, Ramkumar, offered to pay for his education, but he declined, saying he wanted no 'mere bread-winning education'. Instead he devoted himself to prayer. First he worshipped the Hindu goddess Kali, making offerings to her and going on pilgrimages. Then he became a *sannyasin* (monk) and took the name Ramakrishna. Later he learned about Islam and Christianity, and came to the conclusion that all religions were equal paths to the same goal.

He gradually earned a reputation as a wise and spiritual man, and thousands of people came to listen to him speak. Eventually his followers began to collect Ramakrishna's sayings, so that they could be written down and published throughout the world, as well as being preserved for all time. These followers kept his memory alive long after his death, and his lessons became universal. Ramakrishna's wife, Sarada-devi, whom he married when she was five, became a saint and was known as Divine Mother to Ramakrishna's disciples.

Pope John XXIII

Italian pope from 1958 to 1963
Born 1881   Died 1963 aged 81

At the age of 12 Angelo Roncalli went to the school for priests in Bergamo and from there he went to Rome. He was unexpectedly elected pope in 1958, at the age of 76. He visited children in hospital and prisoners in jail, and was especially concerned with helping the poor and with movements for international peace. He also asked the Catholic bishops from across the world to help him solve the problems of the Church. More than 2000 bishops met in Rome between 1962 and 1965 at the Second Vatican Council. Unfortunately, 'good Pope John' died before the council ended.

Ayatollah Khomeini

Iranian religious leader
Born 1900   Died 1989 aged 89

In the 1960s Ayatollah Ruhollah Khomeini spoke out against the shah (king) of Iran, who was using Iran's oil wealth to change the country's old way of life. Khomeini was against giving more freedom to women, and taking land and education out of the hands of religious leaders. In 1964 he was forced to live abroad. He returned in 1979 and although he did not actually govern, little could be done without his approval. In the name of Islam, opponents of his rule were imprisoned, tortured, and executed. Despite this, when Khomeini died in 1989 there were scenes of wild grief in Iran.

Pope John Paul II

Polish-born pope from 1978 to 2005
Born 1920   Died 2005 aged 85

Before becoming pope, John Paul II was called Karol Wojtyla (pronounced Voy-ti-wa). During World War II, Karol was forced to work in a stone quarry. His first ambition was to be an actor, and six of his plays were later published. But in 1946 he became a priest and went to study in Rome. In 1964 he was made Archbishop of Kraków and three years later he became a cardinal.

His election as pope in 1978 was a complete surprise. The pope before him, John Paul I, had died after only a month in office. Wojtyla was chosen because he was only 58, which was young by papal standards. He was strict on sexual morality, wanted priests to stay out of politics, and was strongly opposed to women priests.

Pope Benedict XVI

German-born pope from 2005
Born 1927

The German cardinal Joseph Ratzinger was elected pope after the death of John Paul II in 2005. He was born into a Bavarian farming family, although his father was a policeman. Like all young Germans he was obliged to join the Hitler Youth in the 1930s, which caused some controversy when he was made pope.

He is known for his uncompromising views, which became clear when he was a cardinal, and his strong belief in the traditional values of the Church. He upset many people when he quoted an ancient Byzantine emperor in saying that the Prophet Muhammad had brought the world evil.

⬇ Pope Benedict XVI visiting the site of a former concentration camp at Auschwitz in Poland in May 2006.

Desmond Tutu

Archbishop of Cape Town from 1986
Born 1931

Desmond Mpilo (meaning 'life') Tutu was the son of a primary-school headmaster and a domestic servant. He soon discovered what it was like to be black and poor in South Africa. He trained to be a teacher, but in the 1950s the South African government decided that black children should only be given a basic education. Tutu could not accept this decision, so he abandoned teaching to become a priest in the Anglican Church.

In the 1960s and 1970s he and his family spent some time in Britain. They were amazed at the civilized way they were treated compared to their experiences in South Africa. This gave Tutu the courage to speak out against apartheid (the policy of racial separateness and discrimination) when he later returned to his own country.

In 1975 he was created dean of Johannesburg and he would have been allowed to live in an area reserved for whites. Instead he chose to live in Soweto, a crowded township that was home to more than a million black people.

In 1984 he was awarded the Nobel Peace Prize in recognition of his 'non-violent struggle against apartheid'.

See also **Nelson Mandela p. 53, F. W. de Klerk p. 58**

◐ Desmond Tutu, one of the leading figures in the struggle against apartheid in South Africa.

> *Do your little bit of good where you are; it's those little bits of good put together that overwhelm the world.*
> DESMOND TUTU

Dalai Lama

Spiritual and political leader of the Tibetan people
Born 1935

When Tenzin Gyatso was two years old, he was declared to be the reincarnation of the Dalai Lama, who was believed to be the Buddha of Compassion come to Earth. When he was four he went to a palace called Potala in Lhasa, the capital of Tibet. He had to study hard and take many exams in Buddhist philosophy.

When he was 16 the Chinese invaded Tibet, killing many people and destroying the great Buddhist monasteries. For nine years the Dalai Lama tried to coexist peacefully with the Chinese, but in 1959 he made a daring escape to India. He now lives in a small Himalayan hamlet in India, from where he takes care of the 120,000 Tibetan refugees, and tries to get the world to help his people in Tibet. He was awarded the Nobel Peace Prize in 1989.

Saints

Saint Andrew

One of Christ's Apostles and the patron
saint of Scotland
Lived during the 1st century

Andrew was a disciple of John
the Baptist and then became an
Apostle of Jesus. Andrew went
out into the world preaching the
Gospel. The people of Patras in
Greece claimed that he was
crucified there. A later legend said
that in the 4th century, a native
of Patras took Andrew's bones to
Scotland. For this reason, Andrew
was chosen to be the patron saint
of Scotland. (He is also the patron
saint of Greece and Russia.)

Saint Peter

Leader of the 12 Apostles, the first
followers of Jesus
Lived during the 1st century

Peter was originally called Simon,
but Jesus gave him the name
Cephas, which means a stone.
Peter comes from the Greek
equivalent, *petra*. In Matthew's
gospel Jesus says that Peter and
his faith are the rock on which
the Church will be built.

After the crucifixion of Jesus,
Peter preached that Jesus was
alive. He was imprisoned twice,
but escaped and travelled round
the Mediterranean telling people
about Jesus and his teachings.

There is a tradition that Peter
spent the last years of his life,
before being crucified for his
beliefs, as the first bishop of Rome.

» See also Jesus p. 68

Saint Paul

Christian saint and Apostle
Born *c*.3 CE   Died *c*.65 CE aged about 62

Paul was originally named Saul,
after the first king of Israel. He
was Jewish by birth and was also
a Roman citizen. In the years after
the crucifixion of Jesus he joined
others in persecuting Christians.

Saul was travelling to Damascus
one day when he saw a light and
heard the voice of Jesus asking,
'Saul, Saul, why do you persecute
me?' Blinded for a while by the
great light, he was led to
Damascus and there he was
baptized as a Christian.

He spent three years quietly
praying and thinking, and then
joined other Christians in
Jerusalem. This was the beginning
of a life of missionary journeys,
teaching people about Jesus. Paul,
as he was now called, taught and
wrote letters to the Christian
congregations to help them to
understand their new religion.

Paul's life was very difficult. He
was beaten for his beliefs, and often
criticized by those who had been
followers of Jesus right from the
beginning. Roman soldiers arrested
him in Jerusalem after a mob of
people attacked him. He used his
right as a Roman citizen to be tried
in Rome. He was imprisoned for
two years and was probably killed
in the reign of Nero.

» See also Jesus p. 68

↑ This 15th-century fresco shows St Paul (right) visiting St Peter in jail.

Saint Augustine of Hippo

Important early Christian writer
Born 354   Died 430 aged 75

Augustine grew up in a small town in North Africa, which was then part of the Roman empire. At the age of 16 he went to study law at Carthage University. By the time he was 22 he had a mistress and a son, but was able to support himself by teaching. Six years later he moved to Milan in Italy, where he taught the art of speech-making. His beloved mother had been a Christian, but over the years Augustine felt he had grown away from God. Then suddenly one day, when he was looking again at an inspiring passage in the Bible, he decided to give up his career, leave his partner and son, and devote the rest of his life to God. His *Confessions* tells the story of his childhood, youth, and conversion.

> *Habit, if not resisted, soon becomes necessity.*
> ST AUGUSTINE OF HIPPO

When he wrote the *Confessions*, Augustine had just become Bishop of Hippo, a city near his home town in Africa, where he remained until his death. He continued to write and in his most important work, *The City of God*, he urged Christians not to trust in Rome or in anything that it stood for, but to think of themselves instead as belonging to God's city in heaven.

Saint Patrick

Patron saint of Ireland
Born *c.*390   Died *c.*460 aged about 70

Patrick was born into a family of Christians in Roman Britain. At the age of 16 he was captured by Irish pirates. He spent the next six years as a slave in Ireland, where there was no practised religion, before escaping back to Britain. According to his own later writings, he was now a much changed person. He trained to become a priest, and in about 435 he returned to Ireland. From then on he devoted his life to converting the Irish people to Christianity. He worked mainly in the north, where he had his own bishopric at Armagh.

He is still the most popular saint in Ireland, although no one is sure where he died and was buried.

⬆ Among many other legends, St Patrick is believed to have driven the snakes out of Ireland.

77

Saint David

Christian monk and bishop
Lived during the 6th century

We know almost nothing about the life of this saint. His monastery was at 'Menevia', which is now called St Davids, in Dyfed, south-west Wales. Later writers nicknamed him 'the Waterdrinker' because he led a very simple life and refused to drink wine or beer. It is said that he gained a reputation as a great speaker and teacher, and he is believed to have founded ten monasteries in places like Wales, Cornwall, and even in France, as well as the one at Glastonbury in England. The monks in these monasteries led lives of great hardship, and they were not allowed to eat meat or drink alcohol. They spent their days farming and their evenings praying and reading.

Legend has it that David lived for more than 100 years and he was buried at St David's Cathedral. Since the 12th century St David has been the patron saint of Wales. His feast day is 1 March, when the Welsh wear leeks or daffodils in his honour.

Saint Thomas Becket

Archbishop of Canterbury from 1162 to 1170
Born 1118 Died 1170 aged 52

After training as a lawyer, a priest, and a knight, Thomas Becket entered the household of the Archbishop of Canterbury, where he soon attracted the attention of the new king, Henry II. At the age of 36, Becket became the king's chancellor. He was a good statesman and he soon became a favourite of the king because he was talented and trustworthy. At this time, whenever there was a dispute between the Church and the state (represented by the king), Becket normally took the king's side.

All this changed in 1162 when he was offered the position of Archbishop of Canterbury. No one thought Becket would give up his luxurious life at court, but to everyone's surprise, he resigned as chancellor and began to live like a holy man. Saying that his duty to God as archbishop now came before his duty to the king, Becket angered Henry by challenging his claims to power over the Church.

Six years of quarrelling followed between the two men. Becket went into exile in France, but he returned after the pope managed to persuade them to put aside their differences. However, almost as soon as he returned home, Becket excommunicated (cut off from membership of the Church) any bishops whom he felt did not support him. The king flew into a rage, saying 'Will no man rid me of this turbulent priest?'

Four of Henry's knights took him at his word and, believing that the king was asking for Becket to be murdered, they went to Canterbury and slaughtered him at his cathedral altar.

This sensational event shocked the whole Christian world. People saw Becket as a martyr and even compared his death with Christ's crucifixion. In 1172 the pope declared Becket to be a saint. There is a shrine to him in Canterbury Cathedral, which has become an important focus for Christian pilgrims.

↩ This 15th-century panel shows Thomas Becket kneeling before the altar at Canterbury, as he is martyred.

Saint Francis of Assisi

Founder of the Franciscan order of friars
Born 1182   Died 1226 aged about 44

Francis had all the makings of a successful man of the world. Then, when he was 22, he suffered a serious illness and began to feel that helping the poor was more important than making money. He worked for no money, let robbers beat him up, and kissed lepers. He was still searching for a pattern to follow in his life. He found it in the instructions given by Christ to his disciples: 'Go to the lost sheep... Heal the sick... Cleanse lepers... Provide no gold, silver, or copper to fill your purse, no pack for the road, no second coat, no shoes, no stick: the worker earns his keep.'

Francis became a travelling preacher, owning nothing but his coat and living on the food that people gave him. He inspired others to live like him, and in 1210 he set up a new order of 'friars' (brothers), called the Franciscans. Within nine years there were Franciscans all over Europe, but Francis himself was not interested in running such a large organization and refused to be their leader. He travelled to Egypt in 1219 to preach to the Muslims and made other missionary journeys. But for most of his life he stayed near his home town of Assisi with a small group of followers, praying and preaching until his death in 1226.

⬆ This painting by Giotto is entitled *St Francis Preaching to the Birds*.

Saint Bernadette

French girl who saw a vision of the Virgin Mary at Lourdes
Born 1844   Died 1879 aged 35

Marie-Bernarde Soubirous came from Lourdes, a French town close to the Spanish border, where she was the eldest of six children of a miller and a laundry woman.

When she was 14 years old Bernadette announced that she had been visited in a vision by the Virgin Mary and that she had spoken to her. Although neither her parents nor church officials believed her, Bernadette never changed her story. She said that Mary had impressed upon her the need for prayer and penance.

JE SUIS L'IMMACULEE CONCEPTION
U. L. FRAU VON LOURDES

⬅ A souvenir postcard from Lourdes, showing a vision of the Virgin Mary.

Her claims aroused a great deal of public interest, though, so to avoid the publicity she was sent to a boarding-school. When she finally left school she went to live as a nun with the Sisters of Charity at Nevers. Here she was constantly plagued by sickness and suffered from asthma. Even when she was dying she showed considerable courage and good humour, and won the admiration of her friends.

In 1933 Pope Pius XI canonized her as Saint Bernadette. Lourdes is now visited by thousands of pilgrims every year, particularly the sick. Many of them who are dipped in the water of a spring there claim to have been cured. Bernadette said it was faith that was the cure.

Philosophers

John Locke

English philosopher
Born 1632   Died 1704 aged 72

John Locke was one of the most learned men of his time – educated in the sciences, politics, religion, and philosophy. But he was a practical as well as an academic man. He would advise young people to find pleasure in doing useful things like gardening.

His most famous book, *Essay Concerning Human Understanding*, explores the idea that experience is the only source of knowledge. He was also a firm believer in the rights of the individual, and wrote that no one has the right to force another person to take on his or her beliefs.

David Hume

Scottish philosopher and historian
Born 1711   Died 1776 aged 65

Although he was born and died in Edinburgh, David Hume spent several years in France, where he wrote his major philosophical work, the *Treatise of Human Nature* (1739–1740). Doubting the existence of God, Hume directed his investigations towards providing natural and, if possible, scientific explanations for the way in which human beings think and experience the world.

A leader in Scottish intellectual life, Hume extended his reputation beyond philosophy with his best-selling historical works, *Political Discourses* (1751) and *History of England* (1754–1762).

Jean-Jacques Rousseau

Swiss philosopher
Born 1712   Died 1778 aged 66

Jean-Jacques Rousseau's early life was a series of scandals and adventures, all later narrated with gusto in his *Confessions*, which were published after his death. His essay *Discourse on the Arts and Sciences* (1750), in which he praised the natural state of humankind, as opposed to the highly artificial society of 18th-century France, brought him fame.

In 1762 Rousseau published the novel *Emile* and *On the Social Contract*. The latter, with its revolutionary views on civil society, attracted the hostility of the authorities. Rousseau fled to Switzerland and England for some years. His ideas helped to fuel the French Revolution.

Karl Marx

German philosopher
Born 1818   Died 1883 aged 64

In 1843 Marx began a journey round Europe. He moved to Brussels where he met Friedrich Engels. Together they worked for the Communist League, and in 1848 wrote *The Communist Manifesto*. The ideas in this led to Marx having to flee to London, where he continued his work.

Marx wrote that under Communism, people would own all things in common and share them fairly. Marx believed this would happen, but only if working people organized themselves. That is why he became one of the leaders of the International Working Men's Association. By 1869 Marx had published *Das Kapital*, his most important work.

» See also Vladimir Lenin p. 39, Leon Trotsky p. 41, Joseph Stalin p. 42

⬆ Karl Marx, in a poster from about 1920.

Friedrich Nietzsche

German philosopher
Born 1844   Died 1900 aged 55

Born into a strict Protestant family in Saxony, Germany, Friedrich Nietzsche broke with Christianity in his twenties and devoted himself to classical literature and philosophy. The German composer Richard Wagner influenced him greatly at first, but Nietzsche later rejected him and most German culture of the time.

In books such as *Thus Spoke Zarathustra* (1883–1892), Nietzsche challenged cultural values passed down through many centuries from classical, Jewish, and Christian traditions. He held that notions of 'the good', 'the true', and 'the beautiful' are illusions; what matters is 'the will to power' – man's quest for a higher form of existence. (Nietzsche discounted women except as mothers of future 'supermen'.) He was isolated from mainstream philosophy by his extreme views, and suffered ill-health for the last decade of his life.

His philosophy is notorious because the Nazis misused it as justification for their racist policies, even though his ideas and theirs were not really compatible.

>> See also **Richard Wagner p. 188**

⬆ Nietzsche had a permanent breakdown in 1889.

Bertrand Russell

British philosopher, pacifist, and campaigner
Born 1872   Died 1970 aged 97

Bertrand Russell came from an aristocratic family and had a privileged childhood – even though both his parents died before he was two years old.

He studied mathematics and philosophy at Cambridge University and this led to his most important philosophical work. He tried to show that all mathematics was derived from a few simple laws of logic. Later he extended these ideas to show that knowledge was based, via logic, on simple observations. Neither project was completely successful, but his ideas greatly influenced mathematics and philosophy.

Russell was an excellent writer, and he was awarded the Nobel Prize for Literature in 1950. To the public, though, he was best known for his political and social views, and for his many broadcasts. He was a lifelong pacifist, and in 1958 helped to start the Campaign for Nuclear Disarmament (CND), which was very popular throughout the 1960s.

Thomas Hobbes (1588–1679)

When the English Civil War broke out, Hobbes fled to France for 11 years, believing that his theories about the state put him in danger. These theories, set out in his treatise *Leviathan* (1651), say that all power comes from the people; they hand it over to a monarch, who protects them in return for their absolute obedience. Hobbes's opinion that religion too should be subject to the state led to accusations of atheism.

Adam Smith (1723–1790)

Adam Smith published his first major work, *The Theory of Moral Sentiments*, in 1759, but it is *The Wealth of Nations* that has become one of the most important books on economics. In it Smith explained the development of Capitalism and how it made people better off. After completing this major work, Smith became commissioner of customs in Scotland and moved to Edinburgh, where he died in 1790.

Immanuel Kant (1724–1804)

Immanuel Kant's *Critique of Pure Reason* (1781) looked at the basic philosophical question of how we know or experience something: is it because of the qualities of the object itself or because there are some ideas within ourselves that enable us to make sense of that object? Kant said in addition to 'things in themselves', there exist inborn ideas, which he called 'categories'. Kant also wrote other works on subjects such as morality.

Land Explorers
Marco Polo

Italian merchant and traveller
Born c.1254   Died 1324 aged about 70

In the 13th century, Cathay, as people then called China, was a romantic, unknown land to most Europeans. When Marco Polo was 18 he was invited by his father and uncle to go with them to the court of the emperor Kublai Khan at Khanbalik (Beijing).

The three merchants set out from their home in Venice in 1271. They went by ship to the Mediterranean coast of Turkey, and the rest of the way overland. They took the southern branch of the Silk Road, along which merchants from China regularly brought silk to Europe. The whole journey took nearly four years.

Kublai Khan received them warmly and Marco became a travelling diplomat for the emperor. He was sent on many missions, visiting India, Myanmar (Burma), and Sri Lanka.

After 17 years the Polos decided it was time to return home. They arrived back in Venice in 1295 with a fortune in jewels.

Marco spent the last 30 years of his life as a Venetian merchant. At one time he became a prisoner of war in Genoa. While there he dictated the story of his travels. This is not a story of his personal adventures but a description of the almost unknown Mongol Empire. Many readers thought he was making things up. They called him Il Milione, meaning 'he of the million lies'. Later, people realized his account was mostly true.

» See also Kublai Khan p. 11

Ibn Battuta

Moroccan traveller and writer
Born 1304   Died 1368 aged 64

When he was a boy, Ibn Battuta studied the Koran, the Muslim holy book, very thoroughly. By the age of 21 he was an expert in Muslim theology and law, and he set out on a pilgrimage to Mecca. At first he was homesick, but he soon grew to love travelling, and he would journey more than 120,000 kilometres over the next 28 years.

Ibn Battuta travelled to Damascus and joined a pilgrimage there. At Mecca he joined other pilgrims who were returning to Persia (now Iran). He continued to travel in Asia Minor (now Turkey), observing and keeping records of everything he saw, relating tales and wonders. He then travelled north to Kazan on the River Volga, and on to the city of Constantinople.

Ibn Battuta crossed the Hindu Kush mountains and went into service for the sultan of northern India. He remained there for eight years. He was sent to accompany a returning Chinese embassy, but a storm destroyed the fleet of junks before they could leave. After the storm Ibn Battuta was left with only his prayer mat and ten pieces of gold. He eventually reached China in 1344, before finally returning home.

His travels did not end there, though. He journeyed throughout Spain and crossed the Sahara Desert to Timbuktu before dictating a fascinating account of his travels.

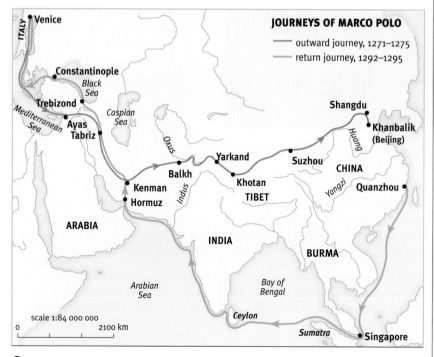

JOURNEYS OF MARCO POLO
—— outward journey, 1271–1275
—— return journey, 1292–1295

Venice • ITALY
Constantinople
Black Sea
Trebizond
Mediterranean Sea
Ayas
Tabriz
Caspian Sea
Oxus
Balkh
Kenman
Hormuz
Indus
ARABIA
Yarkand
Khotan
TIBET
INDIA
Huang
Suzhou
CHINA
Yangzi
Shangdu
Khanbalik (Beijing)
Quanzhou
BURMA
Arabian Sea
Bay of Bengal
Ceylon
Sumatra
Singapore

scale 1:84 000 000
0   2100 km

⬆ The book Marco Polo wrote contained descriptions of the countries he visited.

Francisco Pizarro

Spanish conqueror of the Inca empire
Born c.1474   Died 1541 aged about 67

As a young man, Francisco Pizarro looked after a herd of pigs. He then decided to go to Hispaniola in the Caribbean to take part in several exploring expeditions.

In 1522 he was scratching a living as a landowner in Panama when he heard rumours of the Inca empire in Peru and its fabulous wealth. He made an expedition to check that it really existed, then returned to Spain to ask permission from Emperor Charles V to conquer the land.

In 1532 Pizarro arrived in Peru to find the country split by civil war. He seized the emperor, Atahualpa, and demanded a huge ransom of gold and silver. After the money was paid, Pizarro had Atahualpa executed, saying he was plotting against the Spaniards. Pizarro had conquered the Inca

⬆ Pizarro conquered the whole Inca empire.

empire of several million people with an initial force of just 180 men. He did not enjoy his victory for long, though. In 1541 he was killed by rival Spaniards.

⟫ See also Atahualpa p. 19

Hernán Cortés

Spanish conqueror of the Aztecs
Born 1485   Died 1547 aged 62

Hernán Cortés studied law in Spain, but decided to try to make his fortune in the West Indies. In 1511 he became a soldier and joined an expedition to Cuba. In 1519 Cortés's fleet of 11 ships sailed to Yucatán, on the Mexican coast, to explore the country.

Cortés then marched inland to Tenochtitlán (now Mexico City), the capital of the Aztec rulers of Mexico. He had about 600 Spaniards with him, and several thousand Native Americans who were enemies of the Aztecs. The Aztec ruler, Montezuma, gave the Spaniards a friendly welcome, but he was killed by his own people in a riot, and Cortés and his men had to escape.

The Spaniards returned and besieged the city, bringing with them guns, steel armour and weapons, and horses – all new to the Aztecs. Unknown to both sides, the Spaniards also had an invisible weapon: smallpox. Disease and war killed thousands of Aztecs. By 1521 Cortés had conquered the whole country, and the Aztec civilization collapsed.

⟫ See also Montezuma p. 13

Samuel de Champlain

(1567–1635)

Frenchman Samuel de Champlain made many journeys of exploration to North America. In 1608 he and 32 men founded the colony of Québec. Life was tough and only Champlain and eight others survived the first winter there. He won the respect of the local Native Americans by fighting in their wars. When the English attacked Québec in 1628, Champlain was captured and sent to England, but he returned in 1633, and died there two years later.

Joseph Banks (1744–1820)

English explorer Joseph Banks became interested in botany at school. He later explored the world looking for new plants and animals. His first expedition, in 1766, was to Labrador and Newfoundland. In 1768 Banks set sail with Captain Cook on the *Endeavour*, bound for Tahiti and the South Seas. In 1788 he became President of the Royal Society, the most important British scientific society.

John Franklin (1786–1847)

In 1845 the experienced English explorer Sir John Franklin sailed for the unknown Northwest Passage (a way to the Pacific round the north of Canada) with two ships, *Erebus* and *Terror*. They were never seen again. In 1857, after official efforts to find them stopped, Lady Franklin paid for a further search. The remains of some of the expedition were found on King William Island. A note explained that Franklin had died in 1847, but the cause of his death is a mystery.

Isabella Bird (1832–1904)

When she was 23 British-born Isabella Bird visited Canada and America and recorded much that she saw. Later she travelled to Australia, Japan, India, Tibet, Iran, Korea, and China and wrote successful books about her adventures. She rode great distances and lived under very hard conditions. At the age of 70 she made her last journey – through the Atlas Mountains in North Africa.

Mungo Park

Scottish explorer who located the River
Niger in West Africa
Born 1771   Died 1806 aged 34

Mungo Park studied medicine
but then went to London, where
he was chosen to lead a search for
the River Niger in West Africa.

In 1795 he set out on horseback
from the mouth of the River
Gambia. He travelled inland from
one African kingdom to the next
before being captured by Muslim
nomads, who made him beg for his
food. Park escaped and on 21 July
1796 had his first sight of the
River Niger near Ségou. He
followed it to Sansanding, but
the onset of the rainy season
forced him to return.

In England, his book *Travels in
the Interior Districts of Africa* was
very successful, and in 1805 he
was asked to lead a military
expedition to follow the Niger to
the sea. He set out with 42 British
volunteers, but the rains came and
many of the men died. He built a
boat but by the time he launched
it, only four men remained alive.
Ill and in fear of the Muslim
tribesmen, they travelled down
river firing into the bush. They
were attacked at Bussa and Park
was last seen jumping overboard.

⬇ Mungo Park played an important part in
early European exploration of Africa.

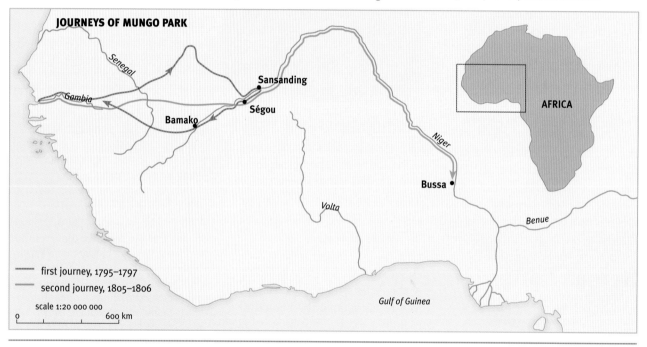

JOURNEYS OF MUNGO PARK

Senegal

Sansanding

Gambia

Bamako

Ségou

Niger

AFRICA

Bussa

Volta

Benue

first journey, 1795–1797
second journey, 1805–1806

scale 1:20 000 000
0   600 km

Gulf of Guinea

Lewis and Clark

Leaders of the first expedition to cross
the American continent
Meriwether Lewis Born 1774
Died 1809 aged 35
William Clark Born 1770
Died 1838 aged 68

In 1803 the US government
bought from France a large piece
of land in North America called
'The Louisiana Purchase'.
President Thomas Jefferson
decided to send an expedition
to explore it and to cross the
Rockies to reach the Pacific Ocean.

Jefferson chose Meriwether
Lewis to lead the expedition,
and he then chose William Clark,
an expert on Native American
Indians, to go with him. With
about 40 other men, mostly
soldiers, they started out in 1804
from St Louis, in boats and canoes
up the Missouri river.

Eventually, they left the river
and climbed a pass through the
Rocky Mountains. They had
many adventures, including close
encounters with grizzly bears,
which no white man had seen
in America before. In November
1805 they reached the Pacific
Ocean. After the winter they
returned by roughly the same
route. The explorers brought
back a lot of information about
the land, the native population,
and the plants and animals.

》 See also Thomas Jefferson p. 30

David Livingstone

Scottish missionary and explorer
Born 1813   Died 1873 aged 60

Although his family was poor, David Livingstone worked very hard and saved enough money to train as a doctor. In 1841 he sailed for southern Africa to join a Christian mission station in what is now Botswana.

In 1853 Livingstone set out to search for new trade routes through Africa. He walked from the middle of Africa to the Atlantic coast, then headed east until he reached the Indian Ocean. He was the first European to see the Victoria Falls. When Livingstone returned to Britain in 1856 he was hailed as a hero because he was the first European to cross Africa from west to east.

Livingstone's second expedition, up the Zambezi River by steamboat, was a disastrous failure. His wife died of fever and many other lives were lost before the expedition collapsed in 1864.

Livingstone's third expedition, to find the source of the River Nile, began in 1866. He vanished and some people thought he had died. But in 1871 the American journalist Henry Morton Stanley found Livingstone on the shore of Lake Tanganyika. 'Dr Livingstone, I presume,' were Stanley's famous words when they met.

Livingstone died in 1873. His body was shipped to England and buried in Westminster Abbey.

🔽 An elephant trumpets a greeting as Livingstone's boat passes by on a voyage along the Shire River in Malawi, Africa.

Robert Peary

American Arctic explorer
Born 1856   Died 1920 aged 63

On 6 April 1909, accompanied by four Inuits (Eskimos) and a black American friend, Matthew Henson, Robert Peary reached the North Pole after a long and very exhausting sledge journey. At least that is what everyone thought. But during the 1980s, when his record books were re-examined, it seems that he got it wrong and probably missed the North Pole by about 80 kilometres.

Peary led many expeditions to little-known areas of the frozen north. Over a period of 20 years he studied Greenland and its isolated inhabitants. He was the first person to prove beyond doubt that it is an island.

Fridtjof Nansen

Norwegian explorer and scientist
Born 1861   Died 1930 aged 68

Fridtjof Nansen made the first crossing of Greenland in 1888–1889. Later he led a more daring expedition. He left his specially designed ship, the *Fram*, drifting slowly across the frozen Arctic Ocean whilst he tried to reach the North Pole on foot. He had to turn back, but had got nearer to the pole than anyone before him.

Nansen then worked as a scientist, becoming first a professor of zoology, and then a professor of oceanography, the study of oceans. In 1921 he was appointed League of Nations High Commissioner for Refugees.

Mary Kingsley

English explorer and traveller in Africa
Born 1862   Died 1900 aged 37

Mary Kingsley's father was a doctor who spent most of his time travelling abroad. Her mother was constantly ill and Mary was never given any schooling. She learned to read and taught herself Latin, physics, chemistry, mathematics, and engineering from her father's library. From his letters and books she learned about countries beyond England that had strange plants and animals.

Her parents died when she was 30 and she was left poor and alone.

However, she was determined to visit the places she had read about. During 1893 and 1894 she travelled in West Africa to collect specimens of fish for the Natural History Museum in London, and to gather information about African religions. She explored the forests north of the River Zaïre (Congo) on foot and by paddling in a dug-out canoe. She wrote two successful books and became a popular lecturer. In 1900 she went to South Africa as a nurse in the Boer War. She died there of fever.

◄ Kingsley was one of the most famous travellers in Africa during the 19th century.

Robert Scott

English Antarctic explorer
Born 1868   Died 1912 aged 43

Robert Falcon Scott was placed in command of a British Antarctic expedition, and in 1901 he sailed south in the ship *Discovery*. He reached further south than anyone else at that time.

In 1910 Scott again travelled to the Antarctic, this time in an attempt to be first to the South Pole. The expedition was dogged by bad planning and bad luck. Captain Scott set out on the final stretch with four colleagues: Oates, Wilson, Bowers, and Evans. They reached the South Pole on

18 January, only to find that the Norwegian explorer Roald Amundsen had beaten them by a month. They turned back, but were overtaken by blizzards, and died from starvation and exposure.

The bodies of Scott and his colleagues were recovered eight months later. Their notebooks, letters, and diaries described the brave but grim events. The gallant manner of Scott's failure was much admired by the British people.

> *Great God! This is an awful place.*
> ROBERT SCOTT (COMMENT ON THE SOUTH POLE IN HIS DIARY)

Roald Amundsen

Norwegian explorer and the first man to reach the South Pole
Born 1872   Died 1928 aged 55

Roald Amundsen began a career studying medicine, but gave it up to go to sea. Soon he became excited by the idea of polar exploration. He set out on his first expedition in 1903 aboard a small vessel with a crew of six. It took just over three years for Amundsen to become the first person to sail north from the Atlantic to the Pacific through the Arctic Ocean, north of Canada.

Amundsen decided to try to reach the North Pole next, but on hearing that an American, Robert Peary, had already done this, he sailed for Antarctica instead. The journey to the South Pole ended up as a race between Amundsen and a British expedition led by Captain Robert Falcon Scott, which had set out earlier than the Norwegian team. Amundsen and four companions, using sledges hauled by teams of dogs, reached the South Pole on 14 December 1911, almost a month before Scott's party. It was another first for Amundsen.

One of Amundsen's later adventures came in 1926, when he circled the North Pole twice in an airship. In 1928 Amundsen went to search for a friend who had gone missing on another airship flight over the North Pole. Amundsen's plane was never seen again. It is thought that it crashed into the sea.

❯❯ See also Robert Peary p. 85, Robert Scott p. 86

Hillary and Norgay

Mountaineers who were the first men
to climb Everest
Edmund Hillary Born 1919
Died 2008 aged 88
Tenzing Norgay Born 1914
Died 1986 aged 71

⊕ Edmund
Hillary and
Tenzing Norgay
on their way
to conquering
Everest in 1953.

Edmund Hillary worked as a bee-keeper before taking up mountain-climbing. After climbing in the New Zealand Alps and the Himalayas, he became a member of the British Everest expedition in 1953. When almost at the summit, it was left to Hillary and Tenzing Norgay, a Sherpa tribesman from Nepal, to make the final ascent. This they did on 29 May. News of their success reached Britain on the day of Queen Elizabeth's coronation. Hillary was knighted by the new queen in July 1953.

Since then Hillary made other trips to Everest, becoming a good friend to the local Sherpa people. For them he worked on schemes for building new schools and hospitals.

He died in New Zealand in 2008 equally beloved in his home country and Nepal.

Ranulph Fiennes

English explorer
Born 1944

Ranulph Fiennes began his career in the army, but he left life as a soldier in the 1960s in order to become an explorer. He first led an expedition up part of the Nile in Africa on a hovercraft. Later he followed the Earth's polar axis overland around the whole world, becoming the first man to travel to both poles by land.

In 2000 he tried to make the first solo, unsupported trek to the North Pole. It almost ended in disaster when his sleds fell through thin ice. Fiennes pulled them out, but in doing so he suffered severe frostbite to his hands and had to abandon the trek. The tips of his fingers later had to be amputated.

Ann Bancroft

American polar explorer
Born 1955

As a child Ann Bancroft was fascinated by stories about the famous explorer Ernest Shackleton. When she was only eight she would lead her friends and family on mini expeditions in the countryside around her home in Minnesota. She decided she wanted to be a polar explorer, even though at that time explorers were mostly men.

In February 2001, Bancroft achieved her dream of crossing Antarctica, with another woman, the Norwegian Liv Arnesen – the first women to do so. It took them 94 days to complete the 2,747-kilometre journey.

Sea Explorers

John Cabot

Italian discoverer of North America
Born c.1450   Died c.1498 aged about 48

John Cabot had an adventurous early life, during which he learned navigation. He settled in London in 1484. In 1496 King Henry VII of England heard of the expedition of Christopher Columbus to the West Indies and realized he was missing out on a chance of wealth and new colonies. So he instructed Cabot and his three sons – Lewis Sebastian, and Santius – to sail in search of 'all heathen islands or countries hitherto unknown to Christians'.

The Cabots set off in 1497 in a tiny ship, the *Matthew*, with a crew of just 18 men. They reached the American coast after a voyage of 53 days, thus becoming the first Europeans to reach the North American mainland. However, Cabot thought that he was in north-east Asia!

On their return, Cabot's report was so encouraging that the king sent him off on another expedition with a fleet of five ships. But Cabot found none of the gold or spices he was hoping for.

See also Christopher Columbus p. 89

Bartolomeu Dias

Portuguese navigator and explorer
Born c.1450   Died 1500 aged about 50

Nothing is known about the early life of the Portuguese explorer Bartolomeu Dias except that he was an experienced sea captain, and a knight at the court of the Portuguese king, João II.

In 1487 João sent Dias on an expedition to sail south along the west coast of Africa. The king was hoping Dias would find a sea route to India. During the voyage, a storm blew Dias and the three little ships under his command out to sea, until his crews feared they would fall off the edge of the Earth.

When the storm subsided Dias turned east, then north, and reached the African coast at Mossel Bay. After sailing as far as the Great Fish River on the south-east African coast, his men insisted on going home. However, Dias had seen that the coast of Africa turned northwards, leaving the passage to India clear. Dias named the south-western point of Africa the 'Cape of Storms', but King João changed the name to the 'Cape of Good Hope'.

Henry the Navigator (1394–1460)

Henry was the son of King John I of Portugal. Although he did not go on any voyages, he devoted his life to exploration. He provided ships and money for the captains who were pushing further and further down the coast of Africa and into the Atlantic. As a result, Portugal become a powerful sea-trading nation, seeking new countries to trade with and new products to bring back to Europe.

John Cabot departs from Bristol in 1497 in search of unknown lands.

Christopher Columbus

Italian explorer who travelled to the Americas
Born 1451   Died 1506 aged 54

Christopher Columbus, a skilled sailor, thought the easiest way to reach Japan was to sail west around the globe. He persuaded Queen Isabella of Spain to pay for his expedition to prove this.

He sailed with three small ships, *Santa Maria*, *Niña*, and *Pinta*, and about 90 men. On 12 October 1492 a look-out sighted land. This was one of the Bahama islands but Columbus was convinced it was the Indies and that he was very near Japan.

The *Santa Maria* was wrecked off the island Columbus named Hispaniola, so he decided to leave 40 men there to form a colony. He returned to Spain, where he was hailed as a hero.

He set off again in 1493, but when he arrived at Hispaniola Columbus found that all 40 of the men had been murdered. He founded another colony, and also visited Jamaica. On his third expedition in 1498, he set foot on the mainland of South America.

In 1502 he made one more voyage. While exploring the coastline of Central America, he became convinced he was near the mouth of the Ganges in India. He returned to Spain and died shortly after, still believing he had reached the Orient.

⊙ On sailing west across the Atlantic, Columbus came across America, a land unknown to Europeans at the time.

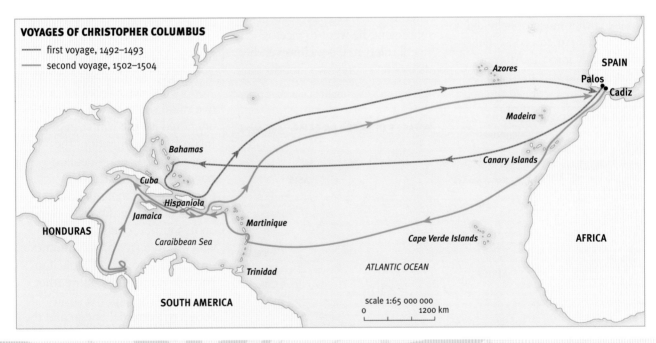

VOYAGES OF CHRISTOPHER COLUMBUS
— first voyage, 1492–1493
— second voyage, 1502–1504

SPAIN
Palos
Cadiz
Azores
Madeira
Canary Islands
Bahamas
Cuba
Hispaniola
Jamaica
HONDURAS
Martinique
Caraibbean Sea
Trinidad
Cape Verde Islands
AFRICA
ATLANTIC OCEAN
SOUTH AMERICA
scale 1:65 000 000
0   1200 km

Amerigo Vespucci (1451–1512)

Vespucci was a navigator who made maps of the lands discovered by Columbus. He sailed across the Atlantic Ocean from Europe, and also explored the South American coast. He realized he was looking at another continent, not parts of Asia as Columbus had believed. In 1507 a map was published in which the newly discovered land was given a name – America, because the mapmaker believed Amerigo had discovered it.

Vasco Núñez de Balboa (c.1475–1519)

In 1501 Balboa sailed across the Atlantic Ocean to make his fortune. He stowed away on an expedition ship to the coast of Central America. He was eventually made governor of a settlement there. Balboa learned that there was another ocean nearby so, with a party of Spaniards and American Indians, he hacked his way through the jungle until from a hilltop he saw the Pacific Ocean.

Henry Hudson (c.1565–1611)

Hudson first sailed from London in 1607 in search of a sea route to China, but this and a second voyage were unsuccessful. He took a job with the Dutch East India Company and explored the east coast of North America. In 1610 Hudson set sail again, hoping to reach China by way of the North Pole, and he discovered what became known as Hudson Bay. However, his crew mutinied, he was set adrift in a small boat, and was never seen again.

Vasco da Gama

Portuguese explorer, the first European to complete the sea route to India
Born c.1469   Died 1524 aged about 55

Vasco da Gama had already distinguished himself as a brave soldier when he was chosen to lead a voyage to India around the Cape of Good Hope. Since Columbus had failed to find a westward sea route to India, the Portuguese were determined to find the eastward route.

Da Gama sailed in 1497 with four small ships and 170 men. Unlike earlier navigators he did not hug the African coast, but sailed boldly into the Atlantic before turning east to round the Cape. The fleet reached the coast north of the Cape of Good Hope after three months without seeing land. They cruised along the coast, stopping at various places. To their astonishment, they found flourishing Arab towns, and the Sultan of Malindi supplied two Arab pilots to guide him to India.

Da Gama made a peaceful voyage to south-west India. He set up a trade agreement with the local people and returned to Portugal with a rich cargo of spices.

In 1502 he took 19 ships to help the Portuguese settlers in Goa. Then in 1524, after 20 years in retirement, he went as viceroy (local ruler) to Goa. However, he died of fever only two months later.

⟫ See also **Christopher Columbus p. 89**

Ferdinand Magellan

Portuguese navigator and explorer
Born c.1480   Died 1521 aged about 41

Ferdinand Magellan was born into a noble Portuguese family. He worked as a page at the Portuguese court before serving in the army, and then sailing with merchants to Indonesia.

Magellan thought there must be a way around the Americas to the East Indies. However, when he approached the king of Portugal suggesting a voyage of discovery, the king rejected the plan, so instead Magellan offered his services to King Carlos of Spain.

Magellan set sail in 1519 with five small ships. When the fleet anchored for the winter in San Julián Bay in Argentina, the captains mutinied. Magellan hanged one of the ringleaders to prevent any more mutinies.

When the fleet finally continued on its journey, one ship was wrecked in a storm, and another turned back to Spain. Magellan battled against the bad weather conditions through the strait between Tierra del Fuego and the mainland of South America. (The strait is now called the Magellan Strait after him.) He emerged into calm sea, which he named the Pacific (peaceful) Ocean.

The ships still sailed on and eventually reached the Philippines. Magellan had at last succeeded in reaching the East Indies by sailing westwards. However, before he could sail for home he was killed in a skirmish there.

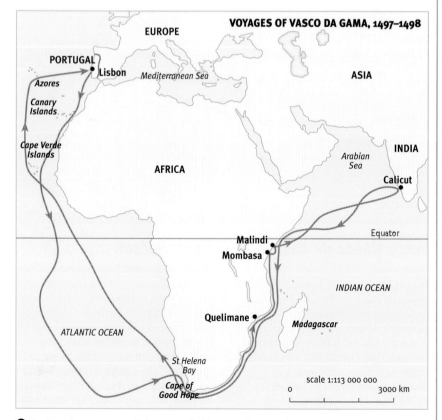

VOYAGES OF VASCO DA GAMA, 1497–1498

EUROPE

PORTUGAL • Lisbon   Mediterranean Sea

Azores

Canary Islands

Cape Verde Islands

ASIA

AFRICA

INDIA

Arabian Sea

Calicut

Equator

Malindi

Mombasa

INDIAN OCEAN

Quelimane •

Madagascar

ATLANTIC OCEAN

St Helena Bay

Cape of Good Hope

scale 1:113 000 000

0   3000 km

🔼 Da Gama's voyage round the coast of Africa to India opened up an important trade route.

Francis Drake

English sea captain, and the first
English person to sail round the world
Born c.1540   Died 1596 aged about 56

At the time of Queen Elizabeth I,
England and Spain were enemies.
Elizabeth I allowed Francis Drake,
an experienced sea captain, to
steal from Spain's colonies, as long
as he did it 'unofficially'. Drake
went on several successful
voyages, seizing treasure from
Spanish colonies in South America
and the West Indies. Drake was
behaving little better than a
pirate, but he was popular in
England for his daring deeds.

Drake set out again in 1577
in his ship the *Pelican*, which was
later renamed the *Golden Hind*.
He plundered many South
American settlements before
sailing up the Californian coast.
From there he crossed the Pacific
Ocean, and returned home
around the tip of Africa. For this
remarkable expedition, Elizabeth I
honoured Drake by
making him a knight.

In 1588 Spain planned
to invade England
with a great fleet of
ships (or armada).
When the Spanish
Armada finally
sailed towards
England, Drake
helped to defeat
the fleet in the
English Channel.

See also
Elizabeth I p. 16

A statue of
Sir Francis Drake.

Walter Raleigh

English courtier and explorer
Born c.1552   Died 1618 aged about 66

Walter Raleigh was an
accomplished soldier who had
fought in France and Ireland,
and helped to prepare England's
defences against the Spanish
Armada. He was also fascinated
by the riches of North America.
He never went there himself, but
expeditions he organized probably
brought potatoes to Britain.

Raleigh was a favourite of
Elizabeth I, but James I, who
became king in 1603, distrusted
Raleigh, and imprisoned him in
the Tower of London for over
12 years. Raleigh wrote a
History of the World while
he was there. In 1616 James
allowed Raleigh to go back to
South America to search for
gold. However, he found no

> I have a long journey to
> take, and must bid the
> company farewell.
> WALTER RALEIGH (LAST WORDS
> BEFORE BEING EXECUTED)

Abel Tasman

Dutch explorer
Born c.1603   Died c.1659
aged about 56

Abel Tasman was a sailor who
worked for a trading company
called the Dutch East India
Company. In 1642 Anthony
Van Diemen, the governor of
the Dutch East Indies, sent
Tasman to explore the seas
further south in the hope of

gold and got into a fight with the
Spanish instead. Raleigh returned
home and was executed in 1618.

Walter Raleigh went in search of El Dorado,
a mythical land said to be full of gold.

finding a route across the Pacific
Ocean to Chile. Tasman set off
and eventually came across a
land he named 'Van Diemen's
Land' (now Tasmania). He carried
on east and found more land,
which he named 'Staten Land'
(New Zealand). Heading back,
Tasman lost his way. He sighted
Tonga and then Fiji before
reaching home. He had also sailed
right around Australia without
knowing it!

91

Vitus Bering

Danish explorer
Born 1681 Died 1741 aged 60

Vitus Bering joined the Russian navy in 1703. He was a skilled navigator and in 1728 Tsar Peter the Great appointed him to lead an expedition to find out whether Asia and North America were connected by land.

Bering sailed northwards along the coast of Asia and, when the coast turned westwards, he concluded that the two continents were separated by sea. In fact, the distance between them, now known as the Bering Strait, is only about 80 kilometres. Five years later he headed the 600-man Great Northern Expedition along the Siberian coast.

In 1741 he sailed west towards America and became the first European to sight Alaska, when he saw an Alaskan volcano. Foul weather and sickness forced him back. He was shipwrecked on a deserted island and died of scurvy with 19 of his crew. The survivors buried him on the island, which was later named Bering Island after him.

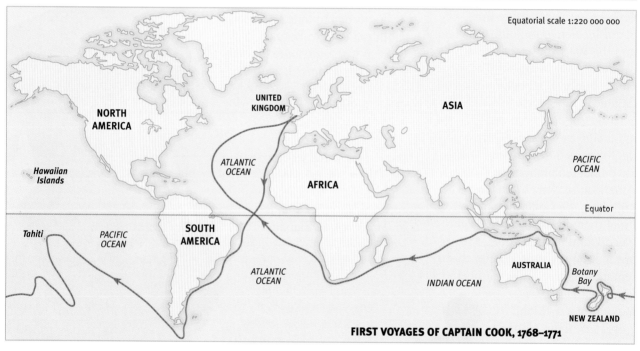

FIRST VOYAGES OF CAPTAIN COOK, 1768–1771

James Cook

English navigator and explorer
Born 1728 Died 1779 aged 50

James Cook went to sea when he was 18 and in 1755 he joined the Royal Navy. He soon proved to be an outstanding navigator and was quickly promoted.

In 1768 the Royal Society organized a scientific voyage to Tahiti. Cook was given command of the ship *Endeavour*, taking on board some famous scientists. On the journey, Cook insisted that the sailors ate plenty of fresh fruit, and so became the first captain to save his crew from scurvy, a disease caused by lack of vitamin C.

Cook became the first European to chart the coast of New Zealand, and to discover the eastern coast of Australia. He named one bay 'Botany Bay' because of its many fabulous plants. It later became a prison colony.

On his second voyage (1772–1775), Cook sailed south to

🔾 James Cook circumnavigated the world on his first voyage.

Antarctica and then charted the Pacific and its many islands.

On his third voyage (1776–1779), he explored a possible sea route around North America from the Pacific. He discovered the Sandwich Islands (Hawaii), explored the Alaskan coast, then passed through the Bering Strait before returning to Hawaii, where he was killed by islanders.

Jacques Cousteau

French underwater explorer
Born 1910 Died 1997 aged 87

In 1943 Jacques Cousteau helped invent the scuba or aqualung, a breathing device that allows divers to spend long periods under water. ('Scuba' stands for 'self-contained underwater breathing apparatus'.) He also developed the first under-

water diving station and an observation vessel known as the diving saucer. Using his observation vessel and his scuba equipment, Cousteau made many amazing films and television programmes about life in the oceans.

In 1960 Cousteau led a campaign to stop the planned dumping of nuclear waste in the Mediterranean. His fame helped swing public opinion behind him, and the plans were dropped. After that he continued to campaign for the conservation of the seabed, writing books and making more fascinating films about what goes on in the ocean depths.

Thor Heyerdahl

Norwegian explorer
Born 1914 Died 2002 aged 87

Thor Heyerdahl always had his own definite ideas about how human civilization might have spread during the world's early history. He was convinced that early progress was spread by people from advanced communities travelling to other parts of the world.

To prove that this might have been so, he and five companions built a simple balsa-wood raft called the *Kon-Tiki*. In 1947 they sailed it from Peru to eastern Polynesia to prove that Indians from South America could once

have made this journey. Their own journey involved great danger but to everyone's delight the *Kon-Tiki* expedition landed safely.

Heyerdahl's next project was to cross the Atlantic from Morocco to the Caribbean, this time in *Ra*, a reproduction of an ancient Egyptian boat made of papyrus. Heyerdahl's idea was to suggest that South America could once have been influenced by ideas from Egyptian civilization. Heyerdahl wrote popular books about both of these expeditions.

While many scholars are still not convinced by his theories, they all admire Heyerdahl's bravery and talent as an explorer and navigator.

⊕ In their papyrus-reed craft *Ra*, Thor Heyerdahl and a crew of six set off from the port of Safi in Morocco in 1969 to cross the Atlantic.

Air Explorers

Louis Blériot

French airman
Born 1872   Died 1936 aged 64

Frenchman Louis Blériot first made a fortune making car headlamps. When he was 30 he turned to aircraft design. In 1908 he created an aircraft control system not unlike that in use today, using elevators on the tail and later ailerons on the wings.

The first crossing of the English Channel by an aircraft was made by Blériot on 25 July 1909. He flew from Calais to Dover – a distance of some 34 kilometres. The flight took 37 minutes and won him a prize offered by the London paper, the *Daily Mail*. Blériot had designed this aircraft, his eleventh. It was a lightweight monoplane with a wooden frame and a fabric fuselage.

🔼 Blériot on the cover of a French magazine.

Richard Byrd

American polar explorer
Born 1888   Died 1957 aged 68

Richard Byrd started exploring when he was in command of American naval aircraft assisting an expedition to Greenland. Unlike many other polar explorers, Byrd believed in using aircraft and modern navigational aids rather than relying just on dogs and sledges. In 1926 he made the first flight over the North Pole. (After Byrd's death, an old friend claimed that this was a hoax.)

Byrd mostly explored the Antarctic. He named a range of mountains 'Rockefeller' after the millionaire John D. Rockefeller, who had financed one of his expeditions. On one occasion, whilst he was out mapping the Antarctic, Byrd was trapped alone in a hut for five months and had to be rescued.

Alcock and Brown

English pilot and navigator who made the first non-stop flight across the Atlantic Ocean
John Alcock Born 1892   Died 1919 aged 27
Arthur Brown Born 1886   Died 1948 aged 62

John Alcock was a motor mechanic but his interest switched from cars to aircraft. He learned to fly and became a flying instructor. During World War I he was awarded a medal for his bravery as a pilot. After the war, Vickers Aircraft recruited him as a test pilot: they wanted someone to make an attempt to fly an aircraft across the Atlantic Ocean.

Amelia Earhart

American pilot
Born 1897   Died 1937 aged 39

As a young woman Amelia Earhart took various odd jobs to pay for flying lessons. She was first noticed by the public when she flew across the Atlantic in 1928, even though she had really only been a passenger. However, she was soon making long-distance flights on her own and in 1932 she flew solo across the Atlantic.

In 1937 she embarked on a trip around the world, with navigator Fred Noonan. All the stops on the route were carefully planned, but one of them was at a small island in the Pacific Ocean. Her advisers were worried about whether she would be able to find it. Their fears were justified. Earhart could be heard on the radio, but she failed to find the island and the plane disappeared into the sea.

At 4.13 pm on 14 June 1919, Alcock took off from St Johns, Newfoundland in a specially adapted Vickers Vimy bomber, with Arthur Brown as his navigator. They landed the next day in a bog in County Galway, Ireland. The flight lasted 16 hours 12 minutes and covered 3025 kilometres at an average speed of 190 km/h. Alcock and Brown received a £10,000 prize and knighthoods. Alcock died in a plane crash shortly afterwards but Brown, who was also a pilot, eventually became a manager in the Vickers company.

⧁ See also Charles Lindbergh p. 95

Charles Lindbergh

American aviation pioneer
Born 1902   Died 1974 aged 72

Charles Lindbergh always had an ambition to fly. After a time in the Army Air Service he took a job flying mail across America.

In 1926 a prize was put up for the first non-stop flight from New York to Paris. Several famous airmen decided to attempt this and some were killed doing so. On 20 May 1927 Lindbergh took off in a specially built aeroplane called the *Spirit of St Louis*. He landed at Le Bourget Airport, Paris, 33½ hours later, having flown 5800 kilometres.

Lindbergh became a hero on both sides of the Atlantic, and went on to be an important adviser during the growth of long-distance air travel. Later he became interested in conservation, and opposed the development of supersonic aeroplanes, believing they would have a bad effect on the Earth's atmosphere.

Amy Johnson

English pilot
Born 1903   Died 1941 aged 37

As a young woman, Amy Johnson joined the London Aeroplane Club. As well as learning to fly, she wanted to know about engines, and she became the first English-woman to be a qualified ground engineer for servicing planes.

In 1930 she became the first woman to fly to Australia. She was disappointed, though, because she had just failed to beat the existing record for the journey, made by another pilot, Jim Mollison. Shortly afterwards she and Mollison were married.

In the early 1930s she made a number of long-distance flights, including trips to Japan, Cape Town, and America. Some of these were made with Jim Mollison and some of them alone. In 1941 her aircraft was lost in mysterious circumstances.

⊙ Amy Johnson photographed in 1930 standing by her aeroplane *Jason I*. This was the plane in which she made her record flight to Australia.

Space Explorers
John Glenn

American astronaut who was the first
American in space
Born 1921

John Glenn was working as an
American air-force pilot, and had
more than 2000 hours of flight
time, when he was picked for
the NASA astronaut training
programme, along with six other
former pilots. The
programme to put
a man into
space was
accelerated after the Russian
cosmonaut Yuri Gagarin made
a successful flight in 1961. John
Glenn was chosen to be the first
American to be launched into
space. His flight was postponed
ten times because of bad weather
and computer failures, but he took
off on 20 February 1962 for a
flight that took him three times
round the Earth.

After retiring from NASA,
Glenn entered politics as a
senator from Ohio and in
1984 tried unsuccessfully to
become the Democratic
presidential candidate.

❷ John Glenn was
the first American
to orbit the Earth.
He did so in the
spacecraft
Friendship 7, in
a flight lasting
five hours.

Neil Armstrong

American astronaut; the first person
to set foot on the Moon
Born 1930

As a young man, Neil Armstrong
was always interested in flying.
He earned his pilot's licence at
the age of 16, even before he
had learned to drive a car. The
following year he became a naval
air cadet, and went on to fly in
the Korean War.

In the 1950s Armstrong became
a test pilot for NASA (America's
National Aeronautics and Space
Administration) before joining the
US space programme in 1962.
President John F. Kennedy had
announced that America intended
to put a man on the Moon by the
end of the decade. In 1969
Armstrong joined astronauts
Edwin 'Buzz' Aldrin and Michael
Collins on the *Apollo 11* mission.
On 20 July he became the first
person to walk on the Moon. As
he stepped off the lunar landing
module, he uttered the famous
words, 'That's one small step for
man, one giant leap for mankind.'

Yuri Gagarin

Soviet cosmonaut; the first man to travel in space
Born 1934   Died 1968 aged 34

Yuri Gagarin was born into a poor farmer's family in a village, now renamed Gagarin, near Smolensk in Russia. While at college, he joined an air club near Moscow and learned to fly. Soon after college he joined the air force and began to fly fighter planes.

Because Gagarin was daring and skilled, he was singled out for space training. Being small also helped, as the first spacecraft did not have enough room inside for tall people.

His spaceship, *Vostok*, was launched from the Baykonur site in the Kazakh desert on 12 April 1961. Although his flight around the Earth took only 1 hour 48 minutes, it was the first human journey into space.

Only seven years later Gagarin was killed while testing a new plane. He was buried with honours alongside the Kremlin wall in Moscow's Red Square.

Valentina Tereshkova

Russian cosmonaut; the first woman to go into space
Born 1937

Valentina Tereshkova spent her childhood on a farm. When she was older she worked in a tyre factory and then in a textile mill. However, young Valentina had an adventurous spirit, and in her spare time she made as many as 163 parachute jumps.

Because of her lack of fear and her dedication, she was picked for space training in 1962. It was only a year later that she piloted a spacecraft, *Vostok 6*, in a group flight that lasted three days. Her spaceship orbited the Earth 48 times during the trip.

Although she was a colonel in the Soviet air force, Tereshkova devoted herself to helping others in many spheres – as a figure in politics, as a diplomat on trips round the world, and as a campaigner for world peace and for women's rights.

> *Once you've been in space, you appreciate how small and fragile the Earth is.*
> VALENTINA TERESHKOVA

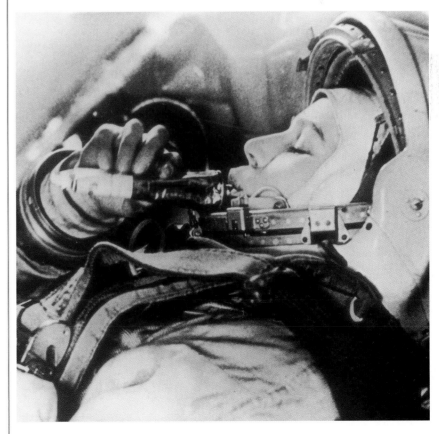

Valentina Tereshkova practises eating in flight conditions before her journey on *Vostok 6*.

Biologists
William Harvey

English physician who discovered how blood travels around the body
Born 1578   Died 1657 aged 79

William Harvey was the eldest of seven sons born into a wealthy farming family. His brothers all did well as merchants in London, but William went off to study medicine. He was a very successful doctor, and became court physician to King James I and then to King Charles I.

Harvey made a careful study of the heart and of blood vessels (veins and arteries) in the dozens of different animals he cut up. For more than 1500 years doctors had followed the writings of the ancient Greek physician Galen, who believed that blood moves backwards and forwards in the vessels that carry it. However, Harvey discovered that valves in the blood vessels allow the blood to move in only one direction.

Harvey showed that blood is pumped from the heart all the way round the body and back to the heart, where it begins its journey again. He was the first person to describe the circulation of the blood accurately.

Carolus Linnaeus

Swedish botanist
Born 1707   Died 1778 aged 70

Carolus Linnaeus was fascinated by plants from an early age and was lucky enough to live at a time when many new plants and animals were being discovered.

When he was older, Linnaeus worked out a method of giving two-part names to every different species. In this way each kind of plant and animal had a unique name. It was said at the time that 'God created; Linnaeus set in order', because his system made it possible for each new discovery to be slotted in with similar species.

Linnaeus was made professor of medicine and then of botany at Uppsala University, Sweden, where he had been a student. In 1753 he became a Knight of the Polar Star in recognition of his work, and later he was made a count.

Wherever he went he collected plants and made notes on all that he saw. He published more than 180 works, the most important of which is *Systema Naturae*, which is still used today by scientists who classify the living world.

Linnaeus was born Carl Linné but became known as Carolus Linnaeus as all his works were in Latin.

⬆ William Harvey (right) demonstrates his theory of the circulation of the blood to Charles I.

Edward Jenner

English discoverer of the smallpox vaccine
Born 1749   Died 1823 aged 73

In Edward Jenner's time there were regular outbreaks of a deadly disease called smallpox, which claimed tens of thousands of lives in England alone. Jenner heard stories of milkmaids who believed that they would be protected from smallpox if they caught cowpox, a mild disease that affected cows. He decided to see if this was true.

In 1796 Jenner took the contents of a blistering pimple from the arm of a milkmaid suffering from cowpox, and injected it into an eight-year-old boy. The boy became ill with cowpox but soon recovered from this mild infection. Jenner then injected him with smallpox. The boy did not become ill; the cowpox had made him immune to smallpox.

In 1798 Jenner published the results of his work, and within three years people as far away as America and India were receiving the new protection from smallpox. Jenner's discovery made him rich; he was rewarded by Parliament with sums totalling £30,000 – an enormous amount of money in those days.

> " *I hope that some day the practice of producing cowpox in human beings will spread over the world – when that day comes there will be no more smallpox.* "
> EDWARD JENNER

Charles Darwin

English scientist, best known for his theory of evolution
Born 1809   Died 1882 aged 73

Charles Darwin began studying classics, but he found that he was more interested in geology and botany. He became the friend of a professor of botany, who suggested that Darwin should go as the naturalist on a naval survey ship, HMS *Beagle*. Darwin set sail on 27 December 1831 on what was to be a five-year journey.

The most important part of the voyage for Darwin turned out to be the few weeks spent in the Galapagos Islands, which lie on the Equator, about 1000 kilometres from the coast of South America. These islands have plants and animals that cannot be found anywhere else in the world. Darwin was surprised to discover that each island had its own particular sort of tortoise. Why, wondered Darwin, should this be?

When he got home, Darwin realized that some of the birds from the Galapagos Islands were also closely related to each other, but differed in the shapes of their beaks. Yet the birds from any one island were similar. They were all rather like some small birds that live on the South American

⬆ A cartoon of Darwin from the magazine *Punch*, in 1881.

mainland, and Darwin decided that some of these must have reached the Galapagos Islands accidentally, and had evolved (changed) in their new home.

Darwin developed his theory of natural selection. This proposed that although most young animals die, the ones that survive are those best suited to their environment. If an animal is born that has some feature that gives it an advantage, it will survive, and so will any of its offspring that share this feature. In this way a process of natural selection enables a particular population to evolve.

Darwin hesitated to publish his ideas, but in 1859 his book called *The Origin of Species* came out. It caused an uproar, as it contradicted the ideas found in the Bible. Even today, some people dispute his arguments.

Gregor Mendel

Austrian monk who developed the
theory of genetic inheritance
Born 1822   Died 1884 aged 61

As a young man Gregor Mendel
became a monk. The monastery
supplied schools with teachers,
and Mendel was sent to university
to train as a science teacher. He
spent his life teaching science in
a local school and living a quiet
religious life in the monastery.

Mendel had his own little
garden in the monastery, where he
grew edible peas as well as sweet
peas with pretty coloured flowers.
He became interested in how the
different characteristics, such as
size and colour, were passed down
from parent plants. He kept
careful records of what all the
parent plants looked like and
what sort of young plants their
seeds produced. He grew many
generations of pea plants and
finally worked out a set of rules
to explain how the different
characteristics were passed down
(the subject we now call genetics).

He published his work in a
local magazine for botanists, but
at the time it went unrecognized.
Then, 16 years after Mendel's
death, the Dutch botanist Hugo
de Vries discovered Mendel's
paper, and Mendel's Laws of
Heredity became the basis of
all studies of heredity.

> " I am convinced it will not
> be long before the whole
> world acknowledges the
> results of my work.
> GREGOR MENDEL "

Louis Pasteur

French scientist who discovered that
bacteria cause disease
Born 1822   Died 1895 aged 72

Louis Pasteur was not a very
clever boy at school, but his life
changed when he began to study
chemistry. He became fascinated
by the subject, worked very hard,
and by the time he was in his
twenties, he had become famous
for his experiments.

In 1856 Pasteur was asked to
help the French wine industry
because much of the wine was
going sour. He showed that this
was caused by a tiny living
organism, a yeast, which could
be killed by heat. This heating
process was named 'pasteurization'
and is still used today.

Pasteur's most important work,
however, was his study of what
causes disease. He showed that
microscopic living organisms –
'germs' (bacteria) – carried disease
from one person to another. He
made a special study of a disease
called anthrax, which kills cattle
and sheep. He isolated the
anthrax bacteria and prepared a
weak form that he injected into
sheep; this gave them immunity
to the disease. Pasteur then made
a life-saving vaccine for treating
and preventing the deadly disease
called rabies. He dedicated his
whole life to his work, and died
a respected and well-loved man.

⬆ Pasteur's scientific achievements included a life-saving vaccine against rabies.

Joseph Lister

British surgeon who introduced
sterilization in operating theatres
Born 1827   Died 1912 aged 84

Joseph Lister trained to be a
doctor and attended one of the
first operations to be performed
under anaesthetic. He was
appalled at the huge number
of people who died after surgery.
At that time, conditions in
operating rooms were very
unhygienic. Surgeons, working in
their ordinary clothes and without
even washing their hands, boasted
that they could cut off a leg in 25
seconds. It is not surprising that
many of the patients died.

Lister began to wonder what
could be done to prevent these
deaths. He tried moving the
patients' beds further apart to
prevent infection, but he found
that the situation did not improve.
Then Lister read Louis Pasteur's
discoveries about bacteria in the
air spreading disease, and he
started to look for something
that would keep operating
theatres perfectly clean.

Lister suggested that as carbolic
acid was used to purify sewage,
perhaps it would kill bacteria in
surgery, too. Carbolic acid was
sprayed into the air during
operations, and heat was used to
kill bacteria on the knives and
instruments that were used for
surgery. At first no one believed
Lister's success, but by 1879,
most hospitals in London were
using his methods, and many
patients lived who would have
died without them.

» See also **Louis Pasteur p. 100**

Robert Koch

German bacteriologist
Born 1843   Died 1910 aged 66

Robert Koch studied medicine
at the University of Göttingen
in Germany. His teacher there
believed that diseases were caused
by microscopic organisms. Koch
spent his life identifying these
organisms. He studied the life
cycle of the tiny bacteria that
cause the animal disease anthrax
and also found the tiny spores
that infect the land where
animals graze. Koch then studied
tuberculosis (TB). Today TB can

↑ Koch was also a teacher, and many of his
students became great scientists.

be prevented by inoculation but it
used to cause thousands of deaths
each year. The bacteria responsible
are extremely small, but Koch
used his superb practical skills to
identify and grow them. This
work enabled others to develop
a vaccine against the disease.

Koch spent the rest of his life
studying other diseases, including
cholera, bubonic plague, and
malaria. He was awarded the
Nobel Prize for Medicine in 1905.

» See also **Edward Jenner p. 99**

Ivan Pavlov (1849–1936)

Ivan Pavlov knew that when a hungry dog is shown food it will immediately start to dribble saliva. This is called a reflex action. In his experiments he cut open the cheeks of his dogs to reveal their salivary glands, so that he could observe the dribbling. He rang a bell every time food was brought to the hungry dogs. After a while, ringing the bell alone was enough to make the dogs dribble. The dogs had learnt to expect food when the bell rang. Dribbling had become a reflex response to the bell ringing. Pavlov's experiments made scientists think more about how animals learn different types of behaviour.

Banting and Best

Frederick Banting (1891–1941) became interested in the disease diabetes and persuaded Professor John MacLeod at Toronto University to let him investigate its causes. A young student, Charles Best (1899–1978), came to help him. Banting and Best carried out a series of experiments that proved the hormone insulin can be used to treat diabetes. In 1922 a 14-year-old boy became the first person to be successfully treated using insulin. Banting and MacLeod were awarded the Nobel Prize for Medicine in 1923. Banting shared his prize money with Best.

Kary Banks Mullis (b.1944)

Kary Mullis trained as a biochemist. In 1981 he was studying small pieces of DNA, the chemical that makes up our genes. Scientists had a big problem with DNA because every piece is different. This meant that when they wanted to study a particular piece they had to copy it, and this was very difficult. Kary realized that it would be possible to use a chemical called a polymerase, which came from bacteria, to make millions of DNA copies quite easily. His idea became the polymerase chain reaction – one of the most important tools in the study of genetics. In 1983 he received a Nobel prize for his work.

Alexander Fleming

English discoverer of penicillin
Born 1881 Died 1955 aged 73

Alexander Fleming trained as a doctor at St Mary's Medical School, London, and spent his entire working life there. He became interested in the infections caused by bacteria that resulted in so much disease. He joined researchers looking for vaccines that would kill such bacteria.

One day in 1928, Fleming noticed that a mould had formed on one of his experimental dishes containing live bacteria. The bacteria next to the mould were dying. Fleming realized that the mould was producing a substance that killed the bacteria. The mould was called *Penicillium notatum*.

Fleming showed that penicillin could kill many dangerous bacteria, but he was

⬆ This stained-glass window, in St James's Church, London, depicts Alexander Fleming at work in his laboratory.

slow to see that it could be used as a medical treatment and, in any case, he found it difficult to produce except in very small quantities.

As a result there was little interest in penicillin until 1941, when Howard Florey, an Australian pathologist, Ernst Chain, a German-born biochemist, and other scientists at Oxford University found a way of making enough penicillin to begin treating patients with serious infections. The results were spectacularly successful. In 1945 Fleming, Florey, and Chain shared a Nobel prize for their work.

➋ The molecular structure of penicillin.

Crick and Watson

British and American discoverers of
the structure of DNA
Francis Crick Born 1916   Died 2004
aged 88
James Watson Born 1928

During World War II, Francis Crick was a physicist working on the development of radar. After the war his interest turned to a new science called molecular biology. Physicists and chemists were working together to try to unlock the secrets of chemicals found in the body. There was special interest in the chemicals we inherit from our parents that make us look like them. This information is contained in tiny structures called chromosomes, which are found in all the cells of the body. These chromosomes are made of a complicated chemical called dioxyribonucleic acid – DNA.

You cannot see the detailed structure of DNA under a microscope. Several scientists, including Maurice Wilkins and Rosalind Franklin in London, investigated DNA by firing X-rays at it. The X-rays produced patterns as they passed through the DNA, but they were difficult to understand.

A young American man called James Watson came to Cambridge and joined Crick in the difficult task of sorting out what those X-ray patterns meant. With a sudden flash of inspiration, Watson realized that a so-called double helix (a spiral within a spiral) could describe the structure of DNA. This led to an understanding of how DNA can make copies of itself. It was the key to all kinds of research on the features that animals and plants inherit from their parents, and in 1962 Crick, Watson, and Wilkins shared a Nobel prize.

◆ DNA is a double helix – rather like a twisted ladder.

↑ Crick and Watson with a model of the double helix-structure of DNA.

> ❝ We wish to suggest a structure for the salt of deoxyribonucleic acid, DNA. This structure has novel features which are of considerable biological interest. ❞
> WATSON AND CRICK

Chemists
Joseph Priestley

English chemist who discovered oxygen
Born 1733   Died 1804 aged 70

Joseph Priestley was a minister in the Unitarian Church and although he had no scientific education, he became very keen on doing experiments.

Priestley's real claim to fame is his outstanding work studying gases, and particularly his identification of oxygen, which he called 'dephlogisticated air'. The importance of oxygen in burning was shown by the great French chemist Antoine Lavoisier.

Priestley was forced to flee to London with his family when a mob burned down his home because of his support for the ordinary French people during the French Revolution. Before long it was not safe for him to remain in England and he quickly left for the United States. He was warmly welcomed and spent the rest of his life working mainly for the Unitarian Church.

Antoine Lavoisier

French chemist who became known as the 'father of modern chemistry'
Born 1743   Died 1794 aged 50

As a young man Antoine Lavoisier became interested in improving street lighting and studied how different fuels burnt in lamps. He went on to conduct careful experiments of burning substances in air, and the work of English chemist Joseph Priestley made Lavoisier realize that air contains two gases; he called one 'oxygen' and the other 'azote', which we now know as nitrogen. He proved that when a substance is burned it combines with oxygen in the air. Lavoisier went on to give chemicals many of the names we now use, and arranged them into family groups.

Lavoisier invested his money in a business called tax-farming. The tax-farmers were paid by the government to collect all the taxes. Many of the people were poor and hated tax-farmers. During the French Revolution they rebelled. Lavoisier was found guilty of being a tax-farmer and was executed.

↩ **This is the apparatus used by Lavoisier in his burning experiments.**

John Dalton

English chemist and physicist
Born 1766   Died 1844 aged 77

When John Dalton was only ten he went to work for a man called Elihu who was interested in science and who taught him mathematics. Dalton later became a lecturer at New College in Manchester, and then went to London to lecture at the famous Royal Institution.

In his early twenties he began to keep a diary, which was mainly notes and theories about the weather. When he died there were 200,000 entries. He suggested – correctly – that auroras, of which there was a specially brilliant display in 1787, were electrical in origin. However, his most important work was the development of his atomic theory. The Greeks of the ancient world had some ideas about atom,s but John Dalton was the first modern scientist to suggest that atoms of different elements had different weights.

Humphry Davy

English chemist, inventor of the miner's safety lamp
Born 1778   Died 1829 aged 51

As a boy Humphry Davy had an extremely good memory and was something of a showman. He used to stand on a cart in the marketplace of his home town and tell Cornish folk-stories to crowds of children. He was later apprenticed to a surgeon, and while he worked making up medicines and pills he became interested in chemistry. When he was 21 he began to study a gas called nitrous oxide, which is sometimes called laughing gas. It was later used to put people to sleep while they had their teeth pulled out.

Scientists today remember Davy because he discovered so many new chemical elements, including sodium, potassium, calcium, and barium. However, he is also remembered for his invention of the miner's safety lamp. In 1813 a dreadful gas explosion occurred in a mine and more than 90 miners were killed. Davy was asked to help prevent such accidents in the future. The safety lamp he invented, which had a flame enclosed in glass so that it could not ignite undetected gases, must have saved thousands of lives in the years to come.

Davy made many scientific discoveries, but he always said that his greatest discovery was a young man who came to work for him and who he influenced: his name was Michael Faraday.

See also Michael Faraday p. 108

Dimitri Mendeléev

Russian chemist who first arranged the 'periodic table' of chemical elements
Born 1834   Died 1907 aged 72

Dimitri Mendeléev was interested in the atomic weights of different elements and made a list of all 63 of the chemical elements known at that time, putting them in order of increasing atomic weight. He then rearranged the list into a continuous pattern of rows and columns, and found that all the elements in the same column were similar to one another. This arrangement of chemical elements is called the 'periodic table'.

Mendeléev found there were gaps, and he predicted that new elements would be

Mendeléev was professor of chemistry in the Russian University of St Petersburg.

discovered to fill these gaps. At first scientists were suspicious of Mendeléev's predictions, but within a few years some of these new elements were discovered.

Linus Pauling

American chemist
Born 1901   Died 1994 aged 93

Linus Pauling was awarded the 1954 Nobel Prize for Chemistry for his work on the structure of molecules. He used information from X-ray diffraction and other techniques to find the lengths of the bonds holding the atoms together and the angles between them. He then used quantum mechanics to explain how the bonds were formed. His ideas explained the shape of simple molecules and helped scientists to understand some very complicated molecules such as proteins.

Pauling was a pacifist and campaigned for many years against the testing of nuclear weapons. He published his views in a book called No More War! and also took a petition, signed by over 11,000 scientists, to the United Nations calling for a ban on weapons testing. He was awarded the 1962 Nobel Peace Prize for his efforts, thus making Pauling one of the few people to receive two different Nobel prizes.

Physicists

Christiaan Huygens

Dutch scientist who developed the pendulum clock
Born 1629   Died 1695 aged 66

Huygens was very good at making things. He made improvements to the telescope, which made it possible to observe the rings around Saturn for the first time. Huygens also built the first pendulum clock, which was more accurate than other clocks at that time. He also studied light, and concluded that it moves in waves that spread out, like ripples on a pond. But many scientists preferred Newton's idea that light is a stream of tiny particles. Huygens's 'wave theory' was ignored for 150 years, until Thomas Young was able to prove that light really does behave like a wave.

⬆ Huygens built the first pendulum clock.

⬆ The original manuscript of Newton's book on the theory of light and colour.

Isaac Newton

English scientist
Born 1642   Died 1727 aged 84

Isaac Newton went to Cambridge University when he was 19, and was already doing important research in his second year. But then, because of the great plague, he had to go home to Lincolnshire for two years until the danger of catching the disease was past.

Many people have heard the story of Newton watching an apple fall from a tree. He was thinking about the movement of the Earth, the Moon, and the planets. He realized that, just as the force of gravity pulled the apple to Earth, gravity keeps the Moon in its orbit. It is rather like a stone tied to a piece of string that you whirl around your head; if the string breaks, the stone is flung away. Without gravity the Moon would fly off into space.

Newton tried to make a telescope to study the stars, but found that if he used lenses the bright images had coloured edges. In trying to find out why this happened, he invented the mirror telescope. This does not give coloured edges, and many of our present-day telescopes are based on Newton's design. He was so persistent in asking questions about the coloured edges that he was the first person to discover that white light is a mixture of all the different colours. Raindrops make a rainbow and a prism makes a spectrum by splitting up the white light. Before Newton, people thought that the raindrops or the prism added the colour.

Newton's greatest book, written in Latin and usually called *The Principia* (1686–1687), has had an enormous effect on the way scientists have thought ever since.

≫ See also Christiaan Huygens p. 106, Gottfried Leibniz p. 116

James Watt

Scottish physicist and designer of a new steam-engine
Born 1736   Died 1819 aged 83

Having trained as a mathematical instrument-maker, James Watt was given a model of Thomas Newcomen's steam-engine to repair. He was intrigued by the machine and studied the model carefully. It was clearly a clever idea to use steam pressure to drive an engine, but Newcomen's design did not work well; it was very inefficient and wasted a lot of fuel.

Watt though he could improve on this design, and over the next ten years he made the steam-engine much more effective.

In 1775 he went into partnership with the businessman Matthew Boulton. Together they began manufacturing steam-engines based on the improved design. Although Watt had not actually invented the steam-engine it was because of his improvements that it became so effective.

See also George Stephenson p. 119, Thomas Newcomen p. 122

Alessandro Volta

Italian inventor of the first battery
Born 1745   Died 1827 aged 82

Luigi Galvani told Volta about a puzzling experiment: he had hung a piece of frog muscle on a brass hook, and when the muscle came in contact with some iron wire it twitched. Volta proved that it was the contact of the brass and the iron that produced the electricity and made the muscle twitch. Volta did many experiments with metals. He made a pile of coins of two different metals, separated the coins with card soaked in salt solution, and produced an electric current – the first battery.

➤ Volta's experiments led to the invention of the battery.

Hans Christian Oersted

Danish physicist who discovered electromagnetism
Born 1777   Died 1851 aged 73

Hans Oersted studied at the University of Copenhagen and, to complete his education, travelled to meet Europe's leading scientists. He learnt a lot and in 1806 was given a job at his old university. At a lecture in 1820, Oersted tried an experiment he had never done before. He put a compass underneath a wire and then switched on an electric current: the magnetized compass needle moved! Up to that time, scientists believed that electricity and magnetism were different forces. Oersted had proved that they were connected.

Study of this 'electromagnetism' led to many important inventions, such as the dynamo and the electric motor.

Robert Boyle (1627–1691)

Irish scientist Robert Boyle did much to establish the method and ideas of modern chemistry. He helped to explain ideas about atoms and elements. He insisted on the importance of doing experiments to test whether scientific ideas were really true. Boyle is best remembered for a law of physics: Boyle's Law tells us mathematically how the volume of a gas will alter when the pressure is changed.

Robert Hooke (1635–1703)

English scientist Robert Hooke studied the way metals behave when they are stretched, and described it in a way that we still call Hooke's Law. He also developed a new version of the microscope, which was more powerful than existing ones and which had several lenses. This was called the compound microscope. He described his invention and many other pieces of apparatus in his book *Micrographia*.

Henry Cavendish (1731–1810)

English scientist Cavendish's first work was helping with his father's experiments. Soon he was making discoveries of his own, particularly in chemistry and electricity. Cavendish found that hydrogen was a component of water, and investigated many of the properties of hydrogen gas. He also calculated the mass and density of the Earth.

Luigi Galvani (1737–1798)

Italian Luigi Galvani began to do experiments to test what electricity would do to muscles. Galvani used a machine to generate electricity and send it through frogs' legs. He noticed that the legs jumped. He then discovered he could do the same thing without the electrical machine. He touched the legs with a copper hook hanging from an iron rail and the legs twitched. He thought he had discovered 'animal electricity', but really he had found the starting point for making a simple battery.

Georg Ohm (1787–1854)

In 1827 German physicist Georg Ohm published a book that contained his famous law, which shows that the current flowing in an electric circuit is proportional to the voltage. This became known as Ohm's Law. Resistance to the current in an electrical circuit is measured in units called ohms. In 1841 the Royal Society of London acknowledged the importance of Ohm's work by awarding him its prestigious Copley medal.

William Kelvin (1824–1907)

British William Kelvin was a pioneer in the study of electromagnetism. He and Michael Faraday put forward the idea of an electromagnetic 'field'. Kelvin also worked in the field of thermodynamics. Most importantly, he put forward the idea of absolute zero – the temperature at which all molecules and atoms stop moving. The scientific unit of temperature is named after him.

Henri Becquerel (1852–1908)

French physicist Henri Becquerel was experimenting with X-rays. He put some uranium crystals on top of a photographic plate wrapped in paper and then left them in sunlight. When developed it showed the outline of the crystals. He left some of the crystals and a photographic plate in a drawer. When he developed it he was surprised to see an image of the crystals. He had found that the effect was not due to sunlight but something coming from the crystals themselves. In fact it was radiation coming from the uranium.

Abdus Salam (1926–1996)

Pakistani physicist Abdus Salam investigated the forces between the tiny particles that make up the parts of an atom. Salam shared the 1979 Nobel Prize for Physics with two others, Steven Weinberg and Sheldon Glashow. Their theories about the interactions between fundamental particles have since been tested by experiments and their predictions confirmed.

Michael Faraday

English scientist
Born 1791   Died 1867 aged 75

Faraday's most important work was with electricity and magnetism. Winding a coil of wire on to a piece of iron, he showed that when electricity was passed through the coil, the iron became a magnet. Then he wound another, separate coil on to the same piece of iron. When he switched on the current in the first coil he found that a current flowed in the second. He had discovered the transformer. Faraday found that if he took a hollow coil and moved a magnet in and out of it, a current flowed in the coil. He had invented the dynamo.

Faraday also had the knack of explaining what he was doing in a simple way, so that people could understand. He started the famous Royal Institution Christmas Lectures in 1826. These public lectures have been held every year since, except during World War I.

James Joule

English scientist who experimented with heat
Born 1818   Died 1889 aged 70

James Joule's father was a wealthy brewer. In his twenties, Joule helped run the brewery, but he always managed to find time for doing experiments. He had no proper education, but taught himself. He measured the amount of heat produced by all kinds of processes. He noticed that doing work always produces heat. The 'work' could be as different as boring a hole in a piece of metal, or pushing a wheel round with water. He found that a certain amount of work always produced a certain amount of heat.

Joule explained that energy is never destroyed – it is just changed into different forms. When you jump up and down you use lots of energy; when you stop jumping the ground you were jumping on will have got hot, and so will you. Your jumping energy has become heat energy. This is known as the 'law of the conservation of energy'.

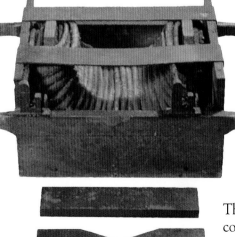

↩ Joule used this electromagnet in some of his experiments.

James Clerk Maxwell

Scottish physicist
Born 1831   Died 1879 aged 47

At 14 James Clerk Maxwell was asked to speak to scientists of the Royal Society of Edinburgh about his work in geometry, and when he was only 24 he became professor at Aberdeen University. He retired ten years later to write about his theories on electricity and magnetism. Then, at the age of 40, he was invited to become the first professor of experimental physics at Cambridge.

Some years before, the scientist Michael Faraday had talked about magnets and electric currents having 'lines of force' and had made pictures of them. Maxwell heard about this and developed a theory that explained it. He suggested that if the magnet moved back and forth it would make waves run along the lines of force Faraday had discussed.

Maxwell then made the amazing suggestion that light is in fact incredibly rapid waves on the lines of force. The waves are called 'electromagnetic waves'. He was able to prove that this is true. His mathematics also suggested that there ought to be other kinds of electromagnetic waves with shorter and longer wavelengths than light. He died before any of the others could be discovered, but we now know that radio, infrared, ultraviolet rays, X-rays, and gamma rays all belong to the electromagnetic wave family.

⊗ See also **Michael Faraday p. 108**

Wilhelm Röntgen

German scientist who discovered X-rays
Born 1845   Died 1923 aged 77

In 1895 Wilhelm Röntgen was doing experiments in which he applied a strong electric current to metal plates inside a glass tube from which most of the air had been removed. His tube was covered with black cardboard and the room was dark. To his amazement, he noticed that a chemical on the bench across the room was glowing. After many experiments he decided that the tube was giving out rays that went through both the glass and the cardboard. He called these rays X-rays. Today, X-rays are commonly used in hospitals or at the dentist to see inside the human body. For his work on X-rays, Röntgen was awarded the Nobel Prize for Physics in 1901.

⊙ This cartoon imagines what a beach scene might look like to the discoverer of X-rays, Wilhelm Röntgen.

Joseph Thomson

English physicist who discovered the electron
Born 1856   Died 1940 aged 83

In 1876, Joseph Thomson went to Trinity College, Cambridge. He stayed there for the rest of his life, becoming one of the university's most famous professors.

Thomson investigated the cathode rays given out when hot metals are placed in strong electric fields (these are the rays used in television tubes). He was trying to prove that these rays were streams of particles and not waves, as other physicists believed. To solve the problem, Thomson built a 'vacuum' tube in which he could bend a beam of rays using magnetic and electric fields. He then calculated the mass and charge of the particles in the beam. In 1897 he announced his remarkable results. At that time scientists believed that the hydrogen atom was the smallest piece of matter: Thomson's 'corpuscles' were about 1000 times lighter! He had found the first subatomic particle – the electron. He was awarded the Nobel Prize for Physics in 1906.

⊗ See also **Ernest Rutherford p. 111, Niels Bohr p. 112**

Heinrich Hertz

German physicist
Born 1857   Died 1894 aged 36

In 1865, James Clerk Maxwell predicted the existence of electromagnetic waves that could travel through a vacuum. Heinrich Hertz was encouraged to find them.

In 1888 he set up his most famous experiment. He used an electrical circuit to make sparks jump across a gap between two metal rods. He noticed that this caused pulses of electricity in a similar circuit some distance away. He had become the first person to broadcast and receive radio waves. The unit of frequency is called the hertz in his honour.

» See also James Clerk Maxwell p. 109

Max Planck

German physicist
Born 1858   Died 1947 aged 89

Max Planck spent much of his early research on thermodynamics – the branch of physics that deals with the transformation of heat into other forms of energy. In 1900 he solved a problem that had troubled scientists for a long time: hot objects radiate heat energy but the energy stops suddenly instead of tapering away gradually. Planck explained this by saying that energy is always transferred in fixed amounts, rather like money. Just as in money there is a smallest-value coin, so energy has a smallest value. It is called a quantum of energy. Planck's 'quantum theory' was one of the most important discoveries of the 20th century.

Marie Curie

French physicist and chemist
Born 1867   Died 1934 aged 66

Marie Curie was born Marya Sklodowska in Poland's capital, Warsaw. Women were not allowed to go to university in Poland at this time, so Marya worked hard as a governess so that she could go to study at the Sorbonne in Paris. When living in France, she changed her name to the French 'Marie'.

In 1894 Marie met a successful chemist called Pierre Curie, and within a year they were married. Working with her new husband, Marie Curie spent her whole life studying radioactive substances. She invented an instrument to measure radioactivity, and found that a substance called pitchblende (the ore from which uranium is extracted) was a thousand times more radioactive than uranium itself.

After several years' work, Marie and Pierre managed to separate the material that made pitchblende so radioactive. They called it radium and received a Nobel prize for their work. After her husband's death, Marie carried on with her work and received a second Nobel prize in 1911.

The dangers of radioactivity were not properly understood at that time, and Marie Curie suffered throughout her life from radiation burns on her skin. She eventually died from leukaemia.

⬆ Marie Curie at work in her laboratory.

Ernest Rutherford

New Zealand scientist who revealed the structure of atoms
Born 1871   Died 1937
aged 66

Ernest Rutherford grew up on his family's small farm in New Zealand. He was very clever and studied at university in New Zealand before going to Cambridge University in England.

At Cambridge he began work on the exciting new subject of radioactivity. He discovered that radioactive substances produce three different types of radiation. At this time, scientists were only just beginning to study the inside of atoms. For more than 2000 years atoms had been thought of as like tiny marbles, but Rutherford's experiments showed that in the centre of an atom there is a tiny, heavy blob – the nucleus – and that most of the atom consists of empty space.

⬆ Ernest Rutherford was awarded the Nobel Prize for Chemistry in 1908 for his work on radioactivity.

Rutherford gathered other brilliant scientists at the Cavendish Laboratory in Cambridge, including James Chadwick (who discovered the neutron) and John Cockcroft (who built an early version of a particle accelerator). The work of these and others, like Marie and Pierre Curie, Enrico Fermi and Niels Bohr, began a new age of physics: the 'nuclear age'. This has resulted in many advances, such as producing radiation for treating cancer, nuclear power stations, which generate electricity, as well as the introduction of nuclear weapons.

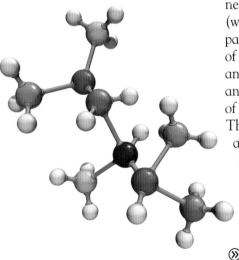

≫ See also Niels Bohr p. 112

Meitner and Hahn

Scientists who carried out important work on radioactivity
Lise Meitner Born 1878   Died 1968
aged 89
Otto Hahn Born 1879   Died 1968
aged 89

Lise Meitner was born in Austria and studied at Vienna University. Afterwards she moved to Berlin to study theoretical physics. Sexual prejudice at that time meant that she was not allowed to use the same laboratories as the men, so she worked in an old carpentry shop. In spite of this, she and her German colleague Otto Hahn did important work on radioactivity. In 1918 she and Hahn announced the discovery of a new radioactive element – protactinium.

After World War I Meitner returned to Berlin, but when Hitler came to power she was forced to flee Germany because of her Jewish origins. She took refuge in Sweden, where she eventually became a citizen. She continued working and in 1939 published a paper explaining how uranium nuclei could split after being bombarded with neutrons. During World War II, many scientists worked on atomic weapons, but Hahn worked on other projects. For their earlier work on radioactivity Meitner and Hahn were awarded the 1966 Enrico Fermi Prize for Atomic Physics. Meitner was horrified that her research had been used to develop the atomic bomb and after the war Hahn became an opponent of further research on atomic weapons.

≫ See also Enrico Fermi p. 113, J. Robert Oppenheimer p. 114

Albert Einstein

German-born physicist
Born 1879   Died 1955 aged 76

As a boy Albert Einstein was very unhappy at school because his teachers thought he was not very clever. But when he was 26, after moving to Switzerland, he published several scientific papers that completely changed the way scientists think. In 1921 he was given the top award in science, the Nobel prize.

Einstein had moved back to Germany, but when the Nazis started to gain power he suffered a lot of abuse because he was Jewish. In 1933 he went to America, where he lived for the rest of his life. He spent much of his time trying to persuade world leaders to abandon nuclear weapons.

Einstein's ideas in science were so new and strange that for many years ordinary people used to say that no one else could possibly understand them. But now his theories about time and space (relativity), and about how very tiny particles like electrons and protons behave (quantum theory) are important parts of the courses that all physics students learn.

🡑 Einstein is probably one of the few people who truly deserve the title 'genius'.

Niels Bohr

Danish physicist who helped discover the structure of atoms
Born 1885   Died 1962 aged 77

Niels Bohr worked with Ernest Rutherford, trying to discover what atoms looked like. Bohr's work showed that atoms have a nucleus at the centre and that electrons are arranged in orbits a fixed distance from the nucleus. In 1922 Bohr received the Nobel Prize for Physics.

During World War II Bohr fled from Denmark to America, where he worked on the atom bomb project. However, he was horrified by the potential effects of such a bomb and began working on peaceful uses of atomic energy.

Erwin Schrödinger

Austrian physicist
Born 1887   Died 1961 aged 73

When he was 39 Schrödinger developed a theory that described subatomic particles as waves. He applied his 'wave mechanics' to the hydrogen atom and got an equation that predicted results that other scientists had found but had not explained. He shared the 1933 Nobel Prize for Physics with Paul Dirac for this work.

Schrödinger tried hard to attach physical meaning to the symbols used in his equations but was never completely successful.

In 1933 he fled from Nazi Germany and eventually found refuge in Ireland, where he became senior professor at the Dublin Institute for Advanced Studies in 1940.

Enrico Fermi

Italian-born American nuclear physicist
Born 1901   Died 1954 aged 53

Enrico Fermi was a physics professor at the University of Rome. In 1932 he heard about James Chadwick's discovery of the neutron, a particle in the centre of atoms. Fermi decided to do some experiments with neutrons himself. He set up a target made of uranium and bombarded it with neutrons, hoping to make a new substance. Although at the time he did not realize it, he had in fact discovered nuclear fission, the basis of nuclear power and atom bombs. For this work he was awarded the Nobel Prize for Physics in 1938. Later, Otto Hahn explained what was happening during nuclear fission.

During World War II, Fermi worked in America developing the first nuclear reactor. It was built in a squash court at the University of Chicago. This work led directly to the making of the atom bombs that were dropped on Hiroshima and Nagasaki in Japan in 1945 towards the end of World War II.

⟫ See also **Meitner and Hahn p. 111**

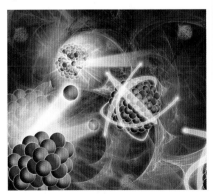

⬆ **This artwork demonstrates nuclear fission.**

⬆ German physicist Werner Heisenberg.

Werner Karl Heisenberg

German physicist
Born 1901   Died 1976 aged 74

Werner Karl Heisenberg studied at the German universities of Munich and Göttingen. Then, from 1924 to 1926, he went to work in Denmark with Niels Bohr. At that time the world's physicists were struggling with the fact that the electron sometimes behaves like a particle and sometimes like a wave. Heisenberg said that it was wrong to think of the electron in this way and suggested that we can only know about it by observing the light that it emits.

Using this idea he put together a method of predicting the behaviour of atomic particles. He was awarded the 1932 Nobel Prize for Physics for this work.

Heisenberg went on to show that we cannot measure an atomic particle's speed and position at the same instant. Each can be measured separately, but measuring one of them alters the other – so we cannot know both exactly. This is known as Heisenberg's Uncertainty Principle.

He was made director of Hitler's atomic bomb programme, but Germany was defeated before the work could be completed.

J. Robert Oppenheimer

American nuclear physicist
Born 1904   Died 1967 aged 62

Julius Robert Oppenheimer was a student at Harvard University before going to study in Europe, where he met the world's leading physicists. He then returned to America to conduct research into subatomic particles.

During World War II, Albert Einstein and others warned that if Nazi Germany developed a nuclear weapon then the rest of the world would be in great danger. In response the American government gathered together a group of scientists to build its own atomic bomb. Oppenheimer set up a laboratory at Los Alamos, New Mexico, and led the project. On 16 July 1945, Oppenheimer's team successfully tested the first atomic bomb. Three weeks later 'A-bombs' were used to destroy the Japanese cities of Hiroshima and Nagasaki, killing thousands of people.

See also Enrico Fermi p. 113

➲ In 1963 Oppenheimer was awarded the Enrico Fermi Award for Atomic Physics.

John Bardeen

American physicist
Born 1908   Died 1991 aged 83

Amplifiers, which make electrical signals stronger, and electronic switches were once big, expensive to operate, and were very easily broken. John Bardeen, along with scientists William Shockley and Walter Brattain, managed to create something much more efficient: the transistor.

Bardeen was born in Madison, Wisconsin, in America. After World War II he went to work at the Bell Telephone Laboratories. There he met Shockley and Brattain and they began doing experiments on how electricity passed through materials called semiconductors. Just before Christmas 1947, one of the scientists spoke into a microphone and the world's first semiconductor transistor amplified the electrical signal to make the words sound louder. For this work, the team won the Nobel Prize for Physics in 1956. The development of the transistor has made it possible to have such things as pocket calculators, digital watches, and laptops.

Bardeen then started work with another team, including J. R. Schrieffer and Leon Cooper. They investigated how some materials resist the flow of electricity whereas others – called superconductors – do not. By explaining how they worked, they earned the Nobel Prize for Physics in 1972. Bardeen was the first person to have won a Nobel prize twice for the same discipline.

Wernher von Braun

German rocket engineer
Born 1912   Died 1977 aged 65

Wernher von Braun was the son of a German baron. He became interested in rockets as a teenager after reading science-fiction books.

It was during World War II that the real importance of rockets was recognized: unmanned rockets could carry bombs to enemy targets. Von Braun, a member of the German Nazi Party, headed a team that developed the first true missile. It was called the V-2 ('V' stood for *Vergeltung*, which means 'vengeance'). This rocket was fuelled with alcohol and liquid oxygen, and had an explosive warhead. It could travel a distance of about 300 kilometres. More than a thousand V-2 rockets hit London during the war.

In 1945, just before the war ended, von Braun and many of the scientists he had been working with surrendered to the Americans. They took him to America, where he was put in charge of a rocket-building programme in New Mexico. This team eventually became part of the new National Aeronautics and Space Administration (NASA), and built the *Saturn 5* rocket, used to launch America's manned missions to the Moon.

> *I have learnt to use the word 'impossible' with the greatest caution.*
> WERNHER VON BRAUN

Stephen Hawking

English physicist
Born 1942

Stephen Hawking, one of the most brilliant thinkers of modern times, has been Lucasian Professor of Mathematics at Cambridge University since 1979 – the same position Isaac Newton once occupied. He is a worthy successor to that great scientist because his research into the nature of black holes, relativity, gravitation, and cosmology has been outstandingly important, influencing the work of many other scientists.

Hawking has travelled and lectured widely. Apart from his technical papers and books, he has also written highly successful publications for the general reader: his *A Brief History of Time* (1988) was a huge bestseller. His lengthy list of fellowships, prizes, medals, and honorary degrees is an acknowledgement of his intellectual service to humankind. To achieve all this he has triumphed over a crippling neurological condition that has confined him to a wheelchair for much of his career.

⬇ In *A Brief History of Time*, Hawking argues that our universe, and an infinite number of universes like it, are all part of one great 'super-universe'.

Mathematicians

René Descartes

French mathematician and philosopher
Born 1596   Died 1650 aged 54

When René Descartes was 25, after studying, travelling, and serving in the army, he decided to devote his life to the study of philosophy and science. He never married, although he had a daughter whose death was said to be his greatest sorrow. He died of pneumonia in Stockholm, where he had gone to teach philosophy to Queen Christina of Sweden.

Descartes made a number of advances in mathematics, including the use of Cartesian coordinates in geometry. In philosophy he explored the certainty of knowledge. In his most famous philosophical book, *Discourse on Method* (1637), he argued that everything should at first be doubted because we can only be convinced of the truth after satisfying our doubts. This proved to him that he at least existed, because if he did not exist he could not think, much less doubt, and so he coined his most famous phrase: 'I think, therefore I am.'

Gottfried Leibniz

German mathematician and philosopher
Born 1646   Died 1716 aged 70

Leibniz was one of the greatest thinkers of the 17th century. He tackled philosophical questions and was devoted to the cause of world peace. He was also a scientist and met Christiaan Huygens and Robert Boyle among others, and suggested new ideas about force, time, and energy.

His greatest discovery was calculus. Scientists use this to deal with quantities that are constantly varying. Newton had developed a similar method for his work on gravity and so there was a bitter row about who had been first. Newton had started work on it in 1665 but Leibniz published his results in 1684, three years before Newton. In fact, they probably discovered the method at the same time.

> " *Two things are identical if one can be substituted for the other without affecting the truth.*
> GOTTFRIED LEIBNIZ "

Blaise Pascal

French mathematician
Born 1623   Died 1662 aged 39

Blaise Pascal was a mathematical genius. By the age of 12 he had worked out the first 32 theorems of the ancient Greek mathematician Euclid. At 16 he published a geometry book about parts of cones called conic sections.

By the time he was 19 Pascal had invented a calculating machine for adding and subtracting numbers, but it was too expensive to make and was never used. Pascal was also very interested in Evangilista Torricelli's work with barometers. He proved that the atmosphere really does have weight by sending his brother-in-law up a mountain with a barometer. The level of mercury in the tube dropped the higher he went.

Ten years before he died Pascal became a devout Catholic, gave up his mathematical work and instead devoted his time to writing about religion and philosophy.

Leonhard Euler (1707–1783)

Swiss scientist Euler was a pioneer of pure mathematics and made major contributions to the fields of geometry, calculus, the theory of numbers, and to the practical application of mathematics. He worked for both Frederick the Great and Catherine the Great. Even went he went blind he did not stop working, and he continued to apply his skills to the fields of mechanics, optics, acoustics, and astronomy.

Pierre Laplace (1749–1827)

By the age of 18 Laplace had been appointed professor of mathematics at the Paris Military School. His work as an astronomer is reckoned by scientists to be second only to Isaac Newton's. Laplace studied the orbit of the Moon, and worked on the shape and rotation of Saturn's rings. He also introduced the nebular hypothesis of the origin of the Solar System: the theory that the Solar System originated from a cloud of gas.

Andrew Wiles (b.1953)

The 17th-century scientist Fermat was supposed to have proved that there are no solutions to a simple set of equations ($xn + yn = zn$), but the proof had been lost. In 1986 Englishman Wiles learned about a connection between Fermat and a more recent problem. He set to work to solve this. In 1993 he thought he had found the proof, but he was mistaken. It was another year before he could say he had solved Fermat's Last Theorem.

George Boole

English mathematician
Born 1815   Died 1864 aged 49

George Boole's father worked as a cobbler but was interested in mathematics and making optical instruments. He passed these interests on to his son who, by the time he was 15, was well-grounded in mathematics and had taught himself Latin, Greek, French, and German. In 1849, although he had no university degree, he was appointed professor of mathematics in Queen's College, Cork, and in 1857 was elected fellow of the prestigious Royal Society. At Cork he wrote 50 mathematical papers and four books, and developed what is still known as Boolean algebra. In this, logical statements are represented by algebraic equations, and the numbers 0 and 1 are used to represent 'false' and 'true'. Boolean algebra is fundamental to the operation of today's modern computers.

A computer-generated fractal image. The pattern of fractal images repeats endlessly.

Boolean mathematics is applied to modern computer science.

Benoit Mandelbrot

Polish-born American mathematician
Born 1924

Benoit Mandelbrot was born in Warsaw, Poland, and moved to Paris with his family in 1936. There he met an uncle who was an important mathematician. His uncle advised him to avoid geometry, but Mandelbrot liked geometry best of all branches of mathematics and continued to study it.

After World War II Mandelbrot moved to America and worked on various projects. He soon became interested in what he called 'fractal geometry' – a term used to describe shapes that are repeated indefinitely, each time smaller. Fractals can be generated on a computer screen and often resemble natural shapes. Because of this similarity, fractals can be used to create models of natural changes, for example how a coastline may change through erosion, or how tree roots branch out. Fractals can also create amazing computer art.

Engineers

Jethro Tull

English agricultural engineer
Born 1674   Died 1741 aged 66

Jethro Tull studied at Oxford University and in 1699 qualified as a lawyer before turning to farming instead.

At that time it was the custom for farmers to sow seed by hand, scattering handfuls as they walked up and down the fields. The crop then had to be weeded by hand. Tull invented a horse-drawn seed drill, which sowed the seed in parallel rows. When the weeds appeared they could be removed by a horse-drawn hoe. He described his method in a famous book called *Horse-Hoeing Husbandry*, published in 1731.

However, mechanized farming was slow to be adopted in England, where labour was then plentiful and cheap, although it quickly became popular in North America, where labour was scarce and expensive.

Thomas Telford

Scottish civil engineer
Born 1757   Died 1834 aged 77

Thomas Telford started working as an apprentice stonemason, but because of his skills, hard work, and constant thirst for knowledge, he became one of Europe's leading civil engineers. His canals, bridges, harbours, and roads can be found all over Britain, still in use today.

In 1793 Telford was given his first big project: to build the Ellesmere Canal, linking the rivers Severn and Mersey. This canal made his reputation. He was an outstanding road builder too, and his road from London to the Welsh port of Holyhead was one of the most important routes in the country. His famous Menai suspension bridge still carries this road to the island of Anglesey.

In 1820 the Institution of Civil Engineers invited Telford to be its first president. He held this post until his death, and his influence greatly helped civil engineering become a respected profession. In 1963 the town of Telford in Shropshire was named after him.

⏷ Telford engineered the Menai suspension bridge, which connects the Welsh mainland to Anglesey.

George Stephenson

English engineer and builder of the world's first public railway
Born 1781   Died 1848 aged 67

As a teenager George Stephenson had various jobs working with mining engines. He never went to school, but he taught himself to read by attending night-classes. He became a colliery engineer, and in 1812 was appointed to be an engine-builder at Killingworth colliery, near Newcastle.

Stephenson spent the rest of his working life designing and building railways and railway locomotives. Between 1814 and 1826 he built railway engines for pulling coal.

In 1823 he was put in charge of building a railway from Stockton to Darlington that would carry people. When it opened in 1825, Stephenson himself drove the engine that pulled the world's first steam-hauled passenger train. Stephenson's successes led to the building of railways throughout Britain. He also won a competition with his design for an efficient locomotive, called the *Rocket*, which was built by his son Robert. He used the money he had made from his inventions to set up schools for miners' children and night-schools for the miners so they could get an education.

> " *The rage for railroads is so great that many will be laid in parts where they will not pay.*
> GEORGE STEPHENSON "

Ferdinand de Lesseps

French engineer and diplomat
Born 1805   Died 1894 aged 89

Between the ages of 21 and 44, Ferdinand de Lesseps worked as a diplomat in several countries. During his late twenties he worked in Egypt. While there, he had the idea for the Suez Canal to connect the Mediterranean Sea to the Red Sea through Egypt. Work began in 1860. Progress was expensive and slow, but in 1869 the canal was opened.

His next project was the Panama Canal linking the Pacific and Atlantic oceans. It was dogged by technical and financial problems, and in 1893 Lesseps was found guilty of bribery. He died shortly afterwards.

» See also Gustave Eiffel p. 120

Isambard Kingdom Brunel

British engineer
Born 1806   Died 1859 aged 53

In 1830 Brunel entered a competition to design a bridge to span the Avon gorge in Bristol. He won, but his design for the Clifton suspension bridge was not completed until after his death.

In 1833 he was made chief engineer of the Great Western Railway Company. His main task was to build a railway between London and Bristol. It was one of the finest achievements of its day.

Brunel then became interested in steamships and he built the first steamship to cross the Atlantic, the *Great Western*, which was launched in 1838. His second ship, the *Great Britain*, had a screw-propeller and was built of iron. It was the largest ship of its time and the forerunner of modern ocean-going vessels.

⬇ Brunel's steamship *Great Eastern*.

John McAdam (1756–1836)

Scottish engineer John McAdam was appalled by the state of Britain's roads. He believed that they should be dug up and remade by laying 25 centimetres of small broken stones, each no bigger than 2.5 centimetres, on a flat, well-drained bed. The wheels of the carriages would then compact the stones until the surface was smooth. McAdam's system worked so well that today the word 'tar-macadam' or 'tarmac' is still used.

Gottlieb Daimler (1834–1900)

German Gottlieb Daimler wanted to improve on the internal combustion engines of the time. Daimler studied the work of other engineers, and in 1883 he built an engine that ran on petrol. It was much more powerful than any other internal combustion engine of the time. In 1885 he used one to make what was probably the world's first motorbike. He later built cars that used his engines.

Karl Benz (1844–1929)

German Karl Benz produced the first road vehicle to use the internal combustion engine, realizing that the engine and the carriage had to be designed together. He went on to build a three-wheeled car that was patented in 1886. He kept on improving his designs and by 1893 he was making four-wheeled cars that many people wanted to buy. He teamed up with Gottlieb Daimler, his former rival, to start the great Daimler-Benz company.

Auguste Piccard (1884–1962)

Auguste Piccard developed a keen interest in ballooning and in 1913 he made a 16-hour ascent. But his dream had always been 'to plunge into the sea deeper than any man before'. This he achieved, with his son Jacques, in a self-propelled diving machine called a bathyscaphe. They descended to over 3000 metres in 1953; Jacques – in a later vessel, the *Trieste* – went down to almost 11,000 metres in 1960.

Henry Bessemer

English pioneer of steel manufacture
Born 1813 Died 1898 aged 85

Henry Bessemer's father was an engineer who fled from France during the Revolution. He established an engineering works in England and it was there that Henry Bessemer, after only a basic education, became an ingenious and skilled engineer. At 17 he founded a small business of his own in London, making a variety of products ranging from graphite for pencils to printing machinery.

He flourished but his great success, in the 1850s, was a process for converting iron to steel by blowing air through it while molten. Steel was then scarce and expensive. By 1898, when Bessemer died, more than a million tonnes per year were being made in Britain alone by his process and it was also widely used abroad. Its only rival was the Siemens open-hearth process. Much of the steel produced by Bessemer's methods went into rails for the rapidly expanding railway system.

Gustave Eiffel

French engineer
Born 1832 Died 1923 aged 91

Gustave Eiffel was born in Dijon, France. He was interested in building with iron girders and he designed several large bridges and structures, including the framework for the Statue of Liberty, which stands in New York Harbor.

In 1889, there was a competition to design a monument for the anniversary of the French Revolution. Eiffel's winning design was an iron tower measuring over 300 metres high. Although it was tall, it took only two years to build (1887–1889) and earned Eiffel the nickname 'magician of iron'. It was meant to last for 20 years but is still there today.

Eiffel also designed lock gates for the Panama Canal (1896). There was a scandal over the money for building it and Eiffel was one of those imprisoned.

⟫ See also **Ferdinand de Lesseps** p. 119

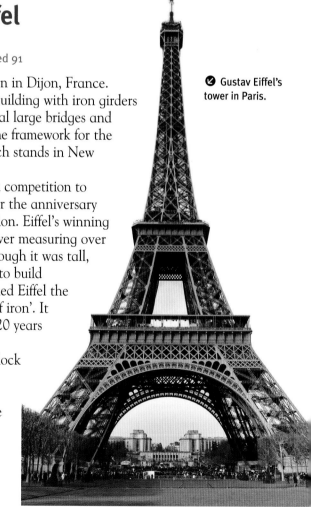

🔍 Gustav Eiffel's tower in Paris.

Robert Goddard

American rocket engineer
Born 1882   Died 1945 aged 62

Robert Goddard joined the Palmer Physical Laboratory, where he began to research radio. His real interest was in rockets, though, and he would spend his evenings trying to work out how to send a rocket beyond Earth's atmosphere.

During World War I the army realized that rocket science might help it develop new weapons and it gave Goddard a grant to help in his research. Goddard and his team set to work, but then the war ended and people were no longer interested in rocket research. Goddard kept working though and in 1926 he tested his first liquid-propelled rocket. Over the next few years he refined the design until he had a rocket that could reach an altitude of 2300 metres.

During World War II Goddard went to the US military and showed them his rocket, convinced that it could be adapted and used as a weapon. The V-1 and V-2 rocket weapons were eventually developed based on his designs.

IN 2 TAGEN NACH NORD-AMERIKA!
DEUTSCHE ZEPPELIN-REEDEREI

Ferdinand von Zeppelin

German airship builder
Born 1838   Died 1917 aged 78

Ferdinand von Zeppelin, a Prussian army officer, designed his first hydrogen-filled airship and launched it in 1900. It did not fly well but Zeppelin improved the design and, before long, his airships were making flights lasting many hours. The German government ordered a whole fleet of them, and in World War I used over a hundred 'zeppelins' to bomb enemy cities, including London.

Zeppelin started the first airship passenger airline in 1909. Although he died before intercontinental airship travel became a reality, by the 1930s huge zeppelins were flying across the Atlantic. The most famous were the *Graf Zeppelin* and the *Hindenburg*. In 1937, though, the *Hindenburg* burst into flames, killing 36 people.

Igor Sikorsky

Russian-born American aeronautical engineer
Born 1889   Died 1972 aged 83

In 1939 Igor Sikorsky built the world's first commercially successful helicopter. Large numbers were made, mainly for military purposes.

Sikorsky had trained as an engineer in Russia and in 1908, after meeting the aeroplane pioneer Wilbur Wright in Paris, he returned home to give serious attention to fixed-wing aircraft. In 1913 he built the first four-engined passenger aeroplane. In 1919 he emigrated to America. There he produced successful 'flying boats', which, in the 1930s, were used for passenger services across the Atlantic and the Pacific oceans. However, he still pursued his dream of a vertical take-off aircraft and this was realized with his VS-300 model in 1939.

» See also **Wright Brothers p. 126**

⬆ Sikorsky at the controls of the Sikorsky VS-300 on 14 September 1939.

Inventors

Johann Gutenberg

German inventor of printing in Europe
Born *c*.1400   Died *c*.1468 aged about 68

Before Johann Gutenberg's invention, most books were handwritten, with a few produced using carved wooden blocks. Both methods were slow, so few books were available and these were very expensive. Only monasteries, universities, and the very wealthy could afford them.

Gutenberg was skilled at working with metals, and invented a mould with which he was able to cast a lot of identical copies of each letter of the alphabet on metal stamps. The stamps could be put together to form words, and arranged to make whole pages. Any number of copies could be made on paper, using a specially built press.

Gutenberg's best-known work is called the Gutenberg Bible. He began to print pages of this in 1452 and it took him until 1456 to finish it and print only 300 copies. He gave up printing altogether in 1460. He had made little money out of it, and died a poor man.

◗ A statue of Johann Gutenberg.

Thomas Newcomen

British inventor of an early steam-engine
Born 1663   Died 1729 aged 66

Thomas Newcomen was a blacksmith. In 1698 he used his skill in working with metal to build a steam-engine. Seven years earlier a military engineer called Thomas Savery had built the first steam-engine. It could be used to pump water out of a mine or well, but it was very dangerous because it required enormous steam pressure, which could easily burst the pipes. Newcomen developed a much safer engine, but it was rather slow

➔ Newcomen's steam engine.

and could not do a lot of work. About 60 years later James Watt found a way of making the engine work much better, and this engine was used to drive machines in many different industries. The steam-engine was one of the important developments that led to the Industrial Revolution.

James Hargreaves

English inventor of the spinning 'jenny'
Born *c*.1720   Died 1778 aged about 58

Spinning wheels have been used for thousands of years to twist the wool fibres from sheep into the long threads or 'yarns' used for weaving. In about 1764 an uneducated weaver from Lancashire called James Hargreaves invented a machine that one person could use to spin several threads at the same time. He called this machine a 'jenny' after his young daughter.

Other spinners thought that Hargreaves' machine would put them out of work because it was so fast. They broke into his house and destroyed his jennies and his weaving loom. This scared him and so he moved his family to Nottingham, where he set up a small mill to spin yarn.

In 1770 Hargreaves received a patent for his invention but he never became rich, even though there were thousands of jennies in use by the time he died.

⟩⟩ See also Richard Arkwright p. 123

Joseph-Marie Jacquard

French inventor of the automatic loom
Born 1752   Died 1834 aged 82

Weaving plain cloth on a loom is easy because the cross-thread (weft) passes over one long thread (warp) then under the next, then over the next, and so on. Making patterned cloth is complicated because the weft passes under a different set of threads each time. If the operator makes a mistake, the pattern is ruined.

In 1805 Joseph-Marie Jacquard invented an automatic loom. This used a chain of cards punched with holes to control needles and hooks attached to the warp threads. Where a card had a hole the needle went through and the hook was lifted up. This lifted the correct set of warp threads. By using a different set of cards a different pattern could be woven.

Local weavers were afraid that Jacquard's loom would put them out of work. They burnt his machines and tried to drown him in the river Rhône. He survived, however, and the French government paid him for his invention. Jacquard's design was so successful that it quickly spread throughout the world and is still used today.

Samuel Morse

American inventor of Morse code
Born 1791   Died 1872 aged 80

Samuel Morse studied painting in London and worked as a successful portrait painter in America for many years. But Morse was also a scientist. On a return voyage to America, a fellow passenger demonstrated some electromagnetic devices. Morse realized he could adapt them to make an electric current put dots and dashes on paper, and he invented a dot-and-dash code for each letter of the alphabet. He used it to send coded messages along a wire to an electrical receiver, which printed the dots and dashes. It was the quickest way to communicate over long

⬆ A telegraph machine, used for sending messages in Morse code.

distances, and more successful than telegraph systems in Europe.

In 1843 Morse constructed a 65-kilometre telegraph between Baltimore and Washington for the American government. Soon other towns and cities were linked, and he became rich and famous.

Richard Arkwright (1732–1792)

Arkwright's claim to fame is his 'spinning frame' – a machine for spinning cotton. He made it with the help of a skilled watchmaker, John Kay. Arkwright went on to invent and improve other machines used in textile manufacture. Many workers found their jobs were taken over by the new machines. They tried to destroy the machines, but Arkwright's factories helped his home county of Lancashire become the centre of the world's cotton industry.

Montgolfier Brothers

Joseph (1740–1810) and Jacques (1745–1799) Montgolfier wanted to make the first passenger balloon. On 15 October 1783, François Pilâtre de Rozier went up in the brothers' tethered balloon. Later, Pilâtre de Rozier and his friend the Marquis d'Arlandes took off in Paris in the Montgolfiers' balloon and travelled nine kilometres in 25 minutes, until the brazier they carried burnt a hole in the balloon.

Nikolaus Otto (1832–1891)

German inventor Nikolaus Otto created the ancestor to the internal combustion engine, which used a four-stroke firing sequence. During the next ten years he sold 30,000 of his engines – the 'silent Otto' – but then his patent was declared invalid. Unknown to Otto the principle of his engine had already been patented in 1862.

John Dunlop (1840–1921)

During the 1880s, bicycles became very fashionable. They usually had solid rubber tyres, but Dunlop had the idea of a hollow tyre with air pressure inside it. He patented his 'pneumatic' tyre in 1888. He never made a fortune out of it, though, because his tyres were stuck to their wheels with glue, making it very difficult to mend punctures. They only became popular when other inventors came up with methods of keeping pneumatic tyres fixed to wheels.

Charles Babbage

English mathematician and inventor
Born 1792 Died 1871 aged 78

Charles Babbage calculated a correct table of logarithms, which meant mathematical calculations could be done very accurately. However, most of his life was filled with his determination to build his own calculating machine. The project was never completed, mainly because the sort of machine that could be built at that time was too clumsy to do the work Babbage wanted it to do. Nevertheless, Babbage is often regarded as the 'grandfather of the modern computer'.

» See also Blaise Pascal p. 116

Alfred Nobel

Swedish inventor of dynamite who left a fund for the Nobel prizes
Born 1833 Died 1896 aged 63

Alfred Nobel's father invented a submarine mine, and went on to manufacture explosives. Alfred became obsessed with what his father was doing. During his own experiments, Alfred's factory blew up, killing his brother, but he later invented a much safer explosive that he called 'dynamite'.

Nobel had hoped that terrible weapons would prevent war because no one would dare use them. He was wrong. In his will he left a fund of over $9 million to give prizes (Nobel prizes) in the fields of literature, physics, chemistry, physiology and medicine, peace, and economics. They have become the highest award anyone can be given.

The inventor of the telephone, Alexander Graham Bell.

Alexander Graham Bell

Scottish-born American inventor of the telephone
Born 1847 Died 1922 aged 75

Like other members of his family, Alexander Graham Bell trained to teach people to speak clearly. He went to America to continue this work and became convinced that he could teach totally deaf people to speak, even though they were unable to hear the sounds they were trying to imitate. He was also interested in other kinds of science, and was offered financial help towards his experiments from the parents of two deaf students whom he had taught to speak. One of his experiments led to his invention of the telephone, and he set up a company to develop and make telephones for sale.

In 1898 Bell became president of the National Geographic Society, and was so convinced that one of the best ways of teaching was through pictures that he started the *National Geographic* magazine, which is now world-famous for its superb colour pictures.

Thomas Edison

American inventor of the phonograph
and the electric lamp
Born 1847   Died 1931 aged 84

Thomas Edison is one of the most famous inventors in history. His mother taught him at home and encouraged his interest in science. By the time he was ten he had made his own laboratory and was conducting scientific experiments.

Edison set up his own company, which he called his 'invention factory'. One of his most important inventions was the world's first machine for recording sounds – the phonograph. The whole of our modern recording industry developed from this.

Edison also invented the electric lamp. It consisted of a wire inside a glass bulb, from which all the air had been taken out to create a vacuum. When an electric current was passed through the wire, called a filament, it glowed white-hot and gave out light. While experimenting, Edison found that a current could also flow across the vacuum to a plate inside the bulb. He did not understand why, but we know today it is due to electrons escaping from the filament: it is known as the Edison Effect. This discovery led to the invention of electronic valves and was the beginning of our modern electronics industry.

> 66 *Just because something doesn't do what you planned it to do doesn't mean it's useless.*
> THOMAS EDISON 99

Lumière Brothers

French inventors of the first films
Auguste Lumière Born 1862
Died 1954 aged 91
Louis Lumière Born 1864
Died 1948 aged 83

↑ The Lumière brothers opened the world's first cinema in Paris to show their films.

Auguste and Louis Lumière's father, Antoine, was an artist and photographer. The boys were extremely clever and when Louis was only 18 they started a factory for making photographic plates.

In 1894 Antoine visited Paris where he saw Thomas Edison's 'kinetoscope', a machine where you looked through a hole at a series of pictures inside a spinning drum. He was amazed by the appearance of movement this created. When he told his sons about it, they immediately set about solving the problem of projecting moving pictures on to a screen. Louis designed a mechanism for holding each 'frame' in front of the light beam for a split second before moving the next one into position.

In 1895 the Lumière brothers demonstrated their *cinématographe* in Paris. Their first film simply showed workers leaving the Lumière factory, but the cinema industry was born.

Wright Brothers

American flying pioneers who built and
flew the first aeroplane
Wilbur Wright Born 1867   Died 1912
aged 45
Orville Wright Born 1871   Died 1948
aged 76

Orville Wright was a champion
cyclist, and so the two brothers set
up a shop where they made and
sold bicycles. Neither of the
brothers had a proper education,
but they had tremendous
mechanical skills. They both
enjoyed the new sport of gliding,
and decided to try to build a
bicycle with wings and a petrol
engine to drive a propeller round.

By 1903 the Wright brothers
had built *The Flyer*. It was a
biplane (with two sets of wings)
and the pilot lay flat across the
lower wing. A series of bicycle
chains and gears connected the
engine to two propellers, which
rotated at about 450 times a
minute. On 17 December 1903,
at Kitty Hawk in North Carolina,
Orville Wright made a 12-second
flight over a distance of 36 metres.

This was the first aeroplane flight
in history. Later that morning
Wilbur flew for nearly a minute.
They carried on building better
planes and in 1905 Wilbur flew
38 kilometres in a half-hour flight.

Wilbur died of typhoid fever in
1912, and his brother Orville gave
up building planes.

> " *No flying machine will
> ever fly from New York
> to Paris.*
> ORVILLE WRIGHT "

⬆ In 1903 the Wright brothers made the first-ever powered flight in their hand-built aeroplane, *The Flyer*.

Guglielmo Marconi

Italian pioneer of radio
Born 1874   Died 1937 aged 63

Guglielmo Marconi began his
experiments in sending radio
signals in Italy before deciding
to move to England.

Marconi realized that if signals
were to travel long distances he
needed to have a very high aerial,
so he began to use balloons and
kites to get the aerial to the
right height.

In 1897 he sent a signal just
over 14 kilometres across the
Bristol Channel. Two years later
he set up his apparatus in two
American ships and was able to
report on the America's Cup yacht
race. This caused great excitement
and Marconi became famous. But
some scientists still did not believe
that you could send signals very
far. They thought the waves
would go straight up and get
lost in space.

In 1901 Marconi finally
convinced everyone that he
was right by sending a signal
all the way from Cornwall to
Newfoundland. It was later proved
that the waves bounced back off
special layers in the atmosphere,
and that was how they were able
to travel round the world.

John Logie Baird

Scottish inventor of the first television
Born 1888   Died 1946 aged 57

John Logie Baird's early ideas flopped and by the time he was 35 he was penniless. But in 1923 he started work on a machine that could transmit pictures, as well as sound, by radio. Soon he was able to send crude images by wireless transmitter to a receiver a few feet away. Then, in January 1926, he gave the first public demonstration of television at the Royal Institution in London.

In 1929 the BBC made the first television broadcast, using Baird's equipment. Baird was also responsible for the first sight and sound broadcast and the first outside broadcast (the Derby in 1931). A rival television system, which made use of cathode-ray tubes, took over from Baird's in 1933 and is still in use today.

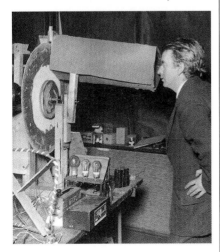

⬆ Baird looking at a picture on the screen of his first television set.

The Gloster E28/39, in which Frank Whittle's jet engine was tested in 1941.

Frank Whittle

English inventor of the jet engine
Born 1907   Died 1996 aged 89

In 1927, as a 20-year-old flight cadet studying at the Royal Air Force College, Frank Whittle wrote a paper on 'Future Developments in Aircraft Design'. He suggested that aeroplanes would soon be flying at more than 800 km/h (the fastest at the time was 300 km/h), at great heights, and with jet engines rather than propellers.

In 1929, Whittle tried to persuade the Air Ministry that jet propulsion was possible. His engine would burn cheap fuel oil; the gases produced would turn turbine blades as they rushed out, and the force of the gases would drive the plane forward. However, the Air Ministry was not interested in his invention, so Whittle went back to flying.

Later, Whittle started a company called Power Jets Ltd. The RAF let him work full-time on his engine, and it was tried, on the ground, on 12 April 1937. A special aeroplane, the Gloster E28/39, was designed to take the engine, and on 15 May 1941 it flew for the first time. It was a great success.

As Whittle had predicted, the jet engine was more efficient than earlier engines when used at high speeds and great altitudes, and by 1944 Power Jets Ltd was producing the first jet fighter. Whittle's jet engine went on to power most modern aeroplanes.

⬇ Frank Whittle's jet engine.

Astronomers
Claudius Ptolemy

Egyptian astronomer and geographer
Lived during the 2nd century

Ptolemy lived and worked in Alexandria from 127 to 151. His great book *The Almagest* was published in about 140. This was an encyclopedia of all that was known in astronomy in Ptolemy's day and was accepted as the truth about the Solar System for about 15 centuries. It taught that the Earth was the centre of the universe, with the Sun, Moon, planets, and stars all revolving about our planet. Ptolemy also published an important book on the principles of geography, in which he dealt with the problems of constructing accurate maps. The book contained a map of the known world.

Ptolemy's books were preserved and much later were translated and studied by Arabian astronomers, who found that they had to modify his theories to fit their more accurate observations. Ultimately Ptolemy's Earth-centred theory of the universe was replaced by Copernicus's Sun-centred theory.

Nicolaus Copernicus

Polish astronomer
Born 1473   Died 1543 aged 70

Nicolaus Copernicus was very well-educated and studied mathematics, law, and medicine, before becoming an astronomer.

At that time everyone believed that the Earth was at the centre of the universe. But Copernicus realized that this picture did not agree with his observations. He worked out that the Sun must be at the centre, with all the planets moving round it. He also said that the Earth takes a year to travel round the Sun, and revolves on its own axis once every 24 hours.

Copernicus wrote his theory in a famous book,

◐ Nicolas Copernicus, holding a model of the celestial spheres.

De Revolutionibus (1543), but he did not publish it straight away. It was only printed just before he died.

Copernicus's ideas were considered very controversial. They challenged the views about the Solar System held since the time of the Ancient Greeks. They also challenged the Church's belief that God created the Earth at the centre of the Universe. In 1616 Copernicus's book was regarded as a source of evil ideas and put on the Index – a list of books that Roman Catholics were forbidden to read. It was not until 1835 that Copernicus's book was removed from the Index.

Tycho Brahe

Danish astronomer
Born 1546   Died 1601 aged 54

At university Tycho Brahe studied philosophy and other subjects. But on 21 August 1560 something happened that changed his life. It was predicted that on that day a small eclipse of the Sun would be seen in Copenhagen. Brahe was thrilled when the eclipse took place at the predicted time. He immediately turned his attention to astronomy and mathematics.

Brahe used various astronomical instruments for measuring the positions of stars and planets, but could only observe with the naked eye because Galileo's telescope was not yet invented. Before he died Brahe passed on his astronomical measurements to his assistant Johannes Kepler, who later used them to produce the first accurate description of the movement of planets in our Solar System.

Brahe was a colourful figure who often courted trouble. He lost his nose in a duel when he was 19.

Galileo Galilei

Italian astronomer; the first person to use a telescope to study the Solar System
Born 1564   Died 1642 aged 77

Galileo Galilei is nearly always referred to just by his first name. He was the eldest of seven children, whose father was a musician and scholar from one of the noble families of Florence. Galileo himself became a good organist and enjoyed playing the lute, but it was his contributions to science that made him famous. His father sent him to the University of Pisa to study medicine, but he was much more interested in mathematics and physics. In 1589 he became a professor of mathematics.

In 1609 Galileo made a small telescope, having heard about this new invention in the Netherlands. Through his observations of the planets, he discovered four moons circling the planet Jupiter, craters on the Moon, spots on the Sun, and rings around Saturn. He also observed that the planet Venus has phases like the Moon's. This could only mean that Venus travelled around the Sun. Galileo became convinced that the Earth

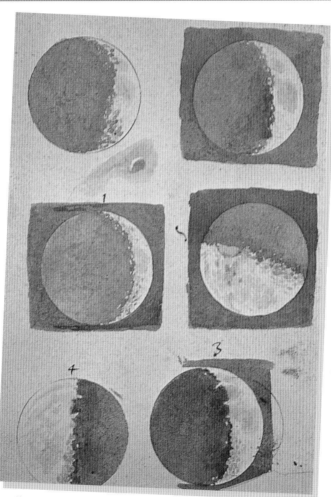

Galileo's sketches of the phases of the Moon.

and all the other planets orbit the Sun rather than the other way round.

At that time the Christian Church thought any idea that the Earth was not the centre of the universe went against the Scriptures. The book published by the astronomer Copernicus in 1543, setting out such a theory, had been officially banned by the Church. Galileo's views on the subject and the books he wrote got him into serious trouble with the Church. As the Church was very powerful in those days, Galileo was forced to say publicly that he did not agree with Copernicus in order to avoid torture or even execution. Although he made this declaration, Galileo never really changed his beliefs about the Solar System.

Johannes Kepler

German astronomer
Born 1571   Died 1630 aged 58

Johannes Kepler was the son of a soldier. His early intention was to be a Lutheran Church minister and he studied theology at university. But it turned out that he had a flair for mathematics, and his interest in astronomy grew.

In 1594 he became a professor of mathematics at Graz, where he settled and married. Four years later the family was forced to flee because of religious persecution, and he went to work for the Danish astronomer Tycho Brahe. When Brahe died in 1601, Kepler got his job. He also inherited a huge number of Brahe's astronomical observations.

⬆ Johannes Kepler discovered three important laws of planetary motion.

Using Brahe's observations of Mars, Kepler proved that the planet's orbit around the Sun is an oval shape and not a circle. Later he worked out two more important laws about the orbits of the planets.

Edmond Halley

English astronomer remembered for his work on Halley's comet
Born 1656   Died 1742 aged 85

While studying at Oxford University Edmond Halley became a good astronomer and mathematician. He was so keen on astronomy that he left Oxford before getting his degree to spend two years on the island of St Helena in the South Atlantic, making charts of the southern sky. Halley also made studies of the Earth's magnetism, tides, and weather.

In 1703 he became a professor at Oxford, and in 1720 was made Astronomer Royal. Halley worked out that a bright comet seen in 1682 was the same one that had appeared in 1531 and 1607. He correctly predicted that it would be seen again in 1758, although he did not live to see it. It is now called Halley's Comet.

❝ *Scarce any problem will appear more hard and difficult, than that of determining the distance of the Sun from the Earth.* ❞
EDMOND HALLEY

William and Caroline Herschel

German-born British astronomers
William Herschel Born 1738
Died 1822 aged 83
Caroline Herschel Born 1750
Died 1848 aged 97

William and his sister Caroline Herschel settled in England in the 1770s and William started to build his own telescopes.

In 1781 he discovered the planet Uranus, the first to be found with the help of a telescope. This discovery changed his life. King George III supported Herschel financially so he could devote himself completely to astronomy.

Herschel directed his energy towards making observations of a much higher quality than anyone had done before. He made catalogues of nebulas and double stars, and discovered moons around Uranus and Saturn.

Caroline Herschel soon became his devoted assistant and an expert herself. She went on to do research of her own, discovering new comets and nebulas.

⬇ This huge mirror telescope was built by William Herschel.

El Greco

Spanish painter
Born 1541   Died 1614 aged 73

Even though Domenikos Theotocopulous was born on the Greek island of Crete, he lived in Toledo, Spain, from 1577 until he died. He became known by his nickname El Greco, which is Spanish for 'The Greek'. Little is known of his youth. He studied in Venice under Titian, and in Rome, but it was in Toledo that he developed his own distinctive style. He mainly painted religious scenes, using distorted figures, which looked longer or shorter than in real life, and great contrasts of colour and light to express the great emotions of the spiritual events he portrayed.

The strangeness of his art inspired theories that he was mad, and people did not really understand his work during his lifetime, but his paintings do express the intense religious feeling of his adopted country of Spain.

> *Artists create out of a sense of desolation. The spirit of creation is an excruciating, intricate exploration from within the soul.*
> EL GRECO

◖ El Greco's paintings, like *The Adoration of the Shepherds* (left), seem more like 'modern' art than those of other artists of his time. His work greatly influenced later artists.

Michelangelo Merisi da Caravaggio

Italian painter
Born 1571   Died 1610 aged 38

Caravaggio went to Rome when he was about 20 and for several years struggled to earn a living. However, his reputation grew and he started to win important commissions from the Church. His paintings were bold and exciting. The people in them looked real and solid because he used real Roman people as models for his saints and madonnas. He had a highly original way of using light and shade, so that the most important parts of the picture stood out dramatically from the background. At the age of 35 he was famous all over Europe, and half the painters in Rome were trying to imitate him. In 1606 he killed a man over a petty argument and fled from Rome.

➔ Caravaggio's *Medusa*.

135

Peter Paul Rubens

Flemish painter and ambassador
Born 1577   Died 1640 aged 62

When he was 14 Peter Rubens became an apprentice painter in Antwerp; seven years later he became a master painter. When he was 23 he travelled to Italy to learn about art and to develop his own extraordinary talents.

He had a charming personality and became adviser as well as court painter to the Spanish rulers of Flanders, and they sent him to Spain and England. He spoke several languages well and combined the two careers of painter and diplomat.

When the demand for his paintings became too great, he set up a studio with several first-class assistants. They kept up a huge output of paintings, which Rubens planned and finished off himself. His paintings (usually on biblical or mythological subjects) are crowded with figures, but seem spacious and light. His work is bold, energetic, full of colour, splendour, and optimism.

At the age of 53, four years after the death of his first wife, he married a 16-year-old girl, Hélène Fourment. His interest in his new young family can be seen in the more domestic paintings of his last ten years.

↑ Rubens' painting *The Kidnapping of Ganymede* is full of movement and colour.

Diego Velázquez

Spanish painter
Born 1599   Died 1660 aged 61

Diego Velázquez produced masterpieces when he was still in his teens. When he was 24 he painted a portrait of Philip IV of Spain. The king was so impressed that he declared that no other artist would be allowed to paint him.

Philip gave Velázquez various court posts, which only left him time to paint about three pictures a year. However, these include some of the finest portraits in the world. He depicted his subjects with great sympathy, whether he was portraying king or commoner.

Rembrandt van Rijn

Dutch painter
Born 1606   Died 1669 aged 63

Rembrandt used his family as models, and mastered the skill of painting facial expressions. He particularly loved to paint portraits and painted himself 60 times. Rembrandt's sufferings began with the death of three of his children, then of his mother and of his wife, leaving him with one son, Titus. His pictures became less popular, and debts made him practically bankrupt.

As he grew older, Rembrandt became extra-sensitive to the real person behind the face he was painting. He no longer bothered with people's clothes or with backgrounds, but concentrated on the true personality. His sombre final paintings reflect Rembrandt's loneliness in his last years.

Jean-Antoine Watteau

French painter
Born 1684 Died 1721 aged 36

Jean-Antoine Watteau was the most important French painter of the early 18th century. He was born in Valenciennes, but when he grew up he moved to Paris to make his living as a painter. He specialized in scenes called *fêtes galantes* (which can be translated as 'scenes of gallantry' or 'courtship parties'). They showed beautifully dressed young people idling away their time in dreamy, romantic settings, and they demonstrate the artist's interest in theatre and ballet.

Watteau's style was exquisitely graceful and charming; it set the tone for the light-hearted approach that was followed by many later 18th-century French artists. However, Watteau was not simply a frivolous painter. His pictures have an underlying feeling of sadness, for the people in them seem to realize that all earthly pleasure is short-lived. Watteau himself died young, of tuberculosis.

Thomas Gainsborough

English painter
Born 1727 Died 1788 aged 61

Thomas Gainsborough was born in Sudbury, Suffolk, and he loved the local East Anglian countryside. Landscape painting was his greatest joy, but he could make more money by painting portraits, so he reluctantly devoted most of his time to that. He worked in Ipswich and Bath, and in London where he settled in 1774. His only real rival as the leading British portrait painter of his time was Sir Joshua Reynolds. They were completely different in temperament (Gainsborough was easygoing and often unpunctual in his work; Reynolds was sober-minded and the complete professional), but they enjoyed a great mutual respect.

Gainsborough painted some of the most graceful and dignified

⬆ *Giovanna Baccelli* by Gainsborough.

portraits (particularly of beautiful women) in the history of art, and although landscape remained a 'sideline' for him, he was an inspiration to his great East Anglian successor, the landscape artist John Constable.

Anthony van Dyck (1599–1641)

Anthony van Dyck worked as an assistant to Rubens for two years, and then branched out. He lived in Italy from 1621 to 1628, but settled in England in 1632 as court painter to Charles I. Charles was a great art lover and van Dyck painted many portraits of him and his family. Van Dyck also painted religious scenes and landscapes, but it is as a portraitist that he ranks among the greatest painters of all time.

Jan Vermeer (1632–1675)

Not very much is known about Jan Vermeer's life and he did not become famous until 200 years after his death, when his paintings were recognized as masterpieces. He worked extremely slowly and produced only about 40 paintings. He painted Dutch people doing ordinary domestic jobs, but he handled light and colour so cleverly that his figures are solid and strong, yet serene and gentle.

Katsushika Hokusai (1760–1849)

Katsushika Hokusai is the most famous Japanese artist of all time. He produced a huge number of paintings, prints, and drawings – about 30,000 works in all. He made his living mainly through coloured prints made from engraved woodblocks; his most famous work is the set of prints *Thirty-six Views of Mount Fuji* (1826–1833), showing Japan's sacred mountain in a marvellous variety of views and weather conditions.

Francisco de Goya

Spanish painter
Born 1746 Died 1828 aged 82

Francisco de Goya spent most of his career in the Spanish capital, Madrid. There he worked mainly for the court, and in 1799 he was appointed King Charles IV's principal painter. He painted many portraits of the royal family and courtiers, designed tapestries for the royal palaces, and produced religious pictures for churches.

His most original works, however, are of a much more unusual kind. When he was 46 he suffered a mysterious illness that temporarily paralyzed him and left him deaf. This experience made him think about human suffering and inspired him to paint scenes involving terror or the supernatural.

After Spain was invaded by Napoleon's armies in 1808, Goya also produced a number of anti-war paintings and prints.

J. M. W. Turner

English landscape painter
Born 1775 Died 1851 aged 76

At the age of 14 Joseph Mallord William Turner became a student at the Royal Academy schools, and at 16 his work was first exhibited to the public. After a sketching tour in Italy, Turner became particularly interested in colour and light. His subject,

⬆ *The Fighting Temeraire*, one of Turner's many dramatic works set at sea.

nearly always landscape, seems to be a magical world of lighting effects, threatening weather, and mysterious shadows.

Turner produced about 500 oil paintings and more than 20,000 watercolours and drawings. In his will, he left the majority of his paintings and his drawings to the British people.

⬆ Goya was a talented portrait artist.

Camille Pissarro

French painter
Born 1830 Died 1903 aged 73

Camille Pissarro was one of the leading Impressionists – the artists who revolutionized painting with their bright colours and sketchy brushwork. He was the oldest of the group, and the others tended to regard him as a kindly father figure. Like the other Impressionists, he endured great

poverty early in his career, and it was only in the last ten years of his life that he achieved any great financial success.

By this time, however, his eyesight was failing and he had to give up painting landscapes out of doors: many of his late pictures were views of Paris that he painted while looking out of windows. Eventually he became completely blind.

⬇ See also Claude Monet p. 140

Edouard Manet

French painter
Born 1832   Died 1883
aged 51

Edouard Manet came from a wealthy family, and no one looked less like a 'bohemian' artistic rebel than he did. He was every inch a gentleman. However, he had unconventional ideas about art. Most painters of his time followed tradition, but Manet liked to look at everything freshly. He chose subjects from everyday life that no one had thought of painting before, and he painted with broad, sketchy brushstrokes, rather than with fine detail as was the current trend. Many art critics were outraged. However, a group of up-and-coming young artists – known as the Impressionists – loved his work and he became associated with them. By the end of his career the critics had come to appreciate the sparkling beauty of his paintings. Two years before his death Manet was made a member of France's Legion of Honour – a great distinction.

⬆ Manet's paintings were mainly of everyday life, such as this one of a couple at a Parisian café.

⏩ See also Camille Pissarro p. 138, Claude Monet p. 140, Pierre Auguste Renoir p. 141

> *There are no lines in nature, only areas of colour, one against another.*
> EDOUARD MANET

Eugène Delacroix (1798–1863)

Eugène Delacroix's new style of painting shocked those who felt that his work was not in the great tradition of French classical painting. It may not seem at all outrageous to us, but at the time his use of bright colours and free handling of paint shocked the art world. His subject matter ranged from lively animal studies to scenes from African, Arab, and Jewish cultures, and to portraits and exciting stories from literary subjects.

Dante Gabriel Rossetti (1828–1882)

Rossetti's father was an Italian political refugee who fled to England. He named his son after the poet Dante, but he was known as Gabriel. In 1848 he and some friends founded the Pre-Raphaelites, aiming to revive the freshness of early Italian paintings. Rossetti was obsessed with Jane Morris, who was married to his business partner, William Morris. His love for her broke up their friendship.

William Morris (1834–1896)

Morris started work as an architect, but gave this up to become a painter. Later he set up his own firm of fine-art craft-workers who designed furniture and wallpaper. In 1883 he joined the Social Democratic Federation, and travelled England to speak at meetings and lead marches. He then started another party, the Socialist League. Five years before he died he began the Kelmscott Press, which published beautiful books.

Edgar Degas

French painter
Born 1834   Died 1917 aged 83

Edgar Degas was born into a wealthy Parisian banking family. He wanted to be an artist from a young age, and his family had no objection to such an insecure life. Degas was able to spend his time painting without worrying about money, because his rich family supported him until he was well-known and established.

Degas exhibited with the Impressionists, such as Monet and Renoir, but he was always an individualist rather than a member of a group. He realized that picture designs could break all the usual rules and that the artist need not place the main subject in the middle of the picture or show it complete. A picture showing just parts of people could look just as lifelike. He loved to paint scenes from unexpected angles, particularly ballet-dancers, because their bodies made exciting and unusual shapes. He was also a fine sculptor, making figures in wax that were then cast in bronze. His sculptures portrayed moving figures, mainly ballet-dancers.

➲ Degas' *Danseuses au Repos* ('Dancers at Rest').

Paul Cézanne

French painter
Born 1839   Died 1906 aged 67

Paul Cézanne's early pictures were not popular and people said they were unskilled. After studying art in Paris, he returned to his birthplace, Aix-en-Provence, in southern France. He did not need to rely on selling his pictures to live and this gave him unusual freedom to develop his skills. By careful mixtures of colour and tone, he made his brushstrokes 'model' a hill or a figure without using an outline. His style of painting greatly influenced other artists.

Claude Monet

French painter
Born 1840   Died 1926 aged 86

When he first became an artist, Monet struggled in poverty while his art was ignored and considered the work of a lunatic. He insisted on working outdoors to make on-the-spot pictures, but because the weather continually changed he had to work quickly, energetically applying pure, bold colour straight on to the canvas. His pictures did not attempt to copy a scene; they gave an impression of it, concentrating on the effects of light and atmosphere.

From his mid-fifties, Monet was regarded as the famous grand old man of Impressionism. His output of paintings was enormous. He particularly liked to paint the same subject many times in different weather conditions and seasons. He painted the Thames in London in different lights, and at home in his garden he made a series of wonderful pictures of water-lilies. In fact, his garden at Giverny, 65 kilometres northwest of Paris, provided the greatest single inspiration for Monet's artistic work for over 40 years.

》 See also Camille Pissarro p. 138, Edouard Manet p. 139

Pierre Auguste Renoir

French painter
Born 1841   Died 1919 aged 78

Pierre Auguste Renoir was the son of a tailor, and grew up knowing that good craftsmanship was essential in the making of quality work. At the age of 13 he was apprenticed to a porcelain manufacturer to produce hand-painted designs. He later moved over to painting fans and then to decorating blinds.

However, Renoir became dissatisfied with this work, and began to study figure drawing and anatomy at evening classes. He worked in a famous studio where he met other young artists who were interested in capturing the dappled effects of light and shadow in their paintings. With them he founded the group of painters known as the Impressionists, who tried to give an impression of the subject using light and colour, rather than painting clear outlines.

Renoir's early work suffered ridicule, but he soon became successful as a portrait painter. He also enjoyed painting busy scenes of ordinary people in bright colours, using bold brushstrokes without fussy detail. He continued to work up until his death and produced more than 6000 paintings.

》 See also Edouard Manet p. 139

> *You come to nature with your theories, and she knocks them all flat.*
> PIERRE AUGUSTE RENOIR

Georges Seurat (1859–1891)

Unlike many artists, Seurat never had to worry about earning a living and could work how and when he pleased. He loved Impressionist paintings, but he thought that he could take these ideas further. He devised a method of completely covering the canvas with tiny dots of pure, bright paint. From close up they looked like abstract patterns, but when viewed from the right distance the patterns blended together perfectly to create a scene that sparkled with light and colour. This technique was called 'Pointillism', from the French word 'point', meaning 'dot'.

Henri de Toulouse-Lautrec (1864–1901)

Henri de Toulouse-Lautrec was the son of a French aristocrat. He had two childhood accidents that damaged the bones in his legs and this left him stunted. His large head made him look a grotesque figure, but he accepted his misfortune without bitterness. His father and uncle were amateur artists, and when he was 21 he was given money to set up his own studio in Paris. He became famous for his pictures of life in dance-halls, theatres, cafés, circuses, and brothels. He was also a brilliant poster designer for many of the stage stars of his time.

Georges Braque (1882–1963)

Georges Braque's father was a skilled painter-decorator. He was trained in this profession himself, but later took up art seriously. At first he painted colourful landscapes, but in 1907 he met Pablo Picasso and this dramatically changed his outlook. Together, he and Picasso created the style known as Cubism. They specialized in still-life pictures and painted objects as if the viewer was seeing them from several angles at once. Their partnership come to an end during World War I. Braque was wounded during the war, but he recovered and had a long and distinguished career as one of France's greatest painters.

⬆ *The Luncheon of the Boating Party* by Pierre Auguste Renoir.

Marcel Duchamp (1886–1968)

Marcel Duchamp was a French artist and sculptor. He was originally influenced by Cubist paintings like those of Picasso and Braque, but later he became associated with Dada and Surrealism, and was a pioneer of the new avant-garde movement. Among his most famous pieces of art are his sculptures that are known as the 'ready-mades' – ordinary items such as a bicycle that are displayed as works of art.

Georgia O'Keeffe (1887–1986)

Much of US artist O'Keeffe's work was influenced by the landscapes of New Mexico and south-west America. She was considered avant-garde (innovative) because she adopted an abstract style for her subject matter, usually based on plant-life and landscapes. Her paintings are very expressive, and include huge flower paintings which seem to magnify the structure of petals and stamens, gently revealing the most intimate parts of the plant.

M. C. Escher (1898–1972)

Dutch artist Maurits Corneille Escher mastered several techniques of printmaking, especially woodcut and lithography. The most famous of his prints are the ones that represent 'impossible' buildings, featuring visual tricks as staircases that lead both up and down in the same direction. Escher's prints have been studied by psychologists interested in understanding how the brain interprets what the eye sees.

Mark Rothko (1903–1970)

Mark Rothko was born in Latvia but emigrated to the United States. He moved to New York in 1923 and became part of an artistic group called The Ten. His early work showed figures in strange shapes, but he later developed a style that has become known as Abstract Expressionism. His paintings often included large rectangles of two or three colours, and he often did not give them a title. He committed suicide in 1970.

Paul Gauguin

French artist
Born 1848   Died 1903 aged 54

↑ Gauguin usually painted the Tahitians and their island in bright, strong colours.

Paul Gauguin was born in Paris but he spent his childhood in Lima, Peru. He eventually settled in France and became a businessman. When he was 35 years old, he decided to devote all his time to his hobby: painting.

He became convinced that European artists had forgotten how to express true feelings in simple, direct ways. At first he studied peasant art in Brittany, but finally he left Europe to find his own way of painting.

He went to Tahiti, an island in the South Pacific Ocean. There he painted the local people going about their daily tasks and developed a distinct style. When his paintings were shown in Paris, he was proud that many people were shocked by what they saw.

Gauguin died in the Marquesas Islands, after years of ill health, disappointment, and poverty.

Vincent Van Gogh

Dutch painter
Born 1853   Died 1890 aged 37

Vincent Van Gogh was taught that a meaningful life meant devoting oneself to others. He trained to be a missionary, but his moody personality prevented him from being successful in the Church or in other jobs.

Van Gogh then taught himself to draw and paint. His dark and sombre early paintings show the miserable lives of the working poor. Later he went to France, where he experimented with clear, bright colours. His technique of excited, bold brushstrokes shows deep emotion and a sort of frenzy even when the subject itself is peaceful. His pictures are of the ordinary things: his bedroom, a chair, a bunch of sunflowers.

Van Gogh spent the last two years of his life in southern France. He suffered periods of insanity, during which he once cut off his ear. After only ten years of painting, he committed suicide. He died having sold only one painting during his lifetime.

⊘ Van Gogh's painting of *The Church at Auvers-sur-Oise*.

Alphonse Mucha

Czech painter and designer
Born 1860   Died 1939 aged 78

Mucha spent much of his working life in France, where he became known for his Art Nouveau style. This used lots of patterns based on flowers and plants as well as more abstract patterns. Mucha designed stage sets and posters for theatre shows. In 1897 he opened his own design school and he taught there until 1904. He went back to Czechoslovakia in 1910. When the country gained its independence in 1918, Mucha was asked to design the new Czechoslovakian stamps and banknotes.

Edvard Munch

Norwegian painter
Born 1863   Died 1944 aged 80

Edvard Munch had a miserable childhood – his mother died when he was five, his sister when he was 11 – and the sufferings he had seen affected his paintings. He depicted people, showing their fears and anxieties. At first, people could not understand his strange pictures, but gradually he was recognized as a genius. At the age of 44 he had a mental breakdown – he had been working too hard, drinking too much, and was unhappy in love. When he recovered, he had a much more cheerful outlook. He gave up his scenes of death and sickness in favour of subjects such as landscapes. However, his 'madness' was part of his genius, and he never quite recaptured the magic of his early work.

Wassily Kandinsky

Russian artist
Born 1866   Died 1944 aged 77

At the age of 30 Kandinsky gave up a promising career teaching law and went to art school in Munich. Since childhood he had been fascinated by colour, and later on was drawn to science and music. Once he became an experienced artist, he began to make experimental pictures in which colour was all important.

Kandinsky is famous as the first artist to paint pictures that did not look like anything recognizable: he was the first 'abstract' artist. He decided that painting recognizable objects harmed his pictures. Instead he wanted to make his pictures seem somehow like music: they did not mean anything in particular but they had a deep effect on the viewer. Just as musical sounds affect people deeply, Kandinsky believed colours and forms could also express and inspire emotions. These 'colour music' pictures astonished the world.

Although Kandinsky was always strongly influenced by his Russian background, he travelled widely around Europe, becoming first a German and later a French citizen. His thoughts, teachings, writings, and artwork caused an artistic revolution.

> " *Of all the arts, abstract painting is the most difficult… It demands that you be a true poet.* "
> WASSILY KANDINSKY

Henri Matisse

French artist
Born 1869   Died 1954 aged 84

Henri Matisse developed a colourful free style, often considered shocking. He made a famous portrait of his wife, nicknamed 'Green Stripe' because he boldly painted green shadows on her face!

The human figure dominated Matisse's drawings, prints, book illustrations, paintings, and sculpture. Later he used North African patterns and shapes in his pictures, and later still cut and pasted paper to create coloured pictures of simplified shapes.

Matisse said that for more than 50 years he had not stopped working for an instant.

⬆ Henri Matisse used shapes cut from paper in his later pictures.

Piet Mondrian

Dutch painter
Born 1872   Died 1944 aged 71

Piet Mondrian was one of the most important painters in the creation of abstract art – art that does not represent anything, but exists purely for the sake of its shapes and colours.

Until he was about 50 he had little financial success, for his kind of painting was slow to win admirers. He used only right-angled shapes and the most basic colours – blue, red, and yellow, and black and white. Gradually, however, people realized that his pictures had a beauty and elegance of their own, and many other artists imitated him. He lived in Paris for most of his career, but left in 1938 because of fears about impending war; he spent two years in London, then settled in New York in 1940.

Paul Klee

Swiss painter
Born 1879   Died 1940 aged 60

Paul Klee is one of the best-loved artists of the 20th century. He produced a huge amount of work (oils, watercolours, drawings, prints), but he had a very vivid imagination and never repeated himself. Some of his paintings are purely abstract, but most of them are based on the things that he saw around him. They are full of radiant colours and a joyous love of life.

Klee spent most of his career in Germany, where he was much admired as a teacher of art, as well as for his work as a painter. When Hitler came to power in 1933, however, he opposed all modern art and Klee was forced to give up his teaching post in Dusseldorf and return to Switzerland. In the last five years of his life he suffered from a painful illness and was depressed by political events as Europe headed for war. He continued to paint superb pictures, but in them a grim humour often replaced the playful wit of his earlier work.

Pablo Picasso

Spanish painter and sculptor
Born 1881   Died 1973 aged 91

Pablo Picasso showed an exceptional talent for art when very young. By the age of 11 he was writing and illustrating art magazines as a hobby. He hated school and never learned to write well, but he loved painting. He often helped his father, a painter, with his work. One evening his father left Picasso to finish a picture of pigeons. On his return, he saw an astonishingly lifelike painting. He gave his son his own palette and brushes and never painted again.

Picasso wanted to do things in his own way, even if he disappointed those who expected him to become a traditional painter. As his talents developed, he was constantly breaking the rules of artistic tradition; he shocked the public with his strange and powerful pictures. He intentionally avoided 'copying' real life in his paintings, but designed new forms to give fresh ways of seeing things. He made drawings, paintings, collages, prints, theatre sets, sculptures, pottery, and ceramics. His style changed many times, but he is probably best known for his 'Cubist' pictures.

➲ Pablo Picasso with his son Claude.

Marc Chagall

Russian painter
Born 1887   Died 1985 aged 97

Marc Chagall was brought up in the Jewish district of the small Russian town of Vitebsk. The people who surrounded him as a child, the stories they told, and the lively music they played, crop up again and again in his paintings.

As a young man he went to Paris, where he was influenced by all the changes in painting, writing, and music. He went back to Russia, but his painting was not popular with the authorities, and he finally settled in Paris in 1923.

His work is highly imaginative, and blends reality with fantasy. Sometimes the figures in his paintings seem to be floating across the picture. He used clear, bright colours that shimmer on the canvas and glow in the stained-glass windows and tapestries that he designed in later life.

Joan Miró

Spanish painter
Born 1893   Died 1983 aged 90

Apart from Picasso, Joan Miró was the greatest Spanish painter of the 20th century. His most famous pictures are dreamlike fantasies featuring strange insect-like creatures with human expressions. They are colourful, bizarre, and amusing. Miró said they were inspired by hallucinations brought on by hunger when he was a poor young artist. He also worked with many other art forms including stained glass and pottery.

Miró was extremely versatile and hardworking. He was still learning new techniques when he was in his eighties and worked up to the day of his death. From 1919 to 1940 he lived mainly in Paris, and after that on the island of Majorca, but he always kept strong links with his birthplace, Barcelona.

➲ Surrealist painter and sculptor Joan Miró. His style includes simple forms, bright colours, and a sense of fun.

René Magritte

Belgian painter
Born 1898   Died 1967 aged 68

Magritte was one of the most famous Surrealist painters. These paintings often look more like dreams than representations of the real world. Once the novelty of this style had worn off, many such paintings looked contrived, but Magritte seemed to have limitless imagination. His paintings are full of bizarre images, including enormous rocks that float in the air and fish with human legs, all presented with a kind of deadpan humour, but also a sense of mystery.

Salvador Dalí

Spanish painter
Born 1904   Died 1989 aged 85

Dalí was a brilliant, very talented, and ambitious young man. He believed that his name, Salvador, meaning 'saviour', meant that he was expected to save the true art of painting, which he defined as 'an instant colour photograph that you can hold in your hand, of superfine images'.

Dalí's paintings are very realistic – that is, objects look as real as he could make them. Yet what he painted, his subject matter, is bizarre. His interest in Freudian psychology led him to create extraordinary paintings that extend the boundaries of the imagination. For example, some of his paintings show strange and eerie dream worlds (sometimes nightmare worlds) inhabited by burning giraffes, tiny people, huge insects, and monstrous figures. People react very differently to his paintings: some people are horrified by what they see, while others are amused.

Dalí is one of the most famous artists of the 20th century. He has influenced the film world, fashion, and particularly the world of advertising.

David Hockney was part of the Pop Art movement that had its heyday in the 1960s.

Jackson Pollock

American painter
Born 1912 Died 1956 aged 44

Jackson Pollock was the most famous representative of a style of painting known as Abstract Expressionism. In this, the artist virtually attacks the canvas with paint to express emotions directly and powerfully. Pollock also often laid his canvases on the floor and dripped paint on to them, a form that would become known as 'Action Painting'.

Abstract Expressionism is now recognized as one of America's most original contributions to art, but Pollock endured poverty and mockery before he achieved success – one magazine article even dubbed him 'Jack the Dripper'.

> On the floor I am more at ease. I feel nearer, more a part of the painting, since this way I can walk around it.
> JACKSON POLLOCK

Andy Warhol

American artist
Born 1928 Died 1987 aged 59

Andy Warhol was the son of Czech immigrants to America. In the 1950s he was a successful commercial artist, winning prizes for his shoe advertisements and earning huge sums. In 1962, he became an overnight sensation when he exhibited pictures of Campbell's soup cans, and was hailed as a leader of Pop Art, which took its subjects from advertising, packaging, and TV. He produced his pictures by the commercial process of silk-screen printing, which meant they could be duplicated as many times as he wanted. His fame grew rapidly with brightly coloured portraits of Marilyn Monroe. He also made films, often with a documentary feel, and wrote books, including *Popism* (1980). Opinions on him are divided. To some he was a genius, to others merely a brilliant con-man.

David Hockney

English artist and photographer
Born 1937

David Hockney studied at the Bradford School of Art until 1957 and later went to the Royal College of Art in London. Early in his career he was influenced by artists such as Pablo Picasso and Henri Matisse, and tried to imitate a style similar to that of the Impressionists in his photographs.

His early paintings show subjects such as a wave or a drop of water. Hockney believed that people lived such busy lives that they had stopped noticing the beauty in simple things, and he wanted to show this in his art. Later he began to paint in a more abstract style similar to the Pop Artists, who were very popular in the 1960s. He continues to use both photographs and paint to create a unique art form that is still very popular today, although he has since returned to more realistic styles of painting.

147

Sculptors

Michelangelo Buonarroti

Italian sculptor, painter, poet, and architect
Born 1475   Died 1564 aged 88

Michelangelo dissected corpses at a hospital to discover how the body worked and this enabled him to paint, draw, or sculpt figures with great accuracy. The painting that he did on the ceiling of the Sistine Chapel turned out to be one of the most astonishing creations in the history of art. In his later sculpture his forms merge into each other. They are very emotional compared to the serenity of his earlier work, such as the huge statue of *David* made between 1501 and 1504.

⬆ The Sistine Chapel.

Auguste Rodin

French sculptor
Born 1840   Died 1917 aged 77

Auguste Rodin was influenced by the statues of Michelangelo and he visited Italy to see more of them. His own figures became famous for their lifelike quality and sense of movement. Rodin discovered that sculpture need not look entirely finished to be effective or powerful. However, his work caused quarrels amongst his critics and changes often had to be made before they were placed in public.

➲ Rodin's *The Thinker*.

Jacob Epstein

American-born English sculptor
Born 1880   Died 1959 aged 78

Jacob Epstein was born in New York, but he came to Europe as a young man and lived in England for most of his life. He was the most controversial sculptor of his time and his statues were often savagely attacked by journalists and critics. Some of them thought that Epstein's nude figures were obscene, and others thought that his work was clumsy and ugly. It was unconventional, for he was more concerned with creating figures that were bold and full of life than with making them look detailed and realistic. However, he was much praised for his portrait busts (some of the most famous men and women of the 20th century were portrayed by him), and by the end of his career he was regarded by many as the 'Grand Old Man' of British sculpture.

Jean Arp

French sculptor and artist
Born 1887   Died 1966 aged 78

Jean Arp studied in both Weimar, Germany, and in Paris, and then moved to Munich. There he became part of the Blue Rider group of artists that included Wassily Kandinsky. However, when he moved to Paris he met Pablo Picasso and started to work in the Cubist style that Picasso had pioneered. Later he moved to Zurich in Switzerland, and married the painter Sophie Taeuber.

In 1916 Arp founded the Dada group, which attracted many artists who were disillusioned by the death and destruction that was taking place in World War I. Their work was often dark with a strong political message, but Arp made sculptures that showed a lighter side, depicting natural curved shapes made out of wood, bronze or marble.

Henry Moore

English sculptor
Born 1898   Died 1986 aged 88

By the time he was 11, Henry Moore had decided to become a sculptor. After fighting in World War I he returned to Yorkshire, where he had been born. He started teaching but disliked it so much that he enrolled at Leeds School of Art. After a scholarship to study at the Royal College of Art in London, he travelled to Italy in order to widen his understanding of sculpture.

Henry Moore's work was always based on nature: rock formations, stones and bones, landscape itself, and the human figure. He never tried to copy precisely the source of his ideas, but rather to suggest a likeness.

He was 50 before he was internationally recognized. He had exceptional energy, finally completing about 800 sculptures in wood, stone and bronze, 4000 drawings and 500 prints.

⊙ Henry Moore used nature's forms in his sculptures – including the human figure – and his works have a smooth, fluid feel.

Donato Donatello (1386–1466)

Donato Donatello was the first sculptor to explore new ideas about perspective. He sculpted, carved, and decorated in marble, bronze, and wood. Later he learnt to deliberately distort figures to make their impact more powerful. In his carved and painted figure of the aged *Mary Magdalene* he chose to make her very ugly in order to emphasize the dramatic appeal of his subject.

Marie Tussaud (1760–1850)

Marie Grosholtz was just six years old when she was taught how to work in wax. By the time she was 20 she was working as art teacher to Louis XVI's sister. During the French Revolution she was called upon to make models of the severed heads of aristocrats. She married François Tussaud, and in 1802 she received permission from Napoleon to take her waxwork collection to England. In 1835 she set up a permanent exhibition in London.

Alberto Giacometti (1901–1966)

For most of his life Giacometti lived and worked in Paris. However, it was an exhibition of his work in New York in 1948 that made him famous. He showed sculpture in a new style he had created. His figures were tall and extremely thin, with a gaunt, wasted look. World War II had only recently ended and many people thought that Giacometti's strange, tragic figures captured the spirit of the time in a moving way.

Barbara Hepworth (1903–1975)

Barbara Hepworth went to Leeds School of Art and then to the Royal College of Art in London. Her work progressed from basic carving of stone or wood to using bronze, sometimes curving metal into shapes joined by thin metal rods. Much of her work is abstract; it focuses on shape, texture, size, and surface. After World War II she gained an international reputation as one of the greatest modern sculptors, and carried out many commissions for public places.

Photographers

Joseph Niepce

French pioneer of photography
Born 1765   Died 1833 aged 68

Joseph Niepce was interested in the reproduction of pictures by lithography. This led him to study possible methods of making permanent photographs (he called them heliographs) on a pewter plate, and later on paper. To develop his invention Niepce went into partnership with Louis Daguerre in 1826, but ultimately he contributed little more.

Louis Daguerre

French inventor of the first practical camera
Born 1789   Died 1851 aged 61

As a young man, Louis Daguerre worked as a tax collector and then became an artist. But what he really wanted to do was to produce an exact copy on paper of the world around him. Daguerre was familiar with the camera obscura, where sunlight entered a dark box through a pin-hole and produced on a screen an image of what was outside the box. In the 1830s Daguerre designed a box in which the image fell on a flat metal plate; the plate was coated with a chemical called silver iodide, which turned black in sunlight. The bright part of the picture became dark and the darker parts of the picture were left lighter. Although it took a long time to produce a rather fuzzy picture, these were the first photographs.

Man Ray

American photographer and artist
Born 1890   Died 1976 aged 86

Man Ray studied art in New York and was already becoming quite well-known for his abstract paintings when he met Marcel Duchamp in 1915. Duchamp was a leader of the art movement known as Dadaism and Ray was very influenced by this. He started making pictures that combined different mediums such as objects and photographs.

He began experimenting with photographic methods, trying to achieve different and unusual effects. He created a special type of photograph that he called a 'Rayograph', which was made without actually using a camera. Instead, he placed objects on pieces of special paper and then exposed them directly to light. The resulting image was full of strange shapes and textures.

Later in his life Man Ray was associated with the Surrealists and exhibited his art and photographs in this style. He continued to experiment with photography until his death in 1976.

» See also Marcel Duchamp p. 142

↑ Man Ray was both an artist and photographer, and his work combined different mediums.

Cecil Beaton

English photographer and set designer
Born 1904   Died 1980 aged 76

Cecil Beaton became interested in photography at an early age. As he grew up he began to copy the style of photographs that he saw in fashion magazines, which often used a soft focus to flatter the subjects and to give them a dreamlike quality.

After three years at Cambridge University, Beaton started to build a reputation as a photographer and was commissioned to take several portraits. He wanted to make his subjects look as beautiful as possible, but he did not like the traditional style of portrait photographs. To change this, Beaton would make his subjects sit in unusual poses and would create a wonderful background so that the person was only part of the whole composition. As a result, his photographs were considered to be works of art in themselves.

As his reputation grew and spread abroad, many film stars of the day wanted to be photographed by Beaton. Among the famous people who sat for him were Gary Cooper and Marlene Dietrich. Eventually he was asked to take a series of pictures of Queen Elizabeth II. The queen was so impressed by Beaton's work that he was later created official portrait photographer of the royal family.

As well as being a photographer, Beaton was also interested in designing stage sets and costumes, and he won Oscars for his work on the films *Gigi* and *My Fair Lady*.

Henri Cartier-Bresson

French photographer
Born 1908   Died 2004 aged 95

Henri Cartier-Bresson was celebrated for capturing significant moments of events on film. He became interested in photography after training as a painter. From 1933, when he held his first photographic exhibition, he covered the world's great events for the media, and published many books of camera studies. As a young man he worked with the great French film director Jean Renoir.

Cartier-Bresson used mainly black-and-white film and a hand-held camera. He rarely resorted to the complex photographic equipment favoured by other

⬆ Henri Cartier-Bresson's style made an art form of news photography.

photographers. He recorded 'the decisive moment' (also the title of one of his books), relying on his own skill and experience.

David Bailey

English photographer
Born 1938

As a child David Bailey was fascinated by cinema and wanted to capture the glamour of Hollywood in photographs. He taught himself photography and started working as an assistant to the fashion photographer John French. Later he worked as a photographer on the magazine *Vogue*, where his unusual and dramatic style attracted much attention. His spontaneous portraits of some of the most famous people of the era – including musicians, actors, and models – came to represent the 1960s, and many books of his photographs were published.

In the late 1960s he began to move into other areas, directing television commercials and documentaries. He is still one of the most sought-after photographers in the world.

Architects

Palladio

Italian architect and writer
Born 1508   Died 1580 aged 72

When he was 27 Palladio was befriended by a group of scholars and he began to learn about the architecture of Ancient Rome. He was particularly interested in the measurements and proportions that ancient Roman architects had used and in the kinds of buildings they had designed. The houses (villas) that he designed in the countryside outside Venice are based on Roman country houses and farms. Palladio wrote four books, which have influenced architects ever since, particularly in 18th-century Britain, where a 'Palladian' style was invented.

Inigo Jones

English architect and designer
Born 1573   Died 1652 aged 78

Inigo Jones studied painting in Italy and designed two palaces for the king of Denmark before he returned to England. He then began designing stage sets for the court of James I. Later he was made Surveyor of Works, which meant he was in charge of the construction of the king's buildings. His most famous project is the Banqueting House at Whitehall Palace. In 1630 Jones designed Covent Garden, the first square in London, with the magnificent St Paul's Church. Because of this, Jones is considered a very important figure in town planning.

Christopher Wren

English mathematician, astronomer, and architect of St Paul's Cathedral
Born 1632   Died 1723 aged 90

After studying at Oxford University, Wren became a teacher there. In London, in 1662, he helped to found a club of men keen to explore the world through science. King Charles II was very interested in it, and it was called 'The Royal Society'. Many outstanding men were members, including Isaac Newton.

Wren began to design buildings, and proved to be brilliant at that as well. The chapel at Pembroke College in Cambridge and the Sheldonian Theatre in Oxford were among his earliest buildings. Then, in 1666, the Great Fire destroyed most of London. Wren drew up a plan for rebuilding the entire city. Sadly this was never used. However, Wren was chosen to design the new St Paul's Cathedral. The construction of his magnificent plan was completed in 1710.

Wren worked very hard: he rebuilt 52 London churches destroyed by the fire, and the list of other buildings he designed seems endless. He was knighted in 1672, and became president of The Royal Society in 1680.

St Paul's Cathedral is considered one of Wren's greatest achievements.

Antoni Gaudí

Spanish architect and designer
Born 1852   Died 1926 aged 74

Antoni Gaudí was proud of his family of coppersmiths. From them he learned to appreciate craftsmanship and to use it in all his buildings. He also passionately loved his native country (the part of Spain called Catalonia) and was inspired by its Gothic and Arab-influenced architecture.

Gaudí's church of the Holy Family (the Sagrada Familia) in Barcelona is one of the most extraordinary buildings in Europe. Gaudí worked on it for 43 years – over half his lifetime – but the huge church is still unfinished. A forest of tall openwork towers soars above walls encrusted with plants and animals (mostly carved by Gaudí himself) and with colourful pottery mosaics – a Gaudí trademark.

🔽 Gaudí's work is often characterized by the use of detailed mosaics.

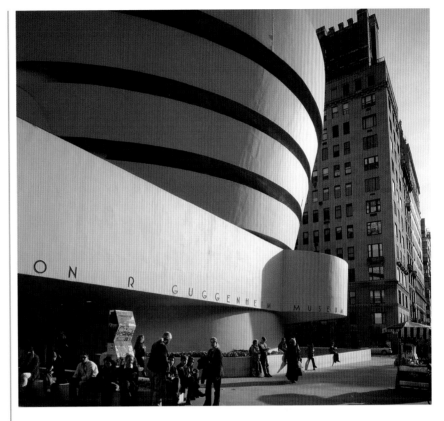

🔼 Wright said his inspiration for the Guggenheim Museum in New York was a child's spinning top.

Frank Lloyd Wright

American architect
Born 1867   Died 1959 aged 91

Frank Lloyd Wright was the most prolific and versatile of the great architects of the 20th century. His career lasted almost 70 years and he designed about 1000 buildings, of which about 400 were erected. He worked in a variety of styles and was highly inventive in his use of materials and architectural forms. Wright also wrote many books and articles, through which he promoted his ideas. His ideal was 'organic architecture', in which buildings harmonize with their environment and their users.

Until he was about 60 most of his commissions were fairly small. From the late 1930s, however, he designed many large public buildings in America, including the magnificent Guggenheim Museum in New York. He was a forceful personality – one of the central figures of modern American cultural life.

❝ *An architect's most useful tools are an eraser at the drafting board and a wrecking bar at the site.*
FRANK LLOYD WRIGHT ❞

William of Sens (12th century)

William of Sens was a French stonemason and architect in the days when the Christian Church was extremely powerful in Europe. He came to Canterbury from the French city of Sens because he had won a competition to design Canterbury's new cathedral in the most up-to-date French style. Three years later he fell from the scaffolding, but although he was disabled, he continued the cathedral choir with the help of another architect, William the Englishman.

Filippo Brunelleschi (1377–1446)

Italian Brunelleschi trained as a goldsmith and did not turn to architecture until he was middle-aged. His own buildings (churches, chapels, and a home for abandoned babies) have pleasing proportions that were quite new in Italian architecture. He also worked out the system for drawing in perspective that is still used today. He was asked to provide Florence Cathedral with the largest dome to be built since Ancient Roman times.

August Pugin (1812–1852)

August Pugin was an English architect best-known for his work on the Houses of Parliament and many churches. The Palace of Westminster had been destroyed by a fire in 1834 and several architects were invited to design a new building. Pugin played a large part in the plans for the new palace (the Houses of Parliament), opened by Queen Victoria in 1852. Many of the buildings he planned still survive all over Britain.

Victor Horta (1861–1947)

Victor Horta was born in Ghent in Belgium, and all his work was for buildings in Brussels. He brought the Art Nouveau style to Belgium. He did not limit himself to only designing buildings, though – he planned out the interiors of many, so that the furniture and decoration suited the style of the whole building. His most famous work is the Maison du Peuple.

Charles Rennie Mackintosh

Scottish architect, designer, and painter
Born 1868   Died 1928 aged 60

Charles Rennie Mackintosh was the son of a police superintendent. As a child in Glasgow he had only one aim – to be an architect. He studied in Glasgow where he became friendly with some painters and designers of stained glass, jewellery, furniture, and embroidery. They became known as the 'Glasgow Group' and Mackintosh became its leading light. He and his friends wanted to combine the best of Scottish art with Art Nouveau from Europe. In his most famous building, the Glasgow School of Art, we can recognize the cragginess of Scottish castles combined with the flowing plant forms of Art Nouveau. Glaswegians flocked to the tearooms that Mackintosh designed for the city. They have now mainly been destroyed.

⬆ The library of the Glasgow School of Art, designed by Charles Rennie Mackintosh.

Mackintosh did not find much success in his lifetime and he gave up architecture when he was only 41 to spend the rest of his life painting. However, he is now regarded by many as a pioneer of modern design.

Walter Gropius

German architect
Born 1883   Died 1969 aged 86

From early on Walter Gropius designed buildings that used only modern materials. In 1914 he built some factories constructed purely from glass and steel. He also borrowed ideas from modern art, sometimes making his buildings look like abstract paintings. In 1919 he founded the 'Bauhaus' in Germany, a school of design that included the most outstanding artists, sculptors, and architects of the day. Students were taught how to use smooth surfaces, bright colours, and three-dimensional design in their buildings.

In 1933 the Bauhaus was closed down by the Nazis. Gropius, who had left the Bauhaus five years before that, moved to England in 1934. After designing more striking modern buildings in Britain, he finally settled in America. There he worked closely with other designers in his search for truly modern architecture fitting for life in the 20th century.

Ludwig Mies van der Rohe

German architect
Born 1886   Died 1969 aged 83

Ludwig Mies van der Rohe tried to incorporate the popular Arts and Crafts style in his architecture, as well as industrial influences. His first important project was the German Pavilion, which he designed for the International Exposition in Barcelona, Spain. This used huge steel columns, with lots of marble and glass. This demonstrated his belief that 'less is more'. Mies van der Rohe was also an important teacher, lecturing at the Chicago School of Architecture after he had designed the building.

Le Corbusier

European architect
Born 1887   Died 1965 aged 77

Le Corbusier – the name adopted by Charles-Edouard Jeanneret – was born in Switzerland. He thought that houses should be on columns, to free the ground underneath, with flat roofs for terraces and gardens. In flats with limited space, Le Corbusier mixed large, open-plan, sometimes split-level rooms, with much smaller rooms for sleeping. In 1925 he designed a workers' city of 40 houses in France. In 1947 he designed a large housing complex for 1800 people in Marseille, which included a school, a hotel and, on the roof, a nursery, open-air theatre, and gymnasium. He had many fresh ideas for housing, but some people still preferred more traditional ideas.

Alvar Aalto

Finnish architect
Born 1898   Died 1976 aged 78

In 1927 Aalto won a competition with his design for a library and this was the start of a long career. He became famous for his belief that buildings should be designed with their surroundings in mind. One of his best-known buildings that fits in with this belief is the Tuberculosis Sanatorium in Paimio, Finland. It is situated among pine trees and the patients' rooms were designed so that they would receive the morning sunlight.

Throughout the 1930s Aalto was asked to exhibit at important shows such as the Paris Exposition of 1937 and New York's Museum of Modern Art in 1938. Later, however, Aalto began to move away from architecture and started designing furniture. This was also a very successful venture.

I. M. Pei

Chinese-born American architect
Born 1917

Ieoh Ming Pei was born in Canton in southern China. When he was 18 he went to America to study architecture and has worked there ever since. Most of his buildings have bold and simple forms, like gigantic pieces of sculpture. Some of them (for instance, his extension to the National Gallery of Art in Washington D.C.) look from the outside like huge blocks of stone or concrete. Others (like the tall and slender John Hancock Tower in Boston) are made of steel and glass, which reflect the sky and the Sun. Pei is most famous in Europe for the pyramids of steel and glass in the courtyard of the Louvre in Paris. They look like sculpture, but they are there to let light into a great underground hall – Pei's new entrance to all the museums in the Louvre.

⬆ Pei's elegant glass pyramids at the Louvre museum in Paris.

Novelists
Miguel Cervantes

Spanish writer
Born 1547   Died 1616 aged 68

The life of Miguel Cervantes reads like a tale of adventure. He spent his childhood travelling around Spain with his father, who supplied medicines for the poor. At the age of 21 he went to Italy and studied the work of the great Italian poets before enlisting as a soldier. He fought the Turks in the great sea battle of Lepanto in 1571, and was wounded three times. Later he was captured by pirates, and imprisoned for five years. He tried to escape, but had to be ransomed in the end.

Back in Spain his luck changed when, in 1605, he published *Don Quixote*. It is a long book that tells the tale of a poor hero who has many adventures, all caused by his own mistakes. The book was such a success that Cervantes could afford to spend the rest of his life writing.

Voltaire

French writer and philosopher
Born 1694   Died 1778 aged 83

The son of a wealthy lawyer, Voltaire was born Francois-Marie Arouet. In 1718 he adopted the pen-name Voltaire, and started to write plays and witty, hard-hitting articles. He was imprisoned for a year for criticizing the power of the French monarchy and the Church. In 1726 he was exiled to England. On his return he unfavourably compared British freedom with the censorship of France, and he finally left Paris in 1734. In 1754 he went to Switzerland, where he spent the rest of his life. He wrote his famous novel *Candide* there in 1758. This describes the adventures of an innocent young man who believes that things always happen for the best. With everything around him getting worse, he finally decides that it is, after all, a dangerous world.

➲ Voltaire was persecuted for his belief that people had a right to think what they liked.

Walter Scott

Scottish writer and poet
Born 1771   Died 1832 aged 61

Walter Scott became one of the most famous writers in Europe. He was so popular that a railway station (Waverley) and a football team (Heart of Midlothian) were named after his novels. Although Scott was lame, he became a great walker and grew to love the Scottish Border countryside with its many legends.

After training in Edinburgh as a lawyer he married and returned to the Borders. He enjoyed collecting the old Border ballads, and wrote poems of his own, such as 'Marmion' and 'The Lady of the Lake'. Their mixture of romance, history, and action was very popular.

His first novel, *Waverley*, mixed real people such as Bonnie Prince Charlie with characters that Scott had invented. It brought history to life in a way that no other writer had ever managed. *Waverley* was an instant success, and so were his other novels such as *Old Mortality*, *The Heart of Midlothian*, *Ivanhoe*, and *Rob Roy*.

Streams of people visited his home and tourists began making trips to Scotland after reading his books. But in 1826 his publishing company collapsed, leaving huge debts. Scott managed to clear the debts by writing, but died after six years of hard work.

Jane Austen

English novelist
Born 1775   Died 1817 aged 41

Jane Austen was the seventh child of a country clergyman. Her father and mother always encouraged their children's imaginative play, converting the rectory barn into a little theatre for plays put on by the family during holidays. By the age of 12 Austen was writing her own stories and reading them out loud to the rest of the household.

She never married but instead moved around with her family, living in several places, including Bath, the setting for many episodes in her books. The family moved to Winchester in May 1817 seeking medical attention for her ill-health, but Austen died two months later. She is buried in Winchester Cathedral.

Her books are famous for their witty insight into human failings and for their humour. The best-known novels are *Sense and Sensibility* (1811), *Pride and Prejudice* (1813), *Mansfield Park* (1814), *Emma* (1816), and *Northanger Abbey* and *Persuasion*, both of which were published in 1818, the year after her death.

Honoré de Balzac

French novelist
Born 1799   Died 1850 aged 51

Honoré de Balzac was extremely hard-working, sometimes working 16 hours at a stretch. His vast collection of novels deals with every aspect of French society, from private life in the town or country to stories with a political or military setting. Taken together, this long series of novels became known as *La Comédie Humaine* ('The Human Comedy'). But Balzac was not really a comic writer; instead, he described a whole society as he saw it, with characters from one novel reappearing in another. Balzac's extraordinary powers of observation and understanding make his characters as believable as the settings in which they appear, which he always describes very vividly.

The sculptor Rodin was commissioned to make this statue of Balzac in 1897.

Jonathan Swift (1667–1745)

Irish novelist Jonathan Swift's best-known satire is *Gulliver's Travels*, which describes the journeys of Lemuel Gulliver. He visits Lilliput, where everyone is tiny, then Brobdingnag, a land of giants. After more journeying, Gulliver arrives at a country ruled by gentle talking horses. These behave so much better towards each other than humans do that Gulliver dreads the return to his own world of poverty and war.

Mary Shelley (1796–1851)

At 16, Mary Shelley ran away with the poet Percy Bysshe Shelley. She married him after his first wife's suicide in 1816. Her novel, *Frankenstein* was published when Mary was only 19. It tells how Frankenstein creates a living creature out of parts taken from dead bodies. Mary also wrote short stories, biographies, and travel literature, including an account of the continental tour she and Percy took when they eloped.

George Eliot (1819–1880)

George Eliot was the pen name of Mary Ann Evans. Her first novel, *Adam Bede*, is rich both in detail and in her under-standing of country people. She then wrote *The Mill on the Floss*, drawing on her own childhood for its descriptions of the growing tension between the heroine and her family. *Middlemarch*, written in 1871, describes a small town society, from rich landowners and clergymen to shopkeepers and labourers.

Alexandre Dumas

French writer
Born 1802   Died 1870 aged 68

Although Alexandre Dumas wrote many historical plays and stories, he is most famous for creating the characters of d'Artagnan, Athos, Aramis, and Porthos in *The Three Musketeers* (1844–1845). Further adventures of the musketeers followed in *Twenty Years After* and *The Vicomte de Bragelone*. His other famous creation was *The Count of Monte Cristo*, written between 1844 and 1845.

His successful writing career began in 1829 with the play *Henri III*. Dozens of works followed as Dumas kept up a hectic pace of writing and travelling. However, he almost never wrote a complete novel himself. He provided the plot and characters and some of the important passages, and then left the main writing to a changing group of literary assistants. This is how he produced so many stories.

Victor Hugo

French poet, novelist, and dramatist
Born 1802   Died 1885 aged 83

By the time he was in his early teens Victor-Marie Hugo was writing poetry and plays. When he was 17 he had already founded a literary magazine and had won three prizes for his poetry. He was also involved in politics and in the 1840s his anti-monarchy opinions led to him being banished from France by Emperor, Napoleon III.

⬆ A poster for the 1939 film version of Victor Hugo's *The Hunchback of Notre Dame*.

He lived in exile from 1851 until 1870, spending most of this time in the Channel Islands.

Hugo produced many novels, poems, and plays but is perhaps best known for the novels *The Hunchback of Notre Dame* (1831), about a deformed bell-ringer and the beautiful woman he falls in love with, and *Les Misérables* (1862), about an innocent man condemned to life imprisonment.

Charles Dickens

English novelist
Born 1812   Died 1870 aged 58

Charles Dickens was born in Portsmouth. His father was a naval clerk who frequently got into debt. When this led to his imprisonment, Charles, then aged 12, was taken out of school and put to work in a factory pasting labels on to bottles of shoe polish.

Later he returned to school, but left at 15 to become a reporter covering debates in the House of Commons. His genius for describing comical characters and his anger about social injustice were soon noticed. In 1836 he began *The Pickwick Papers*. The book was so popular that by the age of 24 Dickens was famous in both Britain and America.

Dickens went on to write such powerful stories that parliament sometimes passed laws to stop the various scandals he described so vividly. For example, after publishing his book *Nicholas Nickleby*, some of the cruel boarding-schools he described were forced to close down.

Dickens also had a wonderful gift for creating larger-than-life characters in his novels: the villainous Fagin in *Oliver Twist*, the bitter Miss Havisham in *Great Expectations*, the drunken nurse Mrs Gamp in *Martin Chuzzlewit*, and the optimistic, unreliable Mr Micawber in *David Copperfield*, a character based on his own father.

When Dickens died of a stroke, he was mourned all over the world, and his books have remained popular ever since.

Brontë sisters

English novel-writing sisters
Charlotte Brontë Born 1816 Died 1855 aged 38
Emily Brontë Born 1818 Died 1848 aged 30
Anne Brontë Born 1820 Died 1849 aged 29

Charlotte, Emily, and Anne were the daughters of a poor Irish clergyman, Patrick Brontë. They lived in Haworth, a small town on the edge of the Yorkshire moors. They had two older sisters, Maria and Elizabeth, both of whom died before they reached adulthood. Their mother died when Charlotte was only five. After that, the sisters and their brother Branwell led their own lives mostly apart from their lonely father.

Later on, the sisters went to boarding school, and then became governesses. However, they hated being apart from one another, and eventually they all returned home, where they started to write. At first they wrote poetry, but they all then started to write novels. In 1847 Charlotte wrote her masterpiece, *Jane Eyre*. This tells the story of a girl called Jane, who goes to a harsh school and later becomes a governess. Jane falls in love with her employer, Mr Rochester. They are just about to marry when she discovers that he has a wife already – a woman who is mad and is kept locked up in a secret room in the same house. Charlotte later also wrote *Shirley* and *Villette*.

Emily also wrote her only novel, *Wuthering Heights*, in the same year. Set in the bleak moors she knew so well, it tells the story of two very different boys, Edgar and Heathcliff, who both fall in love with the same girl, Catherine.

Anne had her novel *Agnes Grey* published in 1847 and then *The Tenant of Wildfell Hall* the following year. The sisters all wrote under pretend names, or 'pseudonyms'. Charlotte was 'Currer Bell', Emily was 'Ellis Bell', and Anne was 'Acton Bell': in those days it was easier to get published if you were a man!

⊘ Laurence Olivier and Merle Oberon in the 1939 film adaptation of Emily Brontë's novel *Wuthering Heights*.

Sadly, all three sisters died young, as did their brother Branwell, who was a painter and a poet, and whom the sisters adored. No other family of novelists has ever achieved so much as the shy and unworldly Brontës, whose books are still read and enjoyed very widely today.

> " It is vain to say human beings ought to be satisfied with tranquillity; they must have action; and they will make it if they cannot find it.
> CHARLOTTE BRONTË "

Gustave Flaubert (1821–1880)

French writer Flaubert's first novel, *Madame Bovary* (1857), was also his greatest. It describes the sad life of a romantic young village girl married to a dull, unsuccessful husband. She has two love affairs, both of which end unhappily. She finally poisons herself, leaving her husband heartbroken. *Madame Bovary* was the most realistic novel of its time, setting a pattern for future novelists all over the world.

Lewis Carroll (1832–1898)

Lewis Carroll was the pen name of Charles Dodgson, a mathematics teacher at Oxford University. Carroll used to take the daughters of his friend, Dean Liddell, for boat-rides on the river. On one of these river-trips he told the story of *Alice's Adventures in Wonderland* to the young Alice Liddell. Later he wrote the story down, and it was published in 1865. As well as this and *Alice Through the Looking Glass* (1872), he wrote poems and another children's book, *Sylvie and Bruno*.

Henry James (1843–1916)

Henry James was born in New York, but went to Britain in 1876 and stayed there for the rest of his life. Altogether he wrote 20 novels and over 100 short stories. He aimed to create characters so lifelike that readers would eventually feel that they knew them as people. In his shorter stories he sometimes described supernatural events, most famously in *The Turn of the Screw* (1898).

Guy de Maupassant (1850–1893)

Guy de Maupassant was encouraged to become a writer by Gustave Flaubert. Maupassant wrote six novels and about 300 short stories, which were immensely popular in his lifetime and remain much admired today. These stories, considered by some to be the greatest of the genre, are written in a direct and free-flowing style, realistically describing the details of the characters' lives.

Fyodor Dostoevsky

Russian novelist
Born 1821   Died 1881 aged 59

Fyodor Dostoevsky first trained as a military engineer before becoming a writer. His early stories described the dreadful poverty then existing in Russia, and in 1849 he was arrested as a suspected political agitator. Condemned to death, he was pardoned while actually facing a firing squad. He then spent four years as a convict in Siberia. Returning to St Petersburg, Dostoevsky lived in poverty.

In 1866 he wrote *Crime and Punishment*, one of the world's greatest novels. It describes a poor student who murders a mean old lady for her money. The student believes that he is justified in doing this because of what he sees as his superiority over his victim. But his conscience finally forces him to confess his crime. Further novels, such as *The Brothers Karamazov* (1880), concentrated on the human struggle to live a spiritual life faced by personality weaknesses and the general despair caused by the corruption in Russia in the 19th century.

Leo Tolstoy

Russian novelist
Born 1828   Died 1910 aged 82

Leo Tolstoy was born into one of Russia's most famous noble families. He did not go to school but was educated at home by a governess. He later studied at Kazan University, but left before finishing his course.

At the age of 23 he became an artillery officer in the Caucasus and took part in the Crimean War. He wrote his first stories during the war, drawing on his own early life. *Childhood* was published in 1852, followed by *Boyhood and Youth*.

During the 1860s and 1870s he spent much of his time and energy on studying education. He also published a magazine and wrote stories for children. It was during this period, 1863 to 1869, that he wrote *War and Peace*, considered by many to be the greatest novel in the world. It gives a picture of Russia just before and during the war against Napoleon in 1812. Next he worked on *Anna Karenina*, about a married woman's tragic love affair with a soldier. By the time the book was finished, Tolstoy was facing a crisis in his life. He was an aristocrat, but he was beginning to reject his life of luxury for the simple life of a peasant. In spite of his marriage and his writing, he felt he was living selfishly. He developed a new religious philosophy based on peace, love, and a humble life.

Finally, one night he felt that he must get away. He left his home secretly, but died of pneumonia at a railway station ten days later.

> *Everyone thinks of changing the world, but no one thinks of changing himself.*
> LEO TOLSTOY

Mark Twain

American writer
Born 1835   Died 1910 aged 74

Mark Twain's real name was Samuel Langhorne Clemens. When he was four, his family moved to the small town of Hannibal on the Mississippi River. He spent his childhood watching the giant lumber rafts and the steamboats on the river. When he was 11 his father died, and Sam left school to do odd jobs to earn money for his family.

At 13 he was apprenticed to a printer, and later began writing for local newspapers. Then, for almost four years, he worked as a pilot on the local steamboats; later he remembered those years as the most carefree of his life. After

> **"** *A person who won't read has no advantage over a person who can't read.* **"**
> MARK TWAIN

trying his luck next as a gold-miner he became a full-time writer, using the pen-name 'Mark Twain', a phrase from his steamboat days meaning 'two fathoms deep'.

He was a great storyteller and wrote in a brilliantly funny way. In *Tom Sawyer* (1876) and *The Adventures of Huckleberry Finn* (1884) he painted a wonderful picture of life on and around the Mississippi, describing it exactly as the boys in the story would see it. He wrote many other novels and also a book about his travels.

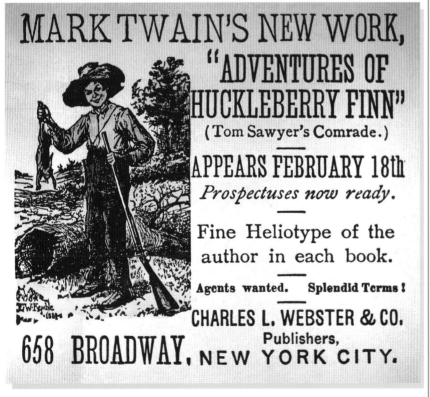

A publisher's advert for Mark Twain's story *Huckleberry Finn* (1884).

A caricature of Emile Zola.

Emile Zola

French writer
Born 1840   Died 1902 aged 62

Emile Zola was one of the greatest figures in the 19th-century French literary world. He was famous not only for his novels, but also for the outspoken way in which he campaigned for social reform and other causes he believed in. His novels, of which he wrote more than 20, paint a carefully detailed panorama of French life at the time. Among the most famous are *Nana* (1880), about a prostitute, and *Germinal* (1885), about the working conditions of miners. In 1898 Zola wrote his famous letter, *J'accuse* ('I accuse'), to a newspaper, denouncing the French justice system for wrongly convicting an army officer, Captain Dreyfus, of treason. Zola had to take refuge in England to escape imprisonment for libel; Dreyfus was later pardoned.

Thomas Hardy

English novelist and poet
Born 1840   Died 1928 aged 87

The son of a stonemason, Thomas Hardy was born – and spent much of his life – in Dorset. He even set many of his novels there and in the surrounding counties (calling the area 'Wessex').

Hardy first worked as an architect and church-restorer in London, but he also began writing novels and poetry at quite an early age. After the success of his fourth novel, *Far From the Madding Crowd* (1874), he returned to his beloved Dorset. This novel was one of many that described the ups and downs of country life in the West Country. However, the good humour running through his early work began to disappear in favour of a sadder approach to life. He increasingly saw his characters as victims of a cruel and uncaring world. For example, in *Tess of the D'Urbervilles* (1891), he describes an innocent girl who is eventually destroyed by a villainous lover and a series of unlucky mishaps.

In 1874 Hardy married, but the relationship was never easy. He described the type of difficulties he and his wife had in his novel *Jude the Obscure* (1895). However, readers were not ready for this sort of honesty about marriage and the tragic consequences it had, and the outcry against him caused Hardy to abandon novels and concentrate on poetry. Hardy experimented with different rhymes and verse forms; his *Collected Poems*, published two years after his death, contains more than 900 poems.

The death of his wife in 1912 led to some beautiful poems in which Hardy expresses his regrets about their past unhappiness together. In 1914 he married again and lived quietly until his death in 1928.

↺ A drawing of Thomas Hardy from an 1892 edition of the magazine *Vanity Fair*. At that time he was a very popular and successful novelist.

Arthur Conan Doyle

Scottish writer
Born 1859   Died 1930 aged 71

Arthur Conan Doyle trained as a doctor, but he was never very successful in this profession. Soon he discovered that he could earn more money by writing books, so when he was 32 he gave up medicine and took up writing full time.

Doyle wrote all sorts of books, from historical romances to adventure stories. But it was his detective stories, with the brilliant Sherlock Holmes as their hero, which brought him financial success and fame. *A Study in Scarlet* (1887) was the first book that introduced the character of Sherlock Holmes. Doyle also wrote some very successful short stories in *The Adventures of Sherlock Holmes* (1891–1893). Nearly all these stories are narrated by Holmes's assistant Dr Watson.

Later, Doyle became tired of writing about Sherlock Holmes. He tried to kill him off in a deadly struggle with the arch-villain, Moriarty. However, Doyle's readers complained so much that he had to write another story, in which Holmes reappears.

> " *The temptation to form premature theories upon insufficient data is the bane of our profession.*
> SHERLOCK HOLMES
> IN *THE VALLEY OF FEAR*
> BY ARTHUR CONAN DOYLE "

Rudyard Kipling

Indian-born English author
Born 1865   Died 1936 aged 70

When Rudyard Kipling was only six years old he was sent by his British parents from their home in India back to England. At boarding school he was quickly noticed as a budding young writer.

At 16 he returned to India and began writing short stories and poems describing the lives of the British and Indian people. In 1894 he wrote *The Jungle Book*, which includes stories about an Indian child, Mowgli, brought up by a family of wolves. Kipling next wrote the *Just So Stories*: a series of fables describing how the leopard got its spots, the camel its hump, and many others. His novel *Kim* appeared in 1901. Kipling won the Nobel Prize for Literature in 1907.

⬆ An illustration by Kipling for one of his *Just So Stories* – 'How the Elephant Got His Trunk'.

André Gide

French novelist
Born 1869   Died 1951 aged 82

André Paul Guillaume Gide was born in Paris in 1869. His father, who died when he was only 11, was a professor of law at the Sorbonne, the University of Paris. Gide was an only child and had a lonely youth. He was educated at home and then in a Protestant secondary school.

Gide loved all kinds of literature and could turn his hand to writing poetry, biography, fiction, drama, travel journals, and literary criticism. He rejected his strict Protestant upbringing in his life and work, and for young people living in France in the years after the end of World War I, he symbolized their rebellion against conventional attitudes.

Gide's work is almost entirely autobiographical, and includes novels such as *The Immoralist* (1902), *Strait is the Gate* (1909), *The Counterfeiters* (1926), and an almost lifelong *Journal* that was published in four volumes between 1947 and 1951. André Gide was awarded the Nobel Prize for Literature in 1947.

Robert Louis Stevenson

(1850–1894)
Stevenson was brought up in Edinburgh but he travelled widely and his first books described his tours. His adventure story about pirates, *Treasure Island*, was published in 1883 and was an instant success. Three years later his fame soared with the horror story *The Strange Case of Dr Jekyll and Mr Hyde*. In 1889 Stevenson and his family settled on the Polynesian island of Samoa.

H. G. Wells (1866–1946)

Herbert George Wells became well-known as a novelist of science fiction. In his books he described air and submarine travel long before anyone believed such journeys were possible. Wells also wrote his massive *An Outline of History* (1920) as well as popular works about science and politics. *The Time Machine* (1895) and *The Invisible Man* (1897) have proved to be particular favourites with many filmmakers.

Franz Kafka (1883–1924)

Franz Kafka was born in Prague but he wrote in German. In his lifetime he published only a few stories, and he left instructions for his unpublished works to be destroyed. However, the person in charge of his will, Max Brod, disregarded these instructions. Two of Kafka's novels, *The Trial* (1925) and *The Castle* (1926), published after his death, gained him a reputation as one of the most powerful and original writers of the 20th century.

Marcel Proust

French author
Born 1871   Died 1922 aged 51

Marcel Proust suffered from asthma throughout his life, and his growing ill health led him gradually to withdraw from people into his own company. However, by this time he had wide knowledge of the ways of rich French society, which he used in the writing of his massive, seven-part novel *Remembrance of Things Past*.

Proust's work is not easy, and was originally refused by so many publishers he eventually had to pay for its publication himself. But over the years *Remembrance of Things Past* has come to be seen as one of the great classics of literature, full of revealing ideas about human thoughts, feelings, and relationships.

James Joyce

Irish novelist
Born 1882   Died 1941 aged 58

Joyce's popular book *Dubliners* (1914) contains some of the best short stories ever written. Two years later he wrote an auto-biographical novel, *A Portrait of the Artist as a Young Man*. This also proved popular, although it seemed shocking to some people. This was nothing compared with the scandal following *Ulysses* (1922), which deals with one day in the life of an unsuccessful Irish businessman. With its publication, Joyce became one of the most famous 20th-century novelists.

Virginia Woolf

British novelist
Born 1882   Died 1941 aged 59

Virginia Woolf had a brilliant intelligence that was revealed in her essays and stories. An early believer in women's liberation, she was also fascinated by the act of writing itself.

In her novels, she breaks away from normal storytelling techniques in favour of a style closer to how we all actually think from moment to moment. In their thoughts, her characters often pass from the present to the past as one memory piles on another. This does not always make Woolf's writing easy to read, but she is always interesting and original.

➲ Among Woolf's novels are *Mrs Dalloway* (1925), *To The Lighthouse* (1927), and *Orlando* (1928)

Although she was a successful author, Woolf was not always happy. She finally committed suicide when she felt she was slipping again into depression.

Agatha Christie

English author of detective stories
Born 1890   Died 1976 aged 85

As a child, Agatha Christie did not go to school at all. During World War I she worked in a hospital dispensary, and learned details of chemicals and poisons that later proved useful when she wrote her detective stories.

She was married twice, once to Colonel Archibald Christie, from whom she was divorced in 1928, and then to the archaeologist Max Mallowan. His care with fragments of evidence and her detective skills combined well together when she helped him in his excavation of sites in Syria and Iraq.

Agatha Christie wrote several plays and more than 70 detective novels. Her books are excellent stories that make the reader desperate to know what will happen next. Since her death, several of her books have been successfully turned into films and television series. Her two most famous detectives are Miss Marple and Hercule Poirot.

> " *The best time to plan a book is when you're doing the dishes.*
> AGATHA CHRISTIE "

J. R. R. Tolkien

South African-born English novelist
Born 1892   Died 1973 aged 81

When John Ronald Reuel Tolkien was three years old he and his younger brother returned from South Africa with their mother to live in the countryside around Birmingham, England. His father died before he could join them, and when Tolkien was 12 his mother died too. She left the boys in the care of a priest, Father Francis Morgan.

Tolkien became very interested in old languages and they remained a fascination for him throughout the rest of his life.

He read Classics at Oxford University, and, after serving in the army during World War I, he returned to become a professor at the university from 1925 to 1959. However, he became most famous for the stories he made up to amuse his children. He invented creatures, like elves and hobbits, with their own languages, and gave them adventures. His first fantasy novel, *The Hobbit*, appeared in 1937, but it took him another 12 years to complete the three volumes of *The Lord of the Rings*. Since then, his books have sold millions of copies in hundreds of languages, and have been read by people all over the world.

F. Scott Fitzgerald

American novelist and short-story writer
Born 1896   Died 1940 aged 44

Francis Scott Key Fitzgerald lived the sort of life that he described in his novels – one of glamour and success. He achieved instant fame with *This Side of Paradise* (1920), and shortly after married the glamorous Zelda Sayre. Their pleasure-seeking lifestyle made them symbols of the high-living young generation of the 'Roaring Twenties'. Among Fitzgerald's most famous novels are *The Great Gatsby* (1925) and *Tender is the Night* (1934), which analyze the mood of the times.

⬆ F. Scott Fitzgerald at his writing desk.

Ernest Hemingway

American writer
Born 1899   Died 1961 aged 62

Much of Ernest Hemingway's writing is based on his own life. He drove an ambulance in World War I and was a war correspondent in World War II and the Spanish Civil War. *A Farewell to Arms* (1929), dealt with his experiences in World War I; *Death in the Afternoon* (1932) was a study of bullfighting; *For Whom the Bell Tolls* (1940) was set in the Spanish Civil War; and *The Old Man and the Sea* is about an aged fisherman trying to catch a huge marlin. His writing skills were rewarded with the Pulitzer Prize in 1953 and the Nobel Prize for Literature in 1954.

Yasunari Kawabata

Japanese novelist
Born 1899   Died 1972 aged 72

After leaving Tokyo University Kawabata wrote *The Izu Dancer* (1924), an autobiographical novel containing many powerful descriptions. He was influenced by ancient Japanese poetry, and his most famous novel, *Snow Country* (1956), has the atmosphere of a long poem, with one event running into another as if in a dream. In his work Kawabata often conveys an image of beauty but there is also a feeling of loneliness and a constant interest in death. He was awarded the Nobel Prize for Literature in 1968 but committed suicide four years later.

John Steinbeck

American writer
Born 1902   Died 1968 aged 66

Most of John Steinbeck's writing explores America's agricultural society and the relationship between people and the land. This is hardly surprising considering that Steinbeck grew up in a farming region in California.

By 1935 Steinbeck had written several books and stories, but it was his novel *Tortilla Flat* that gave him his first popular success. This was followed by *Of Mice and Men*, a touching story of two very different farm workers. In 1939, Steinbeck's greatest work was published. *The Grapes of Wrath* is the story of a poor fruit-picking family migrating from America's dust bowl to California during the Great Depression. Steinbeck's detailed and sympathetic portrayal of this family helped bring the problems suffered by homeless farmers to the public's attention.

Steinbeck's later writing included novels, short stories, and screenplays, as well as several non-fiction works. He was awarded the Nobel Prize for Literature in 1962.

⬆ The plight of poor families like this inspired Steinbeck's novels.

George Orwell

English novelist
Born 1903   Died 1950 aged 46

George Orwell, the pen-name of Eric Blair, was a great journalist, but he only became famous as a novelist in the last few years of his life. In 1945 he wrote *Animal Farm*, describing how some farm

George Orwell working as a radio journalist in 1945.

animals get rid of their harsh master, only to suffer worse cruelties from their ruthless pig-rulers. In fact, Orwell was really attacking the way that the Russian Revolution of 1917 was betrayed by the tyrant Stalin.

Four years later Orwell wrote *Nineteen Eighty-Four*, a novel set in what was then the future. It described a bleak world where workers must exercise every day in front of a 'tele-screen' which also spies on them. Anyone showing any signs of independence is caught and executed. It is a powerful novel describing the horrors of dictatorship.

Jean-Paul Sartre

French philosopher, playwright, and novelist
Born 1905   Died 1980 aged 75

Jean-Paul Sartre, who worked first as a teacher, gained attention as a philosopher with his book *Being and Nothingness* (1943). This became the most important French statement of existentialist philosophy – the philosophy that believes there is no such thing as inherited character and that in order to go from 'nothingness' into 'being', people must choose who they want to be and what they want to do. In short, Sartre believed that human beings have to 'make' themselves by making conscious decisions.

Sartre joined the French Resistance against the invading German forces during World War II, when France was occupied and ruled by Germany. His long novel *The Roads to Freedom* (1945–1949) draws on his experience of the French defeat that occurred at the beginning of the war.

Sartre's existentialism continued to find expression in concerns over human relationships in plays such as *In Camera* (1944). In his later literary and political projects, Sartre usually worked with his long-time lover, the writer Simone de Beauvoir.

> *As far as men go, it is not what they are that interests me, but what they can become.*
> JEAN-PAUL SARTRE

Albert Camus

French novelist
Born 1913   Died 1960 aged 47

Albert Camus was born in Algeria, of French and Spanish parentage. He grew up in North Africa where he had various jobs – he even played in goal for the Algiers football team for a while!

When he moved to France he took up journalism and politics, and fought against the German occupation during World War II. After the war he decided to concentrate on writing. His most famous novels, *The Outsider* (1942) and *The Plague* (1947), express his idea of the 'absurd', the view that human life is meaningless and that happiness is only possible if we accept that life has no meaning except what we give it.

Camus was awarded the Nobel Prize for Literature in 1957. He was killed tragically in a road accident only three years later.

> *It is a kind of spiritual snobbery that makes people think they can be happy without money.*
> ALBERT CAMUS

Maya Angelou

American writer and performer
Born 1928

Marguerite Annie Johnson was born in St Louis, Missouri in the United States. She suffered a traumatic childhood and did not speak for several years. After moving to California, she gave birth to a son when she was only 16 years old.

Before becoming a writer, Angelou was a performer and singer. In the 1940s she toured Europe and Africa in the opera *Porgy and Bess* before returning to America to work as a singer in a nightclub.

Angelou tells the story of her early life in *I Know Why the Caged Bird Sings* (1970), the first part of her much acclaimed three-part autobiography. Her other writing includes plays, poetry, songs, articles, and fiction. Angelou is now professor of American Studies at Wake Forest University in North Carolina.

← Many of Maya Angelou's autobiographical works tell of her struggles growing up as a black woman in the American South.

Jean Cocteau (1889–1963)

From boyhood, French writer Cocteau was attracted to all kinds of theatre, from circus to classical drama. Friends organized a performance of his poems when he was only 16 and his first book of poems was published at 19. In collaboration with Picasso and composer Erik Satie he came up with the ballet *Parade* to music that incorporated typewriters and other unusual sounds. Novels, plays, and movies followed.

Graham Greene (1904–1991)

Graham Greene was the son of a headmaster and attended his father's school. This may be why in novels like *Our Man in Havana* (1958) or *The Honorary Consul* (1973) he describes characters split between conflicting duties. Some of his novels can be read like detective stories. Others, like *Brighton Rock* (1938), take on important issues like belief in God or how far the poor and oppressed should rebel.

William Golding (1911–1993)

After many initial rejections from publishers, English writer Golding's first novel, *Lord of the Flies* (1954), quickly became a classic. In it Golding describes a group of schoolboys stranded on an island. Although they agree among themselves on some things, quarrels between them soon lead to disaster. Other novels by Golding explore the best and worst in human nature, including *The Inheritors* and *Pincher Martin*.

Gabriel Garcia Marquez

Latin-American writer
Born 1928

Born in a poor town in Colombia, Garcia Marquez still managed to study law and journalism at university. He soon began writing short stories that mixed close attention to detail with dream-like descriptions of magical events.

His mosrt famous novel is *One Hundred Years of Solitude* (1967). This describes the adventures of a family settled in a new town in the middle of a South American jungle. Myth and legend combine with ordinary human affairs in an unforgettable way.

This magical-realism style has since encouraged many other novelists to experiment with fantasy in their own books. Garcia Marquez is not always popular with his government for criticizing the huge gaps between rich and poor in South America. He was awarded the Nobel Prize for Literature in 1982.

⬆ Gabriel Garcia Marquez's mixture of myth and realism has inspired many writers.

Chinua Achebe

Nigerian novelist
Born 1930

Born in eastern Nigeria, Chinua Achebe worked in broadcasting and the civil service before becoming a novelist.

In his first and most famous novel, *Things Fall Apart* (1958), Achebe describes the breakdown of African tribal life after the arrival of the British, who colonized the area during the last century.

In his memorable description of a traditional family, Achebe demonstrates an understanding of the way the different cultures and rituals of Africa so often seem to puzzle outsiders.

Another novel, *A Man of the People* (1966), describes a dishonest African politician who wants to make as much money as he can while he has the chance. This is a funny but sad story, pointing out how difficult it can be for a country that is unused to political power to run itself properly during the first years of independence.

Achebe has since written several children's books and has greatly helped younger African writers to get their books published.

> " *Art is man's constant effort to create for himself a different order of reality from that which is given to him.*
> CHINUA ACHEBE "

Storytellers

A. A. Milne

English writer
Born 1882 Died 1956 aged 74

Some writers are less famous than the characters they create. This is certainly true of Alexander Alan Milne, the creator of Winnie the Pooh and Christopher Robin. In real life, Christopher Robin was Milne's son (also called Christopher) and the stories that Milne wrote about Christopher's teddy bear (Pooh) and other toys have become classics.

Winnie the Pooh was published in 1926 and *The House at Pooh Corner* followed two years later. Milne also wrote two books of verse for children: *When We Were Very Young* (1924) and *Now We Are Six* (1927).

⬆ A. A. Milne with his son Christopher.

Enid Blyton

English author of children's books
Born 1897 Died 1968 aged 71

Enid Blyton began her career as a teacher, but soon switched to journalism. Her first book was a collection of poems for children. In the late 1930s she started publishing the *Noddy* stories, for very small children, and adventure stories such as the *Famous Five* and the *Secret Seven*, for older children. It was not long before she was writing her school story series, like *Malory Towers* and *The Naughtiest Girl*.

Enid Blyton wanted to educate her readers, and to give them a clear idea of right and wrong behaviour. Her stories have been enjoyed by many children, although some people have said that the plots are too simple.

C. S. Lewis

English author
Born 1898 Died 1963 aged 64

Clive Staples Lewis began by writing academic books and science fiction for adults, but then decided to write books and stories for children too. *The Lion, the Witch and the Wardrobe* is the most famous of a series of seven stories that describe the fairyland world of Narnia. In each story the children are faced by a choice between good and evil. The adventures are so exciting that many young readers miss the fact that Lewis is using the stories as an allegory to preach a Christian message. His great hero, Aslan the lion, is a symbol for Jesus Christ.

Roald Dahl

British author
Born 1916 Died 1990 aged 74

Roald Dahl's early life was almost as adventurous as any of his novels. As a young businessman working for Shell Oil, he was sent to work in Africa. After some extraordinary adventures – some involving wild animals – Dahl volunteered for the Royal Air Force when Britain declared war on Germany in 1939. After flying in East Africa, he crashed his plane in flames in the middle of the Western Desert. Despite dreadful injuries Dahl was soon flying again in Greece and Syria, before transferring to the United States in 1943.

After World War II he started writing stories, at first for adults and later for children. His most popular children's book is *Charlie and the Chocolate Factory*, about a poor young boy who wins a golden ticket to visit Willy Wonka's Chocolate Factory. Charlie proves to be the most honest child and inherits the factory.

Charlie and the Great Glass Elevator was the sequel, and was published in 1972. Dahl's other books include *The BFG*, *Revolting Rhymes*, and *The Witches*. During the 1980s he was the most popular children's author in the world.

> *I began to realise that large chocolate companies actually did possess inventing rooms, and they took their inventing very seriously.*
> ROALD DAHL

J. K. Rowling

English children's writer
Born 1965

Joanna Kathleen Rowling wrote her first story when she was six. At school English was her favourite subject, but she also enjoyed foreign languages, and studied French at university.

Joanna wanted to write, but she had to work to earn a living. In 1990 she was working in Manchester, and on a train to London she had an idea for Harry Potter – a seemingly ordinary boy who one day receives an invitation to Hogwart's School of Witchcraft and Wizardry.

The first Harry Potter book was finished in 1994, but it was two more years before it was published. The book was a hit with both children and adults, and won many prizes. Joanna was able to give up work and write full-time. She has now completed all seven books in the Harry Potter series, one for each year Harry is at school.

J. K. Rowling was awarded an OBE in 2001.

Thomas Malory (15th century)

No one knows for sure who Thomas Malory was, but many believe he was a knight imprisoned in London for unknown crimes for 20 years. It was possibly during this time that Malory finished his great book about King Arthur's knights of the Round Table and their quest for the Holy Grail. In 1485 the whole work was published by William Caxton, the first British printer.

Grimm brothers

Between 1812 and 1815 Jakob (1785–1863) and Wilhelm (1786–1859) Grimm published around 200 folk tales; these included *Snow White*, *Sleeping Beauty*, *Cinderella*, and *Little Red Riding-hood*. The brothers said that they wrote down the tales exactly as they heard them, but they probably rewrote most of them to make them longer and more satisfying to readers. They also compiled a huge German dictionary.

Hans Christian Andersen

(1805–1875)

When he was 14 Hans Christian Andersen walked all the way from his home in Odense to Copenhagen to try his luck in the big city. He was tall and clumsy, and was often mocked and bullied. Later in his life, when he began to write children's stories, he used this experience in the famous tale of *The Ugly Duckling*. He wrote his stories in simple language, just as he would have told them to a child.

Beatrix Potter (1866–1943)

Beatrix Potter sent *The Tale of Peter Rabbit* to five publishers, but none of them would publish it. Instead, she had the book printed with her own money, and gave copies of it to children. It became so popular that in 1902 the publisher Frederick Warne agreed to reprint it for her. Thousands of copies were sold. During the next ten years she wrote many more, including *The Tale of Tom Kitten* and *The Tale of Jeremy Fisher*.

Poets
Dante Alighieri

Italian poet and writer
Born 1265   Died 1321 aged 56

Dante Alighieri grew up in Florence, Italy. When he was nine years old he met a girl who was younger than himself, and when he was older he wrote a lot of beautiful poetry about her. Dante called her Beatrice and saw her occasionally when he was a young man, but only with groups of friends.

In 1302 Dante quarrelled with the supporters of the pope in Florence and spent the rest of his life in exile in other cities of northern Italy. His great poem, *The Divine Comedy*, describes his journey through Hell, Purgatory, and Paradise. Throughout, the love of Beatrice directs him, and at the end she herself guides him among the souls in Paradise.

⬆ An illustration of part of Dante's *The Divine Comedy*.

Geoffrey Chaucer

English poet and writer
Born c.1340   Died 1400 aged about 60

When Geoffrey Chaucer was a small child, he was a page in the household of the wife of King Edward III's son, Lionel. When he was older, Chaucer became one of the king's 'squires'.

In the war between England and France (1337–1453) Chaucer was taken prisoner, but in 1360 the king paid a ransom for his release. Later he became a diplomat, travelling to France and Italy on missions for the king.

By 1374 he was made Controller of Customs in the Port of London, but left in 1386, and began writing his best-known work, *The Canterbury Tales*. This is a cycle of linked tales told by a group of pilgrims who meet in London before going on a pilgrimage to Canterbury. By that time he had already written many other long poems, including *Troilus and Criseyde* (1385), a sad love story.

Chaucer was one of the most learned men of his age. He died in 1400 and is buried in Poet's Corner in Westminster Abbey.

» See also Dante Alighieri p. 172

Omar Khayyam (1048–1123)

Omar Khayyam was born in Nishapur, Persia (now Iran). His four-line poems (*rubaiyat*) praise the pleasures of life but also show that he thought deeply about religion. At least 250 of them survive. English poet Edward Fitzgerald had the idea of translating them as though they were one long poem. Since their publication in 1859 as *The Rubaiyat of Omar Khayyam* they have been translated into many other languages.

John Donne (1572–1631)

Already well-known as the author of some of the most passionate love poems ever written in Britain, Donne decided to become a priest in 1615. His poetry changed from its early interest in human emotion to the treatment of more religious themes. But even in this later work, Donne continued to write with immense feeling, in poems that were both complex and also very direct in their use of language.

Matsuo Basho (1644–1694)

Basho became a companion to the son of his samurai lord, and together they studied literature, especially poetry. In 1672 Basho moved to the capital city of Edo (now Tokyo), where he became well-known as a poet. Later he went on several long journeys around Japan. Basho's accounts of these include many of his best and most famous poems. He is regarded as the greatest master ever of the haiku, the 17 syllable poem.

John Milton

English 17th century poet
Born 1608   Died 1674 aged 65

At Cambridge University John Milton first thought of becoming a clergyman, but decided instead to put his great gifts into poetry. One of his first major poems was *Lycidas*, written in memory of a friend who had drowned. Like other poets of the time, he was greatly influenced by Latin and Greek literature, but Milton also brought to this poem his own strongly Christian vision of life. In fact, he created a new form of poetry, one that was both passionate and scholarly at the same time.

When the English Civil War began in 1642, Milton sided with Parliament against King Charles I. He wrote many articles and pamphlets attacking the monarchy and defending people's freedom to choose their own leaders as well as to publish and read what they liked.

Milton's work led to serious eye-strain, and in 1652 he went blind. When Charles II was restored to the throne in 1660, Milton was arrested, but eventually pardoned. It was about this time that he wrote one of the greatest poems in existence, *Paradise Lost*. This is a very long poem retelling the Bible story of how Satan tempted Adam and Eve into disobeying God. Composed entirely in Milton's head and dictated to members of his family, *Paradise Lost* uses poetic language to create an effect that is both magnificent and moving.

William Blake

English poet, engraver, and artist
Born 1757   Died 1827 aged 69

As a boy, William Blake loved poetry and art. When he was 10, he went to a drawing school, and at 14 he was apprenticed to an engraver, learning how to prepare illustrations for books. He also studied at the Royal Academy in London, but returned to engraving.

As a young man, Blake began to write poetry and illustrate it with pictures of biblical visions he had experienced. He etched his poems on copper plates and coloured the printed pages. Much of his poetry is happy and full of tenderness, although his later poems show anger and sadness.

In his lifetime, few people valued Blake's poetry, and a lot of it was thrown away. But he produced so much that today we still have much of his poetry to enjoy.

↑ *Songs of Innocence and Experience.*

Friedrich Schiller

German poet and playwright
Born 1759   Died 1805 aged 45

Friedrich Schiller is best known as a dramatist and poet, but he also wrote historical and philosophical works and translated plays.

Schiller's first important work was the play *The Robbers* (1781); it is an attack on political tyranny and shows a passionate concern for freedom. In 1782 Schiller moved from Stuttgart to Mannheim, where he became playwright for the city's famous theatre. In 1794 he met Goethe and on his recommendation Schiller became professor of history at the University of Jena.

Many of his plays were used as the basis for operas; his most popular play, *William Tell* (1804), was made into an opera by Rossini. His most famous poem is 'Ode to Joy' (1785), part of which Beethoven set to music.

⊗ See also Johann von Goethe p. 181, Gioachino Rossini p. 184

Alexander Pope (1688–1744)

When only 23, English poet Pope wrote *An Essay in Criticism*, a witty poem which includes the now famous line, 'To err is human, to forgive, divine'. He then wrote the mock epic poem, *The Rape of the Lock*. He translated Homer's *Odyssey* and *Iliad*, and wrote many poems that were sharply critical of the writers and politicians of his time. His brilliant poetry gave much pleasure to others, except to those he was attacking.

Robert Burns (1759–1796)

Burns published a collection of poems in 1786, which were immediately popular. He also wrote or adapted traditional Scottish songs, including 'Auld Lang Syne' and 'A Red Red Rose'. His last major poem, 'Tam o' Shanter', was published in 1791. Burns has been translated into more languages than any British poet apart from Shakespeare.

Samuel Taylor Coleridge
(1772–1834)

Samuel Coleridge met Wordsworth as a young man, and moved to the Lake District to be near him. Coleridge suffered from rheumatism and to relieve the pain he took the opium-based drug laudanum, to which he became addicted. Together with Wordsworth he began what came to be known as the 'Romantic' movement in poetry. His most famous poems are *The Rime of the Ancient Mariner* and *Kubla Khan*.

Alexander Pushkin (1799–1837)

Pushkin worked for the government, but also wrote poetry. His political poems angered the government and he was banished to southern Russia. Here he started one of his greatest works, the novel *Eugene Onegin*, which portrayed current trends in Russian life. The tsar, recognizing his popularity, summoned him to Moscow and gave him a personal pardon. But his writing continued to be censored. He died after a duel with a French baron who admired his wife.

William Wordsworth

English nature poet
Born 1770   Died 1850 aged 80

After studying at Cambridge University, William Wordsworth spent some time in France, where he fell in love with Annette Vallon, the daughter of a surgeon. Although they had a child together, Wordsworth left her before they could marry. His money ran out and he had to return to England.

In 1798 he published his first collection of poems, *Lyrical Ballads*, in partnership with his great friend, the poet Samuel Taylor Coleridge. Wordsworth's poems caused a sensation because he wrote about ordinary events in plain language, which had not been done before. This new simplicity was a great contrast to the more showy types of poetry that were popular at the time.

Because both of his parents had died when he was a child, Wordsworth was always close to his sister, Dorothy. In 1799 he moved to the Lake District with his wife Mary, whom he married in 1802, and Dorothy. Coleridge joined them. The Lake District was an area both poets loved and its scenery inspired much of their writing.

≫ See also Samuel Taylor Coleridge p. 174, Alfred, Lord Tennyson p.176

Lord Byron

English poet
Born 1788   Died 1824 aged 36

George Gordon Byron was lame from birth, and rode on horseback whenever he could. When he was ten years old he inherited his great-uncle's estate, and became Lord Byron. He later travelled through Europe on horseback. On his return to London he published *Childe Harold's Pilgrimage*, describing some of the wild landscapes he had seen.

Byron was a mixture of good and bad. He was described as 'mad, bad, and dangerous to know'. People were shocked by his love affairs and he left England. He lived in Venice, where he wrote the long poem *Don Juan*, which describes adventures in extraordinary parts of the world.

In 1823 he went to Greece to help in the Greek struggle for independence from the Ottoman Turkish empire. However, before his soldiers could attack the Turkish fortifications, he caught a fever and died.

① Byron was often regarded as a hero figure.

Percy Bysshe Shelley

English poet
Born 1792   Died 1822 aged 29

Percy Bysshe Shelley was expelled from Oxford University in 1811 for distributing a pamphlet, attacking religious belief, which he had written with a student friend. And no one would publish his long poem, *Queen Mab*, for fear of prosecution over its celebration of free love, republicanism, and vegetarianism, so he published it himself in 1813.

Shelley married 16-year-old Harriet Westbrook in 1811, but left her when he fell in love with another 16-year-old. This was Mary, daughter of William Godwin, the man whose writing had shaped Shelley's own ideas. They married after Harriet's suicide and spent the summer of 1816 on Lake Geneva with Lord Byron. In 1818 they left England for good to travel in Europe. They eventually settled in Italy, and it was here that Shelley wrote some of his greatest works, including *Prometheus Unbound* (1820), 'To a Skylark' (1820), and 'Adonais' (1821), written on the death of Keats. Shelley drowned just a year later when his sailing boat, *Ariel*, overturned in a storm off the Italian coast.

See also Mary Shelley p. 157, Lord Byron p. 174

John Keats

English poet
Born 1795   Died 1821 aged 25

When Keats was 16 he started to train as a doctor, but he really wanted to be a poet, and in 1817 published his first book of poems.

While Keats never doubted his own talents, he never earned enough money from writing alone. Even so, he went on to write some of the best-known poems in the English language, including 'Ode to a Nightingale', 'The Eve of St Agnes', and the mysterious 'La Belle Dame Sans Merci'.

Keats became seriously ill after a walking tour in Scotland, and later died in Rome of tuberculosis.

This picture of Shelley's funeral was painted in 1889, many years after his tragic early death.

Ralph Waldo Emerson

American poet and philosopher
Born 1803   Died 1882 aged 79

Ralph Waldo Emerson was born in Boston, one of five sons of a church minister. His father died when he was eight, leaving his mother and aunt to look after the brothers on a meagre income. He studied theology at Harvard University and became a clergyman at 26. However, he resigned only three years later, shortly after the death of his first wife, because of his unorthodox religious views.

He travelled to Europe and in England made friends with several writers, including Thomas Carlyle with whom he corresponded for 38 years. On his return to America he settled in Concord, Massachusetts, and devoted his life to lecturing all over the country and to writing philosophical essays and poems. His belief that people should rely on their own powers of intuition and his great respect for nature were hugely influential in America.

Edgar Allan Poe

American poet and writer
Born 1809   Died 1849 aged 40

Edgar Allan Poe's mother died when he was only three and he was adopted by a wealthy merchant who took him to England. After going to school in London, Poe returned to America to study at the University of Virginia. He then joined the army, but managed to get himself discharged for neglect of duty in 1831.

By this time, Poe had already published two volumes of poems and he decided to make his living by writing. He edited newspapers and magazines, and wrote stories, verse, and critical essays. Although he was admired as a poet – *The Raven and Other Poems* was published in 1845 – he is most famous for his horror stories, such as *The Fall of the House of Usher* (1839), which tells the tale of a madman who buries his sister alive.

Poe failed to earn much of a living by writing, and became an alcoholic, writing less and less.

⬆ Several of Poe's stories have inspired horror movies.

Alfred, Lord Tennyson

English poet
Born 1809   Died 1892 aged 83

By 1833 Alfred, Lord Tennyson had published two sets of poems that received bad reviews. This was followed by the death of his close friend, Arthur Hallam, and Tennyson suffered depression. In the following nine years, Tennyson wrote many poems but published hardly any.

This changed in 1842 with the successful publication of *Poems*. His elegy for Hallam, *In Memoriam*, was published in 1850 and he succeeded William Wordsworth as Poet Laureate in the same year.

Tennyson continued to enjoy great popularity with works such as *The Charge of the Light Brigade* and *Idylls of the King*, a retelling of the Arthurian legends.

》 See also William Wordsworth p. 174

Walt Whitman

American poet
Born 1819   Died 1892 aged 72

Walt Whitman was born in New York, the third of eight children. Between 1838 and 1850, Whitman took up a series of jobs including teaching journalism and newspaper editing. In 1855 he published *Leaves of Grass*, a book of 12 poems. During the next five years Whitman revised this and wrote further poems. By the third edition of *Leaves of Grass*, there were over 130 poems in the book. This is now regarded as one of the most important books in American literary history and Whitman is known as the greatest American poet of the 19th century.

During the American Civil War, Whitman worked as a volunteer nurse in Washington. His wartime experiences formed the basis of his poems printed in *Drum Taps* and *Sequel to Drum Taps*.

In 1873 Whitman suffered a stroke that paralyzed him. He moved to Camden, New Jersey, where he lived by printing, writing, and through donations from admirers.

Charles Baudelaire

French poet
Born 1821   Died 1867 aged 46

Charles Baudelaire first showed his rebellious side by misbehaving at his senior school in Paris. Deciding to become a writer, he lived in the Latin Quarter of Paris along with other struggling writers and artists, and became addicted to the drug opium. In 1841 his family sent him to India in an attempt to give him a fresh start. But he soon returned to his former life and quickly ran up huge debts. Turning to poetry, Baudelaire wrote about the pleasures and miseries of the life he was leading, but his 1857 collection of poems, *Flowers of Evil*, proved to be very controversial. However, the way Baudelaire expressed the longing for something good to live for, gave these poems enormous power. Modern poets still regard Baudelaire as the first 19th-century poet to explore the inner secrets of the soul with the same sort of openness we expect today.

Rabindranath Tagore

Indian poet, philosopher, and musician
Born 1861   Died 1941 aged 80

Rabindranath Tagore was born into a rich Bengali family and went to England to study law. He began writing poems at a very young age, and published his first poems when he was 17. He also wrote a number of plays and novels.

Tagore won the Nobel Prize for Literature in 1913, and was given a knighthood in 1915. He renounced this title in 1919 in protest against the Jallianwala Bagh incident in India, when a British general ordered troops to fire on an unarmed crowd, killing about 400 people. A song written and composed by Tagore was adopted as the national anthem of India in 1950.

Henry Wadsworth Longfellow (1807–1882)

American Longfellow's works include 'Paul Revere's Ride', 'The Wreck of the Hesperus', and 'Excelsior'. These have strong rhythms and tell their stories in vivid language. His most famous poem is *The Song of Hiawatha*. This describes the life of an Indian brave. Before his own death Hiawatha warns about the coming of the white man. The poem is told in a sing-song rhythm.

Emily Dickinson (1830–1886)

American poet Emily Dickinson lived a largely secluded life, although she had a few close friends with whom she exchanged long letters. She may even have fallen in love with one of the men she wrote to, but no one knows who he was. From the 1850s she channeled all her energy into her poetry. Very few of her 1700 poems were published in her lifetime, so it was only after her death that she was recognized as a gifted poet.

Philip Larkin (1922–1985)

English poet Philip Larkin studied at Oxford University, where he met other poets such as Kingsley Amis, who did not like what they thought to be the overly emotional style of the war poets of a few years earlier. His own poems were more detailed and less sentimental. Larkin wrote some novels but later decided to concentrate on poetry. He became one of the most popular writers of the second half of the 20th century.

W. B. Yeats

Irish poet and dramatist
Born 1865 Died 1939 aged 73

William Butler Yeats went to school in London, but for his holidays he was sent to his grandparents in Sligo on the west coast of Ireland. He loved to listen to people talk of fairies and ghosts, and of the time when great kings and warriors lived there.

When he was older he collected the folklore and myths of Ireland, and helped to found a national theatre in Dublin. He met and fell in love with a woman called Maude Gonne, who inspired much of his greatest poetry but refused to marry him.

In his later years, his poetry increased in power, drawing on the ancient myths and his personal emotions. Many of his best-known poems appeared in *The Tower* (1928), and *The Winding Stair* (1929). He won the Nobel Prize for Literature in 1923.

T. S. Eliot

American poet
Born 1888 Died 1965 aged 76

Although Thomas Stearns Eliot was born in the USA, he spent most of his life in England. His first important poem was *The Love Song of J. Alfred Prufrock*. Using language that is an intriguing mixture of the ordinary and the poetic, it describes the thoughts and feelings of a middle-aged man. In 1922 Eliot published an even more extraordinary poem, *The Waste Land*. Traditional critics hated his modern approach, but younger ones saw it as a breakthrough.

Later, Eliot became more religious. He turned to writing plays, including *Murder in the Cathedral* (about the death of Thomas Becket). In 1939 he wrote the jolly *Old Possum's Book of Practical Cats*, which was the basis for the popular musical *Cats*.

↑ A caricature of T. S. Eliot.

Wilfred Owen

English poet during World War I
Born 1893 Died 1918 aged 25

Wilfred Owen was already a poet when World War I began. After he enlisted in the army in 1915, the atmosphere in his poems soon changed from romance to bitter anger against the slaughter then going on in the trenches. As he puts it himself in his poem 'Anthem for Doomed Youth':

> *What passing-bells for these*
> *who die as cattle?*
> *Only the monstrous anger*
> *of the guns.*

In 1917 he returned to England with injuries from the trenches, but he was sent back to France the following year. He was shot dead one week before the end of the war, on 4 November 1918.

Owen's poems, published after his death, did much to change the notion that many people had that war was still a brave and noble thing. Instead, he painted an unforgettable picture of the pointless waste, stupidity, and cruelty that had led to the deaths of so many young men on both sides in the trenches.

> *Shall life renew*
> *these bodies? Of a truth*
> *All death will he annul,*
> *all tears assuage?*
> *Or fill these void veins full*
> *again with youth*
> *And wash with an immortal*
> *water age?*
> WILFRED OWEN, 'THE END'

W. H. Auden

British poet
Born 1907   Died 1973 aged 66

Wystan Hugh Auden emigrated to America in 1939. As a young man in England, Auden was angered by the society around him. The rise of Hitler's Nazi Party in Germany made him strongly anti-fascist. The books of poetry such as *Look Stranger!* (1936) made him a leader among young left-wing English poets.

After moving to America Auden took American citizenship. Much of his later poetry was complex and intellectually demanding, reflecting his conversion to Christianity. He returned to England from 1956 to 1961 as professor of poetry at Oxford.

Derek Walcott

West Indian poet
Born 1930

Derek Walcott was born in St Lucia and later went to the University of the West Indies. He then lived in Trinidad, founding a theatre workshop and writing plays, which often combined singing with storytelling and dancing. He also experimented with different types of English, including local dialect.

Walcott was always fascinated by the ancient Greek writer Homer and this influence found its way into Walcott's poem 'Omeros' (1989) and his own version of Homer's *Odyssey*, both of which won him much fame. In 1992 Walcott was awarded the Nobel Prize for Literature – the greatest honour a writer can achieve.

Sylvia Plath

American novelist and poet
Born 1932   Died 1963 aged 30

Since Sylvia Plath's death by suicide, she has been one of the most discussed women writers of the 20th century. She has become a feminist heroine, seen as both a rebel and a victim. In 1956 she married the English poet Ted Hughes, but they separated in 1962 and she lived alone in London. Shortly before her death, her only novel, *The Bell Jar* (1963), was published; it tells of a woman student's emotional breakdown. Plath also published two volumes of poetry in her lifetime, but it was the collection published after her death, *Ariel* (1965), that made her reputation.

Her best-known poems deal hauntingly with personal pain and tragedy, but she wrote tender and witty poems as well.

↑ Sylvia Plath committed suicide in 1963 when she was only 30.

Playwrights

William Shakespeare

English playwright and poet
Born 1564 Died 1616 aged 52

A miniature of Shakespeare, painted in 1588.

William Shakespeare was the eldest child of the mayor of Stratford-upon-Avon. In 1582 he married Anne Hathaway. Their first child, Susannah, was born the following year and twins, Hamnet and Judith, followed in 1585. Hamnet died when he was 11.

Nobody knows what Shakespeare was doing for a living in his early twenties, but by 1592 he was earning money as an actor and playwright in London while his family stayed in Stratford. He soon became a leading member of a theatrical company called the Lord Chamberlain's Men, later the King's Men. Between 1599 and 1613 their main base was the Globe Theatre on the south bank of the River Thames, and in 1609 they acquired the Blackfriars Theatre.

Shakespeare seems to have taken little or no interest in the printing or publication of his work, and one or two of his plays may have been lost. A complete collection was not published until seven years after his death. This so-called First Folio included all his plays except *Pericles*. The number of plays that are wholly or mostly written by Shakespeare is generally agreed to be 37. He also wrote 154 sonnets.

Shakespeare's most famous plays are probably the four great tragedies, *Hamlet*, *Macbeth*, *Othello*, and *King Lear*. He also wrote popular comedies, such as *A Midsummer Night's Dream* and *Twelfth Night*, and many history plays, including *Richard III* and *Henry V*, about English kings. Other favourites in the theatre are *The Merchant of Venice*, *Romeo and Juliet*, and *The Tempest*.

> " *What are these,*
> *So withered and so wild*
> *in their attire,*
> *That look not like*
> *th'inhabitants o' the earth*
> *And yet are on it?*
> WILLIAM SHAKESPEARE,
> MACBETH "

Molière

French playwright and actor
Born 1622 Died 1673 aged 51

Molière was the son of a successful upholsterer. His real name was Jean-Baptiste Poquelin. He first studied law at university, then left home to become an actor, adopting the stage name Molière. He toured France with a group of friends and began to write plays for this new company.

In 1658, after about 12 years of touring, the group was given a permanent theatre in Paris by King Louis XIV. From that time on, Molière wrote many more delightful plays. Although most of these were comedies, they often had a serious side too, attacking human failings such as snobbishness, hypocrisy, and meanness. One of his funniest plays is called *Le Malade Imaginaire* ('The Imaginary Invalid'). This is about someone who always thinks he is more ill than he really is. Tragically, one night Molière, who was acting the main part in this play, collapsed on stage and then died only a few hours later.

Johann von Goethe

German poet
Born 1749   Died 1832 aged 82

Johann Wolfgang von Goethe is considered to be the founder of modern German literature, and in his old age people would make pilgrimages to his Weimar home to visit him. His writings show that he was influenced by many people, such as great philosophers, as well as other playwrights and poets like William Shakespeare and Lord Byron, folk singers, and, not least, by the many women he fell in love with.

Goethe was amazingly versatile: he made important discoveries in science; he was a good actor, and also a theatre director. But he is best remembered for his great plays, his novel *The Sorrows of Werther* (1774), his many songs, and above all the poetic drama *Faust* (1808), in which the hero sells his soul to the devil in exchange for enjoying all that the world can offer him in his lifetime.

A scene from Goethe's drama *Faust*. Faust is guided by the devil, who takes the form of Mephistopheles (seen right).

Henrik Ibsen

Norwegian playwright
Born 1828   Died 1906 aged 78

Henrik Ibsen planned to go to university but failed the entrance exam. He turned to journalism and also began writing poetry and plays. In 1851, he was given a job as stage director and resident playwright at the Norwegian Theatre. Here he began to have ideas about the psychological development of characters.

Ibsen wrote several plays that established him as the founder of modern drama. These include: *A Doll's House* (1879), *Ghosts* (1881), and *Hedda Gabler* (1890). He was forced to abandon writing after suffering a stroke in 1900.

Jean Racine (1639–1699)

Jean Baptiste Racine found favour at the French court of King Louis XIV and began to write plays. His earliest were *The Thebiad* (1664) and *Alexander the Great* (1665). These were followed by many others, including his masterpiece, *Phèdre* (1677). The subjects for his plays often came from Greek mythology. The plots were simple, but his characters expressed a range of complex emotions.

George Bernard Shaw

(1856–1950)

George Bernard Shaw moved from Ireland to London at the age of 20. His novels were not very successful, but people took an interest in his magazine articles. His first successful play was *Widowers' Houses*, performed in 1892. Shaw went on to write many famous plays, including *Saint Joan* about Joan of Arc, and *Pygmalion* known because of the musical version, *My Fair Lady*. He was awarded the Nobel Prize in 1925.

J. M. Barrie (1860–1937)

When he was six years old, James Matthew Barrie's mother became seriously ill. While she lay in bed Barrie spent many hours with her, reading books or listening to her stories. His first novels were about life in his home town of Kirriemuir in Scotland. Then he began writing plays, and these brought him wealth and fame. His most famous play, *Peter Pan*, was first performed in 1904, and with its mixture of fairies and pirates, it was an immediate success.

Dylan Thomas (1914–1953)

Welshman Dylan Thomas published his first book of poems around the age of 20. He met most of the famous writers of the time, and developed a habit of long drinking sessions with his friends. In 1949 he wrote the radio play *Under Milk Wood*. He was invited to America for a reading tour. However, the effects of alcoholism caught up with him and he collapsed and died while in New York.

August Strindberg

Swedish playwright and novelist
Born 1849   Died 1912 aged 63

August Strindberg is known in Sweden as a novelist and poet, but outside his country of birth he is best-known for his plays. His first novel *The Red Room* was published in 1879.

Throughout his life, Strindberg's works were noted for their honesty, and many thought he was too outspoken. He made many enemies and was even charged with blasphemy. After this, people in Sweden refused to buy or read his works. Elsewhere his plays were performed to rave reviews, but he began to suffer mental illness and his reputation suffered again, although it revived later in his life.

His best-known works are *Miss Julie* and *The Father*, and his plays have been performed throughout the world.

Oscar Wilde

Irish dramatist
Born 1854   Died 1900 aged 46

Oscar Wilde's stories became famous in America as well as in Britain. In the 1890s he wrote a number of brilliant comedies that were wonderfully amusing and sharply critical of the times in which they were written. The best of these was *The Importance of being Earnest* (1895). Sadly Wilde was convicted in the same year of homosexual activities, at that time illegal. The two years he spent in Reading Jail broke his spirit, and he died only three years later.

Anton Chekhov

Russian dramatist
Born 1860   Died 1904 aged 44

Although he was born into a poor family, Anton Chekhov became an eminent doctor, at one time working with prisoners in a remote settlement near Siberia. He soon began writing, starting with short stories which combined humour with a deep understanding of the sometimes comic, sometimes tragic way in which others live their lives. When he was 29 he wrote the first of many plays, where once again he mixed seriousness with the lightest of touches. On stage, his characters talk about their fantasies and failures with honesty and regret. Although they can usually see where they have gone wrong, they generally remain unable to do anything about their mistakes. These plays made Chekhov famous, but at the height of his powers he was struck down with tuberculosis. His last play, *The Cherry Orchard*, is one of the greatest dramas ever written.

» See also Leo Tolstoy p. 160

⬆ Anton Chechov (left), with another of Russia's most famous writers, Leo Tolstoy.

Bertolt Brecht

German playwright and poet
Born 1898   Died 1956 aged 58

After serving in World War I Brecht achieved success with his play *Drums in the Night* (1924). In 1933 he was forced to flee from Germany after Hitler came to power. He returned to East Berlin in 1947 where he founded The Berliner Ensemble, which is now world famous.

Among Brecht's plays that have become classics are *Mother Courage and her Children*, *The Caucasian Chalk Circle*, and *The Resistable Rise of Arturo Ui*.

Tennessee Williams

American writer
Born 1911   Died 1983 aged 71

Tennessee Williams, the adopted name of Thomas Lanier Williams, was born in Columbus, Mississippi, an area that provided the inspiration for many of his plays. After going to university, Williams supported his writing by taking various jobs before winning a grant from the Rockefeller Foundation for his play *The Battle of Angels* in 1940. This was followed by the award-winning play, *The Glass Menagerie* (1945).

Williams continued to confirm his importance as a playwright with *A Streetcar Named Desire* (1947) and *Cat on a Hot Tin Roof* (1955), which both won Pulitzer Prizes. They are notable for their brilliant dialogue and for scenes of high emotional tension.

Arthur Miller

American dramatist
Born 1915   Died 2005 aged 89

Arthur Miller's father was a small New York manufacturer who lost his money in America's economic slump in the 1930s. After working in a warehouse, Miller saved up to go to university and he soon began writing plays. *Death of a Salesman* (1949) is considered to be his masterpiece. It describes a pleasant but weak hero who instead of facing reality lives a false life of public cheerfulness and optimism. When the gap between this fantasy life and his own failures becomes too great, he finally kills himself.

Miller's other great play, *The Crucible* (1962), describes the hysteria that accompanied witch-hunting in 17th-century America. Miller makes a direct contrast here between this fanatical behaviour and the persecution of American Communists in his own time.

In 1956 Miller married the Hollywood actress Marilyn Monroe. They divorced in 1961, and his play *After the Fall* (1964) describes some of the difficulties they encountered in their relationship.

» See also Marilyn Monroe p. 214

⬆ Playwright Arthur Miller with his wife Marilyn Monroe.

Composers

Antonio Vivaldi

Italian composer
Born 1678 Died 1741 aged 63

Little is known of Antonio Vivaldi's early life, except that he was born in Venice and was taught to play the violin by his father. He then trained as a priest and was ordained in 1703. In the same year, he began to teach music at the Conservatorio della Pietà in Venice. The Conservatorio was an orphanage for girls that had a famous choir and orchestra. Vivaldi helped train the girls and wrote music for them to play. As his fame spread throughout Italy, he spent more and more time away from the Conservatorio and finally left there in 1738.

Vivaldi composed all kinds of music, including more than 40 operas, but he is most famous for his concertos. He wrote more than 500 of these, nearly half of them for solo violin. He also wrote concertos for flute, oboe, bassoon, recorder, and mandolin. Some have descriptive titles, such as *The Four Seasons* and *The Hunt*, and their music cleverly conjures up the appropriate atmosphere. As a result, Vivaldi's works are still very popular today.

🔄 This painting from 1723 is the only known portrait of the composer Antonio Vivaldi.

Johann Sebastian Bach

German composer
Born 1685 Died 1750 aged 65

Johann Sebastian Bach taught himself to compose by copying out the music of other composers. When he was 17 he took up his first post as church organist in Arnstadt. He then worked as a court musician. His last and most important post was as organist and choirmaster of St Thomas's Church, Leipzig.

When working as a court musician, Bach wrote mainly chamber and orchestral works, including the six *Brandenburg Concertos*. When working for the church, he wrote organ music, cantatas, and great choral works, such as the *St Matthew Passion*.

Although he was very famous in his day, Bach's music was forgotten after his death. It was not until the 19th century that people began to realize how great it was.

He married twice and had 20 children. Carl Philipp Emanuel and Johann Christian became, for a time, even more well known than their famous father.

Claudio Monteverdi (1567–1643)

Italian Claudio Monteverdi studied with the organist of Cremona Cathedral. In 1592 he entered the service of the Duke of Mantua and worked as a singer, instrumentalist, and composer. His opera *Orfeo* (1607) is regarded as the first great masterpiece of the operatic form that had only just been invented. In 1612 he became Master of Music at St Mark's Cathedral, Venice and he wrote magnificent music for church services.

Henry Purcell (1659–1695)

In 1674 Purcell was made tuner of the Westminster Abbey organ, and in 1677 succeeded Matthew Locke as 'composer to the king's violins'. Two years later he became organist of Westminster Abbey. Purcell wrote many fine choral works for royal occasions, as well as anthems and chamber music. His only real opera, *Dido and Aeneas* (1689), was very dramatic and emotional, and is considered to be his masterpiece.

Gioachino Rossini (1792–1868)

Rossini's career in operatic composition began in 1810, and he found great success with his 1816 opera, *The Barber of Seville*. By 1829, when his greatest serious opera *William Tell* was produced in Paris, he had written no fewer than 39 operas. And then, quite suddenly, he stopped. For the rest of his life he wrote only songs, piano pieces, and a little church music, including the *Stabat Mater* and the *Petite Messe Solennelle*.

George Frideric Handel

German composer
Born 1685   Died 1759 aged 74

George Handel's father wanted him to become a lawyer and he was very unhappy when the boy insisted on studying music instead. When he was 18, Handel went to Hamburg to work as an orchestral player and learn all he could about opera. He wrote two operas. One of them, Almira, was a great success and he was invited to Italy, the home of opera in the 18th century.

He stayed in Italy for nearly three years and wrote many successful works. However, he was still restless. In 1710 he visited London and was so happy there that he decided to make it his home, even though he had already accepted an appointment in Hanover. Fortunately, the Elector of Hanover became King George I of England in 1714 and he forgave the composer, so Handel was able to continue working in England.

Handel wrote orchestral works, such as the *Music for the Royal Fireworks* and the *Water Music* suite, and many fine concertos. However, he is probably best known for his oratorios (a kind of opera without scenery or costumes), including the famous *Messiah* (1742).

What a wonderful thing it is to be sure of one's faith!
GEORGE FRIDERIC HANDEL

Franz Joseph Haydn

Austrian composer
Born 1732   Died 1809 aged 77

Franz Joseph Haydn's father was poor and could do little to help a son who wanted to become a musician. Fortunately a relative agreed to pay for Haydn's education, and in 1740 the organist of Vienna's great cathedral, St Stephen's, took him into the choir, where he remained until he was 17.

Although he did not receive any formal lessons, he learned all he could, and taught himself to compose by studying the music he most admired. In 1759 he obtained his first official appointment, as musician to Count Morzin, and in 1761 he went to work for Prince Esterházy, at the prince's splendid palace at Eisenstadt. Haydn served the Esterházy family for 30 years. He wrote operas for their private opera-house, and church music for their private chapel. He also wrote symphonies and quartets, concertos, songs, and piano music for their day-to-day entertainment.

His fame spread far beyond the walls of the Eisenstadt palace. When the time came for him to retire, his music was known and loved throughout Europe. Haydn's music is ingenious and inventive. Without him, the symphony, of which he wrote 104, and the string quartet might never have become such important musical forms.

Wolfgang Amadeus Mozart

Austrian composer
Born 1756   Died 1791 aged 35

Mozart was composing by the time he was five, and could also play the harpsichord and violin. His father Leopold took young Wolfgang on a tour of Europe to show off his talents. Later, Mozart joined his father as one of the Archbishop of Salzburg's court musicians, but he hated being treated like a servant. In 1781 he went to Vienna where he taught and gave concerts. He was successful at first, but then things began to go wrong, and he died in comparative poverty.

Mozart wrote 41 symphonies and 27 piano concertos, chamber and solo piano music. Finest of all are his operas: *The Marriage of Figaro, Così fan tutte, Don Giovanni*, and *The Magic Flute*.

Ludwig van Beethoven

German composer
Born 1770   Died 1827 aged 56

Ludwig van Beethoven's father and grandfather were both professional musicians, so it was quite natural for him to follow in their footsteps. It was not long before, as a young man, he decided to leave Germany and seek his fortune in Vienna, Austria.

He made influential friends, and was soon in demand as a fashionable pianist and teacher. However, from about 1796 he began to go deaf and by the end of 1802 his deafness was serious.

At first he was in despair, but he pulled himself together and began to concentrate more fiercely than ever on composition. The music he now wrote, including the Third and Fifth Symphonies, was more powerful and dramatic than anything anyone had ever written before. It seemed to tell of a life and death struggle between tremendous forces, ending always in triumph. For example, the heroine of his opera *Fidelio* defends her husband against an evil tyrant; and the *Missa Solemnis* ('Solemn Mass') includes a prayer for deliverance from war.

Some of Beethoven's music was considered to be unplayable at the time, but it was later realized that they were masterpieces. His influence on later composers was enormous.

⊙ Despite his own misery, partly caused by his deafness (his ear-trumpet is pictured here), Beethoven wrote inspiring music.

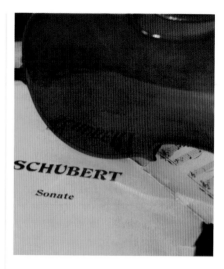

Franz Schubert

Austrian composer
Born 1797   Died 1828 aged 31

As a child, Franz Schubert showed a remarkable talent for music. His father taught him to play the violin, and his elder brother taught him the piano. When he was nine he began to study harmony and counterpoint (the art of adding melody as an accompaniment).

In 1808 he became a chorister of the imperial court chapel. He founded a students' orchestra in which he played and also sometimes conducted. By this time he was also writing music, including quartets for his family to play. When he left college, he became a schoolmaster like his father, although he soon gave it up to concentrate on composing.

In his short life Schubert wrote an amazing amount of music, including nine symphonies, several operas, much fine chamber music, and over 600 songs. He seldom had any money but he lived happily and had many friends who admired his music and encouraged him.

Johann Strauss I and II

Two important members of an Austrian musical family
Johann I Born 1804   Died 1849 aged 45
Johann II Born 1825   Died 1899 aged 73

Johann Strauss I began his musical career as a violinist. Shortly after the birth of his son (Johann II) he formed his own orchestra and played in the inns and dancehalls of Vienna. His fame rapidly spread throughout Europe and he undertook many successful tours.

Johann II began writing music when he was six. However, his father did not want him to take up a musical career and he had to study in secret. It soon became clear that he was very talented. When it came to waltzes, no one could rival Johann II. He was the 'Waltz King' of Vienna. *The Blue Danube* and *Tales from the Vienna Woods* delighted everyone, as did his polkas, quadrilles, and marches. His operettas, such as *Die Fledermaus* ('The Bat', 1874), were equally successful.

Felix Mendelssohn

German composer and conductor
Born 1809   Died 1847 aged 38

Felix Mendelssohn was handsome, intelligent, and born into a very wealthy family. He gave his first public concert when he was nine. By the time he was 16, and had completed his String Octet, it was clear to everyone that he was also a musical genius.

Good fortune followed him through the rest of his life. He became one of the most popular composers of the day in England as well as in Germany. His music, such as the 'Italian' Symphony, The *Hebrides* overture, the music for *A Midsummer Night's Dream*, the Violin Concerto, and the oratorio *Elijah*, pleased everyone. However, he took his duties seriously and worked so hard as a teacher and conductor that he undermined his health. When his beloved sister, Fanny, died, Mendelssohn seemed to lose the will to live and died only a few months later.

Frederick Chopin

Polish pianist and composer
Born 1810   Died 1849 aged 39

It was always clear that Chopin would become a great pianist and composer of piano music. One of his compositions was published when he was seven, and he gave his first public concert a week before his eighth birthday.

Chopin loved Poland, but he realized that he would have to travel if his career was to prosper. Eventually he settled in Paris, but he never forgot his native land. The music he wrote – the brilliant polonaises and mazurkas, the powerful ballades – was Polish through and through. It was an inspiration to the Polish people in their struggle for independence from domination by Russia, Prussia, and Austria. Equally inspiring were his sparkling waltzes and romantic nocturnes. Chopin could make the piano talk. He could make it sing.

Franz Liszt

Hungarian composer and piano virtuoso
Born 1811   Died 1886 aged 74

Music came naturally to Franz Liszt. He began to play the piano when he was only five, and gave his first public concert when he was nine. A group of Hungarian noblemen were so impressed they gave him money to study in Vienna and Paris. By the time he was 12 he was being compared with the greatest adult pianists of the day.

Liszt was also a fine composer. His music was brilliant and very adventurous, and pointed the way to new musical developments. One of his inventions was the symphonic poem, an orchestral work that told a story in terms of music. *Les Préludes*, *Mazeppa*, and Hamlet are examples, but he also wrote vast quantities of music of all kinds.

🔼 Liszt enjoyed great popularity in his lifetime.

Richard Wagner

German composer
Born 1813 Died 1883 aged 69

Richard Wagner was brought up in a theatrical family, and until the age of 15 he seemed more likely to become a playwright than a composer. In the end he did both, by writing the words and music for his own operas.

Wagner studied music at Leipzig University, but he really began to learn his trade when he worked in various German opera houses. His own first attempts at opera failed. Then *Rienzi* and *The Flying Dutchman* were successful and his luck changed.

Wagner was not content with ordinary opera. He wanted to write something that would combine all the arts into a music drama. In 1853 he began to write *The Ring of the Nibelungs*, a cycle (series) of four music dramas based on German legends. This magnificent production confirmed Wagner as one of the greatest musical geniuses the world has ever known. Wagner was as interested in theatre as he was in music. In 1876 he opened his own opera house in Bayreuth, Germany, and it was here that the first performance of *The Ring of the Nibelungs* took place.

> *I have long been convinced that my artistic ideal stands or falls with Germany. Only the Germany that we love and admire can help us achieve that ideal.*
> RICHARD WAGNER

Giuseppe Verdi

Italian composer
Born 1813 Died 1901 aged 87

The wonderful thing about Giuseppe Verdi is that the older he grew, the greater his music became. He wrote his last operas, *Otello* and *Falstaff*, considered to be his masterpieces, between the ages of 74 and 80.

Verdi's parents were poor and his musical education was paid for by a neighbour, a wealthy merchant. Even so, he failed to gain entry to the Milan Conservatory of Music and had to study privately. His first opera, *Oberto*, was quite successful and he was asked to write more. But tragedy struck: his wife and two young children died within two months of each other. Verdi was heartbroken and vowed never to write another note.

Fortunately, he was tempted to write a new opera, *Nabucco*, and its success launched his career. His most popular operas include *Rigoletto* (1851), *La Traviata*

➔ A caricature of Giuseppe Verdi.

Georges Bizet

French composer
Born 1838 Died 1875 aged 36

Georges Bizet began to study at the Paris Conservatoire when he was only nine, and made a deep impression both as a pianist and composer. In 1857 he won the Prix de Rome, which enabled him to study in Italy for three years. On returning to Paris he had a hard struggle to make a living. Although he wrote music of all

(1853), and *Aida* (1871). They are loved for their bold tunes and the way his characters come alive. Verdi also wrote a String Quartet (1873) and a Requiem (1874).

kinds, including a delightful Symphony in C, only performed long after his death, opera was his first love. Some of his operas, such as *The Pearl Fishers* (1863) and *The Fair Maiden of Perth* (1867), were reasonably successful, but others failed. Even his masterpiece, *Carmen* (1875), shocked people by its realism and was coolly received at first. It is now one of the most popular of all French operas. It is lively, colourful, and full of the most glorious melody.

Pyotr Ilyich Tchaikovsky

Russian composer
Born 1840   Died 1893 aged 53

Pyotr (Peter) Tchaikovsky was born into a wealthy Russian family. He was sent to boarding school in St Petersburg when he was eight, and eventually became a law student. It was not until he was 23 that he decided to devote his life to music. He enrolled in Russia's first Conservatory of Music in St Petersburg.

When he was 26 he wrote his first symphony. He also wrote difficult piano works that even top pianists could hardly play. But it is his fairytale ballets that many people know: *Swan Lake*, *Sleeping Beauty*, and *The Nutcracker*.

Tchaikovsky was often unhappy, and he suffered from depression. Nine days after conducting his moving Sixth Symphony, the *Pathétique*, he died. Some mystery surrounds the cause of his death; one theory is he committed suicide.

≫ See also Arthur Rubinstein p. 197

⬆ A performance of *Swan Lake* at the Royal Opera House in Covent Garden.

Antonín Dvořák

Czechoslovakian composer
Born 1841   Died 1904 aged 62

The young Antonín Dvořák would play the violin and join in the music-making in his village. When he was 12 he began to learn how to be a butcher. However, he could not forget music, and eventually an uncle agreed to pay for him to have proper lessons.

When his studies were complete, Dvořák earned his living by playing the violin. He also wrote music, but it was not until he was nearly 40 that people began to recognize his importance.

Dvořák wrote many colourful operas, concertos, chamber music pieces, and nine symphonies, the ninth of which ('From the New World') was composed when he went to teach in America. His music is full of dance-like tunes that seem to have sprung out of the Czech countryside. Dvořák made Czech music famous.

Hector Berlioz (1803–1869)

Hector Berlioz studied music at the Paris Conservatoire. He fell in love with an Irish actress, Harriet Smithson. She rejected him and he recorded his feelings about her in the extraordinary *Symphonie fantastique*. Berlioz made his living as a music critic and conductor while he wrote a series of remarkable works, such as the *Roméo et Juliette* symphony. However, he never quite recovered from the failure of *Les Troyens*, and died a disappointed man.

Johannes Brahms (1833–1897)

German Brahms was a fine pianist but he really wanted to be a composer. His chance came when he met Robert Schumann and his pianist wife, Clara. They did everything they could to encourage him. In 1863 he went to live in Vienna and his composing career really took off. He produced four great symphonies, chamber and piano music, songs, choral works such as the *German Requiem*, and also several fine concertos.

Camille Saint-Saëns (1835–1921)

Camille Saint-Saëns studied at the Paris Conservatoire, impressing everyone with his dazzling gifts as pianist, organist, and composer. His compositions include 13 operas, of which *Samson et Dalila* (1877) is the most famous, ten concertos, three symphonies, sacred and secular choral works, and a great many songs and piano pieces. He was also a great supporter of other composers' works.

Gilbert and Sullivan

Gilbert and Sullivan's operettas, which include *HMS Pinafore* (1878), *The Pirates of Penzance* (1879), and *The Mikado* (1885), were so successful that the theatre manager and producer Richard D'Oyly Carte built the Savoy Theatre especially for their works. But things did not always run smoothly: Gilbert had a quick temper, and Sullivan suffered greatly from ill health. Their partnership ended in 1896.

Nikolay Rimsky-Korsakov

Russian composer and teacher
Born 1844   Died 1908 aged 64

Apart from a few piano lessons, Rimsky-Korsakov was entirely self-taught. He made strenuous efforts with his musical knowledge and eventually became a professor at the St Petersburg Conservatory. He was a great admirer of Russian music and produced his own versions of Borodin's opera *Prince Igor*, and Mussorgsky's opera *Boris Godunov*. His own compositions are distinguished by their brilliant orchestration. They include such operas as *The Legend of Tsar Sultan* (1900) and *The Golden Cockerel* (1907), and the suite *Sheherazade* (1888).

Edward Elgar

English composer
Born 1857   Died 1934 aged 76

Edward Elgar's father ran a music shop in Worcester. He played the violin in local orchestras and wrote music for anyone who asked.

He was a sensitive man and was easily discouraged. It was only when he married, in 1889, that he found someone who really believed in him. In 1899 the *Enigma Variations* for orchestra proved that he was a musical genius. Oratorios, two great symphonies, concertos for violin and cello, and a symphonic poem, *Falstaff*, were further proof.

In 1920 his wife died. Elgar was broken-hearted, and for the rest of his life wrote almost nothing.

Giacomo Puccini

Italian composer
Born 1858   Died 1924 aged 65

Giacomo Puccini was the last and greatest of a long line of composer-musicians who lived and worked in Lucca, Italy. At first it seemed that he would become a church organist like his father, but he was increasingly drawn to opera.

After studying at the Milan Conservatory, Puccini entered a competition for a one-act opera. He failed to win a prize, but so impressed the great music publisher Giulio Ricordi that he was offered a contract to compose a full-length work. Although this first project was not successful, Ricordi still had faith in Puccini, and was rewarded by a series of wonderfully melodious and theatrically effective operas that are among the most popular ever

⬆ Puccini's opera *La Bohème* is famous for its dramatic effect and realism.

written. The most famous are *Manon Lescaut* (1893), *La Bohème* (1896), *Tosca* (1900), *Madame Butterfly* (1904), and *Turandot* (produced posthumously in 1926).

Claude Debussy

French composer
Born 1862   Died 1918 aged 55

Claude Achille-Debussy began studying music at the Paris Conservatoire when he was ten years old. At first he hoped to become a great pianist, but he found that he was not quite good enough so he decided to try composing instead.

> *I love music passionately. And because I love it I try to free it from barren traditions that stifle it.*
> CLAUDE DEBUSSY

As a composer he soon proved that he had genius. Such works as the *Prélude à l'après-midi d'un faune* (1892–1894) startled everyone. Instead of treating harmony according to the old rules, he used it freely, choosing chords for their effect, just as a painter chooses his colours.

Debussy's ideas set music free and opened up all sorts of possibilities for other composers to follow. He is therefore one of the most important composers of his day. Among his other works are the opera *Pelléas et Mélisande* (1892) and two important books of piano Préludes (1909–1910, 1911–1913).

Jean Sibelius

Finnish composer
Born 1865 Died 1957 aged 91

Jean Sibelius wrote his first piece of music when he was ten years old, and began to study the violin in earnest four years later. In 1885 he enrolled at the University of Helsinki as a law student, but turned to music in the following year. His first ambition was to become a concert violinist, but he later decided to try his hand at composing.

Success finally came to Sibelius in 1892 with the symphonic poems *En Saga* and *Kullervo*. Both were based on Finnish legends. This delighted the Finns, who were struggling against Russian domination at the time and were anxious to keep their culture alive.

Sibelius completed the first of his seven symphonies in 1899. These, together with his violin concerto and symphonic poems, brought him international fame and success. However, he gradually became disillusioned with the latest developments in music, and after completing the symphonic poem *Tapiola* in 1926 he gave up composing altogether.

Sergey Rakhmaninov

Russian composer and pianist
Born 1873 Died 1943 aged 69

Sergey Rakhmaninov studied music first at the St Petersburg Conservatory and then (1888) at the Moscow Conservatory. His first opera, *Aleko* (1893), was a success, but despite this, his First Symphony failed completely. He consequently became very depressed, and he even lost faith in his ability to compose. Fortunately, he was helped to recover by a course of hypnosis and he returned to his music.

The success of his second piano concerto (1901) finally restored his confidence. As a pianist he began touring in 1899, visiting America for the first time in 1909. He left Russia after the 1917 Revolution and settled in America, where he pursued the hectic career of a popular concert pianist. Although this greatly reduced the time he

⬆ This drawing of Sergey Rakhmaninov was made when he was 43. His dramatic and emotional style of music thrilled concert audiences.

could devote to composition, he still wrote many fine songs and piano pieces, as well as four piano concertos, *Rhapsody on a Theme of Paganini* for piano and orchestra, and three symphonies.

Gustav Mahler (1860–1911)

German composer Mahler loved writing long, complicated works for orchestras. These include nine completed symphonies. One of his most famous compositions, *Das Lied von der Erde* ('Song of the Earth', 1909), has an alto, a tenor, and an orchestra perform songs based on ancient Chinese poems. His music was mostly ignored for 50 years after his death but he is now praised as a pioneer of modern classical music.

Richard Strauss (1864–1949)

Born in Munich, Strauss developed his own distinctive and bold personal style. He went on to compose many pieces that he called tone poems. His first great success in this style was *Don Juan* (1889). Later, he turned to opera and wrote the startling *Salome* (1905) and *Elektra* (1909). His most popular opera was probably *Der Rosenkavalier* (1911). Strauss also wrote many songs and was a distinguished conductor.

Ralph Vaughan Williams

(1872–1958)

Although he started to compose when he was six, Vaughan Williams developed very slowly. It was only in 1903, when he began to collect and study British folk-song, that his music began to find its own special voice. His music includes opera, choral works, concertos, chamber music, songs, and a series of nine important symphonies. He also wrote music for films.

Arnold Schoenberg

Austrian composer
Born 1874   Died 1951 aged 76

Arnold Schoenberg was a mainly self-taught composer. His highly romantic orchestral work, *Transfigured Night* (1900), brought him a lot of attention. However, before long he found that his music no longer followed the rules that had served composers for nearly 300 years. He looked for an explanation and found it in the development of his own new scale system, where no note was considered more important than any other. He also believed that the notes should always appear in a strict sequence. His ideas appalled ordinary music lovers, but he began to influence other composers.

Because his music met with opposition, Schoenberg was obliged to teach in order to earn a living. When he was forced to leave his teaching post in Berlin in 1933 by the Nazis (he was Jewish), he settled in Paris and then in America, where he taught at the University of California. He is now regarded as one of the most revolutionary composers of the 20th century.

Maurice Ravel

French composer
Born 1875   Died 1937 aged 62

Joseph Maurice Ravel first became well-known as a pianist and a conductor, and he made a number of concert tours. However, apart from these excursions, he led a quiet and retiring life devoted to composing music.

Ravel had studied music at the Paris Conservatoire, under the direction of the composer Gabriel Fauré among others. Ravel turned to many different composers for inspiration, but developed his own uniquely personal style. He often drew on unusual sources, such as fairy tales or magic, for his themes.

His main works are songs and piano pieces, but he also wrote orchestral pieces such as the famous *Boléro* (1928), two piano concertos, ballets, and two short operas. One of his most famous piano works, *Gaspard de la Nuit*, is one of the most difficult to play that has ever been written.

◐ Arnold Schoenberg would often give talks before performances of his challenging musical works to explain what they meant.

Gustav Holst (1874–1934)

Gustav Holst's family came from Sweden. From the age of 18 he made his living as a choir director, a trombonist and playing in an orchestra, and finally as director of music at St Paul's Girls' School and at Morley College in London. Holst's inspiration came from varied sources – English folk music, Hindu scriptures, and from the poems of John Keats, Walt Whitman, and Thomas Hardy. His most famous work is *The Planets*.

Béla Bartók (1881–1945)

After graduating from Budapest's Academy of Music, Bartók became a concert pianist, often performing his own works. Bartók loved Hungary, and when he discovered its folk music he began to collect and study it. In 1940 he emigrated to America, where he wrote two of his best works: the Concerto for Orchestra and the Third Piano Concerto. Bartók's music includes many folk-song arrangements and piano pieces.

Richard Rodgers (1902–1979)

When he was 16, Rodgers met 23-year-old lyric writer Lorenz Hart. 'Fly With Me' (1919), written for Columbia University amateurs, began a 25-year writing partnership. In 1943, the year Hart died, Rodgers found a new lyricist in Oscar Hammerstein II. Among the shows they wrote together are *Oklahoma!* (1943), *Carousel* (1945), *South Pacific* (1949), *The King and I* (1951), and *The Sound of Music* (1959), all filmed by Hollywood.

Igor Stravinsky

Russian composer and conductor
Born 1882   Died 1971 aged 88

Although Igor Stravinsky showed an early talent for music, it was some time before he found his feet as a composer. His first great success came with the ballets he wrote between 1910 and 1913 – *The Firebird*, *Petrushka*, and *The Rite of Spring* made him the most talked-about composer in Europe. However, many people were outraged by *The Rite of Spring* and thought it was nothing more than a horrible noise.

Because of World War I and the Russian Revolution,

⬆ A performance of Stravinsky's controversial *The Rite of Spring*.

Stravinsky decided to leave Russia. He lived first in Switzerland and then in America. His music also took a new turn. It still used interesting harmonies and exciting rhythms, but it was no longer as savage as it had been. As a conductor, he conducted *The Firebird*, which he turned into a concert suite, about a thousand times.

Even at the end of his life Stravinsky was still experimenting with new ways of writing music. When he died, the world lost one of the most adventurous musical explorers of all time.

Irving Berlin

Russian-born American songwriter
Born 1888   Died 1989 aged 101

Irving Berlin was born Israel Baline in Russia. When he was five, his family left to go to New York. His father died when he was young and so, after only two years at school, he had to go to work. He worked as a newsboy, street singer, and singing waiter. Writing song lyrics got him a job with a music publisher and a printer's error gave him the idea for his professional name.

Soon he started to write tunes too, although at the time he could not read music. In 1911 he hit the jackpot with 'Alexander's Ragtime Band', which had sold two million copies by 1915. He wrote music and over 800 songs for shows and movies including *Top Hat* (1935), *Easter Parade* (1948), *White Christmas* (1954), and *There's No Business Like Show Business* (1954), which features stars such as Fred Astaire and Ginger Rogers, Judy Garland, Bing Crosby, Ethel Merman, and Marilyn Monroe.

≫ See also George Gershwin p. 198

⬇ A poster for the 1948 film *Easter Parade*, starring Fred Astaire and Judy Garland.

193

Sergei Prokofiev

Russian composer
Born 1891   Died 1953 aged 61

Sergei Prokofiev had his first music lessons from his mother, who was an excellent pianist. He began composing when he was five, could play Beethoven sonatas when he was nine, and by the age of 11 had written two operas. When he was 13 he went to study at the St Petersburg Conservatory of Music in Russia.

His first important compositions, two piano concertos, caused a great scandal, because they were very different from the kind of music people were used to. They were thought to be far too noisy. However, later works, such as the popular First Symphony (the 'Classical'), helped them to change their minds. Other compositions by Prokofiev include operas, piano and violin concertos, and ballets such as *Romeo and Juliet* (1935).

After the Russian Revolution in 1917, during World War I, and the founding of the USSR, Prokofiev spent many years in America and France. But he could not stay away and returned home in 1927 and again in 1934. One of the first pieces he wrote on his return was the delightful children's tale *Peter and the Wolf* (1936).

➲ Sergei Prokofiev composed seven symphonies, including the popular First Symphony (1917).

Aaron Copland

American composer
Born 1900   Died 1990 aged 90

Although he was born in Brooklyn, Aaron Copland's parents were Russian emigrants whose surname was originally Kaplan. After some time spent in Paris he returned to America in 1924 and supported himself by teaching and playing the piano. He became known as a composer – especially after 1938 when he produced three highly successful ballets on American subjects that made use of folk-songs and jazz rhythms: *Billy the Kid* (1938), *Rodeo* (1942), and *Appalachian Spring* (1944). It was his use of folk-songs and jazz that made him the first composer to develop a recognizably 'American' style.

Dmitry Shostakovich

Russian composer
Born 1906   Died 1975 aged 68

Dmitry Shostakovich's mother was a professional pianist and gave him his first lessons. From 1919 he studied at the Petrograd Conservatoire, but as his family was poor he helped out by playing the piano in a cinema. Success came early. Although his First Symphony was written in 1926 as a graduation exercise, it was hailed as a masterpiece. His career continued to prosper until 1936, when the newspaper *Pravda* suddenly attacked his opera *The Lady Macbeth of the Mtsensk District*, saying it was a disgrace to the Soviet way of life and for a while Shostakovich found himself out of favour.

He was greatly admired during the war years – his Seventh Symphony was composed in Leningrad (now St Petersburg) while the city was under siege by the Nazis in 1941.

As well as operas, ballets, choral, and instrumental works of all different kinds, Shostakovich wrote 15 symphonies and 15 string quartets, which are now considered to be among the most important musical works of the 20th century.

> *A creative artist works on his next composition because he was not satisfied with his previous one.*
> DMITRY SHOSTAKOVICH

Benjamin Britten

English composer
Born 1913   Died 1976 aged 63

Benjamin Britten began writing music when he was only five. His Simple Symphony is made up of tunes he wrote as a child. When he grew up he began to earn a living by writing music for documentary films and concerts. He went to live in America at the beginning of World War II, but could not forget England. When he returned, it was to write the work that made him famous: the opera *Peter Grimes* (1945).

Many of Britten's operas were written for the great opera houses. Others, such as *The Turn of the Screw* (1954), were designed for the festival he started in Aldeburgh, Suffolk. But it was not just opera that made his name. Britten wrote splendid orchestral music, songs, and choral works, none more fine, perhaps, than his great *War Requiem* of 1962.

⬆ Conductor and composer Leonard Bernstein.

Leonard Bernstein

American composer and conductor
Born 1918   Died 1990 aged 72

When Leonard Bernstein was ten, his family acquired a piano. Bernstein began lessons, soon making quick progress. When he was in his mid-twenties he became assistant conductor of a great orchestra, the New York Philharmonic.

From the 1940s Bernstein became known as a composer of musical shows. The most famous and successful of these was *West Side Story*, which opened on Broadway, New York, in 1957 and was later made into a film. It is still popular today. He wrote many kinds of orchestral and choral music, and was a highly respected conductor and pianist.

> *I'm not interested in having an orchestra sound like itself. I want it to sound like the composer.*
> LEONARD BERNSTEIN

⬆ Benjamin Britten studied at the Royal College of Music in London.

Classical Musicians

Yehudi Menuhin

American-born British violinist
Born 1916 Died 1999 aged 82

Yehudi Menuhin was the eldest of a family of remarkable musicians. He began violin lessons when he was four years old, and made his first public professional appearance (in San Francisco) in 1924.

A sensational Paris debut in February 1927, followed by an even greater success in New York in November, launched him on an international career that would last for the rest of his life. Concert tours followed throughout the world, and he began recording in 1927.

In 1959 Menuhin made his home in London (eventually taking British citizenship in 1985). He directed important festivals and appeared frequently as a conductor. In 1963 he established a specialist school to cater for exceptionally talented young musicians. He was knighted by the queen in 1965 and was made a Peer in 1993.

> *The violinist is that peculiarly human phenomenon distilled to a rare potency – half tiger, half poet.*
> YEHUDI MENUHIN

Maria Callas

American-born Greek soprano
Born 1923   Died 1977 aged 53

Maria Callas was born in New York. Her parents were Greek and her real name was Maria Kalogeropoulos. She trained in Athens and made her debut there in 1941, but her international career began in 1947 when she sang Ponchielli's *La Gioconda* in Verona, Italy. Thereafter she appeared in all the major opera houses, specializing in 19th-century Italian opera.

However, her stormy and self-critical temperament, and recurring vocal troubles, cast a shadow over her career. She was also the lover of the Greek shipping millionaire Aristotle Onassis, and for many years they made headline news. At her best, though, Callas was without equal as a dramatic soprano and spellbinding actress. She retired from the stage in 1965, but continued to make records.

🔄 Maria Callas pictured on the cover of a German magazine in 1959. She had the face and gift for dramatic expression and delighted audiences in such operas as *Madame Butterfly*, *Aïda*, and *Medea*.

Luciano Pavarotti

Italian tenor
Born 1935   Died 2007 aged 71

In 1961, after a period of study, Luciano Pavarotti won an international singing competition and made his debut as Rodolfo in Puccini's *La Bohème*. He was first heard outside Italy in 1963 when he went to Holland and London, and in the following year he toured Australia with Joan Sutherland. He made his American debut in 1968, since which time he has appeared in all the world's great opera houses and is widely regarded as one of the greatest tenors of the day.

Pavarotti was very popular, partly because of his larger-than-life personality and remarkable physical appearance. He was closely associated in friendly rivalry with the tenors Placido Domingo and José Carerras.

See also
Joan Sutherland
p. 197

Luciano Pavarotti singing in his usual flamboyant manner, which made him a great favourite with the public.

Kiri Te Kanawa

New Zealand soprano
Born 1944

Five weeks after Kiri was born into a poor Maori family, she was adopted by Tom and Nell Te Kanawa, who named her Kiri, the Maori word for bell.

After winning many singing prizes in New Zealand and Australia, Te Kanawa studied at the London Opera Centre and then joined the Royal Opera Company. She made her Covent Garden debut in 1970, her first major role being that of the Countess in Mozart's *The Marriage of Figaro*.

She has specialized in the music of Mozart and Richard Strauss and made many outstanding recordings of opera and also of American musicals, such as Bernstein's *West Side Story*.

See also Leonard Bernstein p. 195

Nellie Melba (1861–1931)

In October 1887 Melba made her operatic debut, in Brussels, as Gilda in Verdi's *Rigoletto*. Triumphant appearances in London and Paris soon followed, and by 1892 the operatic world was at her feet. She even had two famous foods, Peach Melba and Melba toast, named in her honour! London's Covent Garden Opera House remained especially dear to her, and she made her last appearance there on 8 June 1926.

Pablo Casals (1876–1973)

Pablo Casals was already a capable pianist, organist, and violinist before he took up the cello. His solo career began in 1898, and he was soon regarded as the world's greatest cellist. In 1936 he went into voluntary exile in Prades, in the French Pyrenees, in protest against General Franco's Fascist regime in Spain. In 1950 he founded the Prades annual musical festival, and in 1956 he went to live in Puerto Rico, where he also founded the Casals Festival.

Arthur Rubinstein (1887–1982)

Arthur Rubinstein was a capable pianist when he was three, and after a period of study in Berlin, he began his career. He made his first American tour in 1906. In 1932 he withdrew from the concert platform for a period of intensive study and reassessment. Rigorous discipline was now added to a brilliant technique, and the success of his 1937 American tour swept away any doubts the critics may have had.

Joan Sutherland (b.1926)

Joan Sutherland made her debut in London's Covent Garden in 1952 in Mozart's *The Magic Flute*. In 1959 her performance in the Covent Garden production of Donizetti's *Lucia di Lammermoor* established her as an outstanding soprano. Sutherland and her husband, who is a pianist and conductor, have toured the world's opera houses. She retired in 1990.

Popular Musicians

George Gershwin

American composer
Born 1898   Died 1937 aged 38

George Gershwin was the son of Jewish parents who had emigrated from Russia to New York. Young George did not do very well at school, and showed no interest in music until one day when he was ten he heard another schoolboy playing the violin. He started having piano lessons and made very quick progress.

As a young man he started writing songs for shows. During the 1920s and 1930s he turned out a stream of music, much of which is still sung and played: songs such as 'Somebody Loves Me', 'Fascinating Rhythm', and 'A Foggy Day'. Many of the words of his songs were written by his elder brother Ira. Gershwin always wanted to be a more serious composer, and he wrote orchestral and piano music, and an opera, *Porgy and Bess* (1934– 1935). Sadly, he died of a brain tumour when he was only 38.

≫ See also Richard Rodgers p. 192, Cole Porter p. 199

1950s jazz singer Billie Holiday.

Billie Holiday

American jazz singer
Born 1915   Died 1959 aged 44

Billie Holiday's father played banjo and guitar in a jazz band, and at 15 she was in New York singing in jazz clubs. Her distinctive voice and emotional appeal brought her rapid success. All through the 1940s and 1950s she toured and recorded. Her best-known records are probably 'Strange Fruit', 'Fine and Mellow', 'Lover Man', and 'Violets for my Furs'.

At the time when Holiday was touring, there was still a great deal of prejudice against black people in the American South, and consequently Holiday came across a lot of racism. She also had personal problems, including a drug addiction. This eventually brought about her death, just as she reached the peak of her artistic abilities.

Louis Armstrong

American jazz trumpeter, entertainer, and singer
Born 1901   Died 1971 aged 70

Louis Armstrong had a poor but happy childhood, but one day a silly prank (firing a pistol in the street) ended up with him being sent to a children's home. It was there that he had music lessons and learned to play the cornet.

He left the home as a teenager and gradually started to earn a living as a musician. In the 1920s, he formed various small groups of his own, such as 'The Louis Armstrong Hot Five', and made some recordings.

In 1936 he appeared in his first film, *Pennies from Heaven*. He gradually became a popular entertainer, famous for his cheerful, gravelly singing voice.

Armstrong's most popular songs were 'Hello Dolly' (1964) and 'What a Wonderful World' (1968)

Frank Sinatra

American singer and film star
Born 1915 Died 1998 aged 82

Francis Sinatra was born in a tough neighbourhood in New Jersey, where he may have made the first underworld (organized crime) contacts for which he was often criticized. He started as a singer when he was about 20 and in 1939 was 'discovered' by bandleader Harry James. His style of singing romantic ballads with emotive and characteristic phrasing delighted his teenage fans, but he could also sing witty and moody numbers.

He began acting in films in the 1940s but was not taken seriously until the non-singing role of an American soldier in *From Here to Eternity* (1953). He went on to star in many more films. He continued to sing in live concerts even when he was in his seventies.

B. B. King

American blues guitarist and singer
Born 1925

Riley King was born to sing the blues: he grew up during the Great Depression, a poor black farm boy in the tough southern state of Mississippi. He was always musical, singing in church when he was four, and learning guitar as a teenager. He became known as 'Blues Boy', a nickname he later shortened to 'B. B.' King.

He started recording in 1949, and his distinctive guitar playing on such early classics as 'Please Love Me', '3 o' Clock Blues', and 'You Upset Me Baby' immediately revealed him to be a master musician.

King has remained both popular and influential over the years, and together with his faithful guitar, which he has nicknamed 'Lucille' he is one of the best-known figures in blues music.

⊙ B. B. King's albums include *Blues is King* (1967) and *Lucille Talks Back* (1975).

Cole Porter (1891–1964)

After World War I, American Porter took classes with composer Vincent d'Indy in Paris. His most successful shows were *Anything Goes* (1934), *Kiss Me Kate* (1948), *Can Can* (1953) and *Silk Stockings* (1955). A horse-riding accident in 1937 left him confined to a wheelchair and in great pain. However, this did not stop the flow of songs with their cleverly rhymed lyrics and sparkling tunes.

'Duke' Ellington (1899–1974)

Edward Kennedy Ellington's stylish clothes gained him the nickname Duke. In New York in 1927 he formed a ten-piece band, and became famous playing in Harlem's Cotton Club. Unlike most jazz musicians, he also wrote fully orchestrated works. Many hit records, including 'Don't Get Around Much Anymore' and 'It Don't Mean a Thing', spread his fame worldwide.

Glenn Miller (1904–1944)

Glenn Miller was in demand as an instrumentalist but had less success at forming his own band until he started the Glenn Miller Orchestra in 1937. This 'big band' soon became popular, with compositions such as 'Moonlight Serenade', 'Pennsylvania 65000', and 'Little Brown Jug'. During World War II Miller led the air force band. Returning to London from performances in Paris, his plane disappeared, and no trace of it has ever been found.

Ella Fitzgerald (1918–1996)

At 16 Ella Fitzgerald was dared to sing in an amateur contest in Harlem, and won $25. Then, invited to sing with Chick Webb's band, she found success with hits like 'A-Tisket A-Tasket' (1938). Fitzgerald brought jazz to new audiences as a star singer in the 1950s. Her crystal-clear tones and perfect diction were unrivalled for singing popular songs. Indeed, Fitzgerald's finest achievement is her series of 'songbook' albums recorded in the late 1950s.

James Brown

American soul singer
Born 1928   Died 2006 aged 76

James Brown had a hard childhood. When he was only 16 he
was jailed for armed robbery.
Turning to music kept him out
of trouble, and in 1958 he had
his first million-selling record,
'Try Me', a song in the gospel and
rhythm 'n' blues styles. He soon
added hard, rhythmic guitars
and frantic horns, creating a style
that became known as funk.

His exciting live shows earned
him the title Godfather of Soul.
Hits like 'Papa's Got a Brand
New Bag' (1965) and 'Living in
America' (1986) confirmed his star
status over a period of 20 years.

Ray Charles

American singer and musician
Born 1930   Died 2004 aged 73

Ray Charles Robinson had a
tragic childhood: born in poverty,
he lost his sight through illness at
the age of seven. He attended a
Florida school for blind children
where he learned to write musical
arrangements in Braille. He
became an accomplished pianist.

Recordings such as 'I Got A
Woman' (1954) and 'What'd I
Say' (1959) infuriated churchgoers
because they were rhythm 'n' blues
songs with gospel-style vocals, but
they were later recognized as being
early examples of 'soul' music.

Other hits like 'Georgia On My
Mind' (1960) demonstrated his
ability to play anything from jazz
to country music.

Elvis Presley

American rock and roll singer
Born 1935   Died 1977 aged 42

Elvis Presley was born into a poor
family in Mississippi. As a teenager
he spent much of his time with
black musicians, learning a lot
about blues and gospel music.
In 1953 he paid to make a record
for his mother's birthday at the
Sun Records studios in Memphis.
The owner heard Elvis singing,
liked his unusual mixture of
styles, and offered him
professional recording work.

His first local hit was 'That's
All Right' in 1954, and he
created a sensation on television
by swivelling his hips while
singing. Adults were outraged at
this new dance style, but teenagers
loved it. By 1956 Elvis was a
national star, making huge hits
like 'Hound Dog', 'Blue Suede
Shoes', and 'Jailhouse Rock'.
Known as the 'King of
Rock'n'Roll', Presley eventually
recorded 94 gold singles and over
40 gold albums. He also starred
in 27 films.

He continued touring and
recording during the 1960s.
During the 1970s he spent more
time at Graceland, his huge house
in Memphis. He died there of
heart failure in 1977. Many
thousands of his fans still visit
Graceland every year to pay
tribute to 'The King'.

➜ For many years, Elvis
Presley was the most popular
singer in the world.

Buddy Holly

American singer and songwriter
Born 1936   Died 1959 aged 22

Like many early rock'n'roll musicians, Texas-born Charles Hardin Holley began his musical career by playing country music but, as leader of the group Buddy Holly and the Crickets, he went on to become one of rock'n'roll's greatest songwriters. He was also, in 1956, the first musician to use two guitars, bass, and drums, which became the standard line-up for pop groups in the 1960s. His hits, including 'That'll be the Day' (1957), 'Rave On' (1958), and 'It Doesn't Matter Any More' (1959), have been recorded by many artists and still sound fresh today.

➲ Buddy Holly had an instantly recognizable 'hiccuping' singing style. The music he wrote influenced many later pop musicians.

Tragically, Holly died in a plane crash after playing a concert in Clear Lake, Iowa. Two other popular musicians of the time also died in the crash – Ritchie Valens and the Big Bopper.

Holly was at the peak of his success and only 22 years old when he died.

Marvin Gaye

American singer and songwriter
Born 1939   Died 1984 aged 44

Marvin Gaye was the son of a minister and he learned to love music while singing in church. He joined the Motown record label in 1961, which was famous for recording African-American artists, and which would go on to produce some of the greatest soul music of all time, with musicians including the Jackson 5.

Gaye quickly became one of the most popular soul-pop singers of the 1960s and enjoyed success into the 1970s. His best-known song is probably 'I Heard it Through the Grapevine', but he had several other big hits, including 'How Sweet it is to be Loved by You' and 'Can I Get a Witness'.

As his career progressed, however, Gaye started taking drugs and became very troubled. By the 1980s he had gone back to live with his parents to try and sort himself out. Marvin had a difficult relationship with his father, though, and he was shot and killed by him during an argument one morning in 1984.

Chuck Berry (b.1926)

Born in San Jose, California, Berry did a number of jobs while he tried to become a full-time musician. Once he got a recording contract, he had a string of hits with witty story-lines. These songs mixed country music with rhythm 'n' blues and an irresistible dance beat. His songs, including 'Rock'n'Roll Music' (1957) and 'Sweet Little Sixteen' (1958), are world-famous and have been performed by hundreds of other musicians.

Aretha Franklin (b.1942)

Aretha Franklin was a gospel-singing prodigy at the age of 12. Columbia Records signed her in 1960, but she eventually found her feet at Atlantic Records when she was restyled as 'The Queen of Soul'. A string of hits such as 'Respect', 'Chain of Fools' (both 1967), and 'Think' (1968), established her as possibly the finest female vocalist of her generation. In recent years she has enjoyed chart success singing duets.

Paul Simon (b.1942)

New York's folk-rock duo Simon and Garfunkel had many hit records during the 1960s and 1970s. The best known was probably 'Bridge over Troubled Waters' (1970). They split up after this record. Simon pursued a solo career and his work on albums like *There Goes Rhymin' Simon* (1973) showed him to be a sensitive and intelligent songwriter. In 1986 Simon recorded the album *Graceland* with many African musicians.

Lennon and McCartney

English songwriters and musicians
John Lennon Born 1940 Died 1980 aged 40
Paul McCartney Born 1942

When they met in 1957, John Winston Lennon and James Paul McCartney were just two Liverpool teenagers with a passion for rock 'n' roll. They became the main songwriters in the Beatles, and the incredible success of their songs kept the group at the top of the charts for seven years.

Lennon and McCartney started recording separately in 1970 when the Beatles split up. Neither was as consistent on his own, although McCartney in particular has enjoyed some enormous solo hits. Lennon's peace anthem 'Imagine' (1971) has become a much-loved classic and was widely played at the time of his murder in 1980.

Bob Dylan

American singer and songwriter
Born 1941

Robert Zimmerman was a wild and reckless teenager who ran off to travel across America. He took the name Dylan from Welsh poet Dylan Thomas, and performed as a singer in New York's Greenwich Village coffee bars during the early 1960s. Two of his own songs, 'Blowin' in the Wind' (1962) and 'The Times they are a-Changin'' (1963), became anthems for the Civil Rights movement in the USA. This started a new style, 'protest music', with songs about war, religion, politics, and racism.

Dylan's change from acoustic to electric instruments in the mid-1960s inspired a folk-rock craze, and he was called 'a spokesman for his generation'. His new writing technique was rich in strange images, bizarre characters, and hidden meaning.

After a serious motorcycle accident in 1966, Dylan returned to a simpler style of music. In the late 1970s he became a Christian, which was reflected in his songs of that time on albums such as *Shot of Love* (1981).

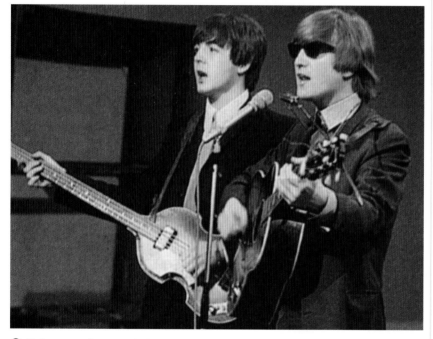

⬆ McCartney and Lennon singing together in the pop supergroup the Beatles.

Joni Mitchell (b.1943)

Roberta Joan Anderson had a talent for painting at school, but then she learnt to play the guitar and became interested in folk music. Her skill as a songwriter was soon noticed, and her songs were sung by others before she recorded them under the name Joni Mitchell. Her early albums *Clouds* (1969) and *Ladies of the Canyon* (1970) contained many of her best-loved songs: 'Both Sides Now', 'Chelsea Morning', and 'Big Yellow Taxi'.

Eric Clapton (b.1945)

Eric Clapton first became interested in American blues music as a teenager attending Kingston Art College. His early recordings with the Yardbirds, John Mayall, and the 'supergroup' Cream helped define the role of the 'guitar hero', and have inspired musicians ever since. In 1970 his band Derek and the Dominos recorded the song 'Layla', one of the greatest rock singles, and Clapton's most inspired performance.

Stevie Wonder (b.1950)

Stevie was blind, but played harmonica, piano, organ, and drums superbly. He had his first No. 1 hit, 'Fingertips' when he was only 13 years old. Twenty hits later he struck out in a new direction, adding funky electronic keyboards to his sound and singing about the problems faced by black Americans. He became even more successful in the 1980s, with hits including 'Ebony and Ivory' (1982), a duet with Paul McCartney.

> *I just hate to be in one corner. I hate to be put as only a guitar player, or either only as a songwriter, or only as a tap dancer. I like to move around.*
> JIMI HENDRIX

Jimi Hendrix

American rock singer and musician
Born 1942   Died 1970 aged 27

James Marshall Hendrix was one of the most exciting, unusual, and imaginative rock guitarists ever. He began his career in his Seattle home by imitating records of blues guitarists. He then played the guitar with many top soul groups. He started his own band in New York, but moved to London in 1966 to form the trio The Jimi Hendrix Experience. He immediately found success with 'Hey Joe' (1967) and, despite the strangeness of his sound, followed it with five more hit singles and three albums before his death in 1970. Many later guitarists have imitated Hendrix, but none play quite like him.

Jimi Hendrix's group, the Jimi Hendrix Experience, disbanded in 1969, but he continued to record and peform until his death a year later.

Mick Jagger

English singer and songwriter
Born 1943

Michael Philip Jagger's father was a PE instructor who stressed the importance of physical fitness. Jagger heeded his father's advice and became one of the most athletic of all musical performers, the unforgettable front man of the rock group the Rolling Stones – one of the most famous bands of all time.

The group emerged from London's thriving rhythm and blues scene in the early 1960s, and at first they were content to copy the blues songs which had inspired them. By 1963, however, Jagger was writing songs with guitarist Keith Richards, and together they produced such rock classics as 'Satisfaction' (1965), 'Jumpin' Jack Flash' (1968), and 'Brown Sugar' (1971).

Jagger has also occasionally acted and made solo records, and in 1985 he duetted with David Bowie on a chart-topping single, 'Dancing in the Street', which raised a lot of money for famine relief in Africa.

See also **David Bowie p. 204**

Bob Marley

Jamaican reggae singer and songwriter
Born 1945   Died 1981 aged 36

Bob Marley was born to a black mother and a white father. He lived with his mother in Kingston, Jamaica, where living conditions were harsh. When he joined the group the 'Wailin' Wailers' he wrote many songs about this. By 1965 the Wailers' reggae music was attracting listeners far beyond Jamaica. A recording contract in the UK brought world fame in the 1970s. He died of cancer in 1981.

David Bowie

English singer and songwriter
Born 1947

David Robert Jones was born in Brixton, London. As David Bowie he remained a star by changing his looks and musical style to keep up with the times.

He was in many groups during the 1960s, but his first big hit was 'Space Oddity' in 1969. That led to a string of over 40 hit records, including 'Let's Dance' (1983) which was No. 1 in both Britain and America at the same time.

Bowie always liked to create a whole new personality for himself on stage, as he did in 1972 as 'Ziggy Stardust'. He also appeared in films and plays, but always returned to music.

Elton John

English singer and songwriter
Born 1947

After college Reginald Dwight played piano in a hotel, then later joined a local group. In 1967 he changed his name to Elton John. He went to America to appear in a concert in 1970, and became an 'overnight success'. His first international hit was 'Your Song' (1971), followed by a string of hit records and sell-out concerts. His involvement with good causes brought him into close contact with Diana, Princess of Wales, and at her funeral in Westminster Abbey he sang a specially written version of his song 'Candle in the Wind' in tribute to her.

⊗ See also Diana, Princess of Wales
p. 27

Sting

English singer and songwriter
Born 1951

Sting was born Gordon Matthew Sumner in Northumberland, England. He became famous as the singer in the rock group the Police in the 1970s, where his gravelly voice and good looks made him a teen idol. The Police broke up in 1984 and the following year Sting released his first solo album *The Dream of the Blue Turtles*. It was an instant hit, and Sting went on to have huge solo success. In 2007 he announced a reunion tour with the Police.

From the 1980s onwards Sting has been heavily involved in many charity activities, including supporting Amnesty International, and performing at Live Aid and Live 8, 20 years later.

Michael Jackson

American singer and songwriter
Born 1958   Died 2009 aged 50

Michael Jackson was hailed as a singing genius from the age of six. In 1970 he and his brothers formed a group called the Jackson Five. In 1971 he began his solo career. Jackson's first album was *Off the Wall* (1979) which sold 19 million copies. This was followed by *Thriller* (1982) which sold 38 million and became the biggest-selling album ever. When Michael Jackson died in 2009, an estimated one billion people watched his memorial service on TV.

Despite his controversial private life, Jackson is celebrated as the biggest-selling solo artist of all time.

◐ Michael Jackson.

Madonna

American singer and songwriter
Born 1958

Madonna Louise Ciccone was the most successful female singer of the 1980s. Born in Michigan, America, she studied dancing, and then combined her dancing skills with pop singing after moving to New York. Some of her outrageous clothes attracted as much attention as her singing. Her hits included 'Like a Virgin' (1986), 'Vogue' (1990), and 'Music' (2000). Her album *True Blue* (1986) was the No. 1 album in 28 countries.

Madonna has also acted in several films including *A League of Their Own* (1992) and *Evita* (1996). She's also written books for children and designed her own clothing line.

Kylie Minogue

Australian pop star
Born 1968

Kylie Minogue started her career as an actress, appearing on the popular Australian soap opera *Neighbours*. By 1987 she had released a single, 'Locomotion', as part of a charity performance and the song proved to be a surprising success. She was signed with the London-based Stock, Aitken and Waterman, who produced thousands of pop hits in the 1980s. Her first single with them, 'I Should be so Lucky', went to

❶ Like Madonna, Kylie managed to change her image and style of music to suit the changing tastes of her fans over the many years of her successful career.

No. 1 in the charts and set her on the path to super-stardom.

In the later 1990s she moved away from synthesized pop and started recording dance anthems, such as 2000's 'Spinning Around'.

In 2005, Kylie was diagnosed with breast cancer and had surgery to treat it. She took some time out from her career while she had further treatment, but burst back on the scene, more popular than ever, in 2006.

Robbie Williams

English pop star
Born 1976

At school, Robbie Williams was always a joker. He was not very good at academic subjects, but he enjoyed sport and acting. Robbie left school at 16 to work as a salesman. One day he saw an advert in a paper for a fifth member of a pop group. He went for an audition and got the job. The band was called Take That.

Take That were not a success immediately, but in 1991 they became hugely popular. From 1991 to 1996 they had a string of hits in the UK. Robbie enjoyed being famous but he didn't quite fit with the band's clean-cut image. In 1996 he fell out with the other members and left the group.

For a year after leaving Take That, Robbie ran wild and most people thought it was the end of his career. But Robbie had other ideas. In 1997 he released a solo album, *Life Thru a Lens*. The single 'Angels' was soon No. 1 in the UK charts, and the album became a bestseller.

A string of No. 1 hits followed and more bestselling albums. Between 2002 and 2006 Robbie won six Brit awards and two MTV awards. He had success in the UK and the USA with the song 'Somethin' Stupid' – a duet with Nicole Kidman.

> *I like listening to good music – I can't stop playing my album.*
> ROBBIE WILLIAMS

Actors
Charlie Chaplin

British-born film actor and director
Born 1889   Died 1977 aged 88

Charlie Chaplin's mother was a music-hall entertainer in London and from the age of five Chaplin took part in her act. When she became ill, the young Chaplin was sent to an orphanage. In 1910 he moved to America and four years later he began to appear in films. He became the best-loved comedian of the silent cinema, famous for his moustache, bowler hat, baggy trousers, and cane. Soon he was writing and directing his own films, and in 1919 he helped to found the United Artists film company.

In his most famous films, such as *The Kid* (1920) and *The Gold Rush* (1925), Chaplin played a sad little tramp who was bullied and confused by powerful people. Usually he bounced back and was always on the side of weaker people. He also made successful talking pictures such as *The Great Dictator* (1940), a fierce but amusing attack on Adolf Hitler and his Nazi followers.

Buster Keaton

American star of silent films
Born 1895   Died 1966 aged 70

Joseph Keaton's parents were comedians. They trained him when he was very young to perform in their stage act. He was given his name 'Buster' when he fell down the stairs and survived unhurt. When he was 21 he joined the comedian Roscoe 'Fatty' Arbuckle in making short films.

From 1919 he started making his own films, such as *Our Hospitality* (1923) and *The Navigator* (1924), in which he escaped from one disaster after another with hardly a change of expression. He was nicknamed 'Great Stone Face' because of this. In his greatest film, *The General* (1927), he played an engine-driver caught up in the American Civil War. Sadly, his career ended with the arrival of talking pictures.

⬆ Buster Keaton in the 1925 film *Go West*.

Marx Brothers

Each of the Marx Brothers had a distinctive character. Zeppo (1901–1979) played straight, romantic roles. Groucho (1890–1977), with his cigar and funny walk, was always cracking jokes. Harpo (1888–1964) never spoke. Chico (1887–1961) spoke with an Italian accent and was often seen playing the piano. Most of their films concentrate on the three most famous and comical of the brothers: Chico, Harpo, and Groucho.

Rudolph Valentino (1895–1926)

Rudolph Valentino was born in Italy. At 18 he travelled to America, where he worked as a dancer and a film 'extra'. He became a star during the 1920s, acting in films such as *The Sheik* (1921), *Blood and Sand* (1922), and *Son of the Sheik* (1926). He was adored by film fans for his handsome appearance in such romantic roles. His early death attracted thousands of fans to his funeral to mourn this glamorous leading man.

Fred Astaire (1899–1987)

Fred Austerlitz had a successful stage career dancing with his sister Adele from the age of seven. Later, Fred looked for work in films. By 1933 he had changed his name to Fred Astaire and teamed up with Virginia ('Ginger') Rogers in *Flying Down to Rio*, the first of nine films they made together. Through films such as *Top Hat* (1935) and *Swing Time* (1936) they became cinema's most famous dancing couple.

Johnny Depp

American film actor
Born 1963

Johnny Depp made his name in the America television series *21 Jump Street*, but his first real film role came earlier, in *A Nightmare on Elm Street* (1984). His television role made him a teenage idol, and more film offers came flooding in. He began a long association with director Tim Burton when he played the hero of *Edward Scissorhands*, and he went on to star in many of Burton's films. Although not all his films of this period were box-office hits, Depp has always taken parts that interested him personally rather than because he knew they would be big successes. This is a philosophy he still sticks to, although he is Hollywood's hottest property and almost anything with Depp is guaranteed to be a success. He cemented his superstar status with his role as Jack Sparrow in *Pirates of the Caribbean* – one of the most successful film franchises ever. Depp is much respected for his professionalism and his individuality.

➲ Johnny Depp as Captain Jack Sparrow.

Clark Gable (1901–1960)

At first Clark Gable appeared in films as a villain, but in 1934 he found success with the romantic comedy *It Happened One Night*, for which he won an Oscar. During the 1930s he was the most popular 'leading man' in Hollywood films. His greatest role was as the handsome Rhett Butler in *Gone with the Wind* (1939). He was still acting in films at the time of his death.

Gary Cooper (1901–1961)

Gary Cooper began his working life drawing political cartoons for a newspaper, but he did not make much money, so he started working an as extra in western films. From there he went on to become a leading man. His best-known performance was in the western *High Noon* (1952). He won an Oscar for this, and for his earlier role in *Sergeant York* (1941).

Jean Gabin (1904–1976)

Frenchman Jean Gabin began his acting career as a cabaret artist, working in French music halls such as the Moulin Rouge. His popularity there had led to film work by the 1930s. At first these were small parts in French films, but his appearance in Jean Renoir's *La Grande Illusion* brought him international recognition and he moved to the USA during World War II. Gabin made more than 50 films in his career, as well as continuing his stage work.

Tom Hanks (b. 1956)

Tom Hanks acted in his first film in 1979, but it was his role in *Splash* (1984) that brought him to international attention. He had mixed success for the next few years, but *Big* (1988) and *Sleepless in Seattle* (1993) were huge box-office successes. In 1995 he became only the second person ever to win the Oscar for Best Actor two years running. He won it in 1994 for his role as a man with AIDS in *Philadelphia*, then in 1995 for his role as the slow-witted hero of *Forrest Gump*.

Actresses

Sarah Bernhardt

French actress
Born 1844   Died 1923 aged 78

When she was young, Sarah Bernhardt enrolled in acting school and got a place in the French national theatre company. She was sacked for slapping a senior actress and it was some years before she became a leading actress famed for her musical 'silvery' voice. She was worshipped by her fans as 'The Divine Sarah' and travelled the world with her own company. Her most famous roles included the title role in Racine's play *Phèdre*, and Marguerite Gautier in *The Lady of the Camellias*. She also played male roles, including Hamlet.

She was the first great actress to appear in movies. During the making of the film *Tosca* she injured her knee while jumping from some battlements. In 1915, after years of pain, her leg had to be amputated – but she went on acting nonetheless.

➔ A theatre poster showing Sarah Bernhardt.

Greta Garbo

Swedish-born American film actress
Born 1905   Died 1990 aged 85

Greta Gustafsson grew up in Stockholm, Sweden, and worked as a model before she started acting in films. She travelled to Hollywood and became a star in romantic silent films such as *The Torrent* (1926). When talking pictures came in, her Swedish accent meant that she was given roles as distinguished European ladies, such as the great Swedish queen in *Queen Christina* (1933) and the tragic heroine of *Anna Karenina* (1935). She was famous for her beauty and for her serious expression, but she was also very private and disliked publicity. She made her last film in 1941.

⬆ Garbo was known for her serious expression.

Marlene Dietrich

German-born American actress and singer
Born 1904   Died 1992 aged 88

Maria Magdalene Dietrich was born in Berlin, Germany. She first attracted attention for her appearances in the German and American versions of the film *The Blue Angel* (1930). She decided to stay in Hollywood, becoming a US citizen in 1937, and she starred in such famous films as *Blonde Venus* (1932), *Destry Rides Again* (1937), and *Judgement at Nuremberg* (1961).

Not only was she an actress but she was also a singer, famous for her husky voice. She performed in cabarets for many years. She would often appear in trouser-suits, which was considered quite daring at the time.

Bette Davis

American film actress
Born 1908   Died 1989 aged 81

Ruth Elizabeth Davis came from Lowell, Massachusetts, and studied acting in New York. Film directors did not think she was beautiful enough for romantic roles, but in the 1930s she established herself as a powerful actress playing forceful women. She won Oscars for her roles in *Dangerous* (1935) and *Jezebel* (1938).

In films such as *The Little Foxes* (1941) and *All About Eve* (1950) she played cruel and selfish characters. In others, like *Now, Voyager* (1942), she played more likeable women, but her strong personality always shone through. In later life she scared audiences of *Whatever Happened to Baby Jane?* (1962) when she terrorized her sister, played by Joan Crawford.

⊘ Bette Davis in a still from the film *Jezebel* (1938).

Katharine Hepburn

American film actress
Born 1909   Died 2003 aged 96

Katharine Hepburn's first film, *Bill of Divorcement*, made her an instant star in 1932. She was then identified with witty comedies, such as *Bringing Up Baby* (1938) and a series of movies with Spencer Tracy (her partner in private life). She also triumphed in mature roles, in *The African Queen* (1951), *The Lion in Winter* (1968), and later in life as the elderly mother in *On Golden Pond* (1981), for which she was awarded one of her four Academy Awards (Oscars). This was despite a trembling caused by Parkinson's disease and an eye ailment, the result of dunkings in a Venice canal for scenes in *Summer Madness* (1955).

> ❝ Sometimes I wonder if men and women really suit each other. Perhaps they should live next door and just visit now and then. ❞
> KATHARINE HEPBURN

Ingrid Bergman

Swedish film actress
Born 1915 Died 1982 aged 67

Swedish actress Ingrid Bergman made her first film, *Liliom*, in 1940. She became an overnight success because of her blonde good looks. She was recognized as a perfect leading lady of the times.

Bergamn starred opposite Humphrey Bogart in the classic wartime film *Casablanca* (1942), which cemented her success and made her a Hollywood icon. She made several other films during World War II.

While she was filming *Stromboli* in 1949 she fell in love with the director, Roberto Rossellini, and although she was already married, she had a child by him. This caused a great deal of scandal in 1940s Hollywood. Their daughter Isabella Rossellini has also become a famous actress.

The scandal surrounding her affair forced her to take a break from film acting for a while, but in 1957 she appeared in the movie *Anastasia*. This saw a triumphant return and it seemed as though she had been forgiven as it was a great success. She continued with stage, film, and later, television work, until she lost her long battle with cancer in 1982.

See also **Humphrey Bogart p. 207**

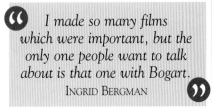

I made so many films which were important, but the only one people want to talk about is that one with Bogart.
INGRID BERGMAN

Marilyn Monroe

American screen idol
Born 1926 Died 1962 aged 36

Marilyn Monroe was born Norma Jean Mortenson. She had a miserable childhood in Los Angeles foster homes because her mother was mentally ill.

After working as a model and in minor film roles, Monroe starred in her first big role in *Niagara* in 1953. Two of her best-known films, *Gentlemen Prefer Blondes* (1953) and *Some Like it Hot* (1959), show she was a fine comic

➡ Marilyn Monroe – the Blonde Bombshell.

actress. However, she also took serious, dramatic roles in films like *The Misfits* (1961), her last film.

She was married three times, including to baseball star Joe DiMaggio and playwright Arthur Miller, who wrote *The Misfits* for her. She died from a drug overdose in 1962. Even now, many years after her death, she is remembered as one of the most beautiful stars of cinema history.

See also **Joe DiMaggio p. 236**, **Arthur Miller p. 183**

Elizabeth Taylor

British-born American film actress
Born 1932

Elizabeth Taylor was born in London, but grew up in Hollywood as a child actress.

She appeared in films from the age of ten and enjoyed great success in *National Velvet* in 1944.

Taylor was very beautiful, with violet eyes that became world famous, and it was not long before she was one of the most glamorous stars of the 1950s and 1960s. She also attracted much attention because of her several short-lived marriages. She was married twice to the great Welsh actor Richard Burton, with whom she acted in *Cleopatra* (1963). She played the title role in this film and had to make 65 costume changes. Her most memorable performances are of strong-minded women. She won Oscars for playing such women in *Butterfield 8* (1960) and *Who's Afraid of Virginia Woolf?* (1966). Recently Taylor has fought through several illnesses, including cancer.

◐ Elizabeth Taylor in a Hollywood publicity shot.

Julia Roberts

American film actress
Born 1967

As a child Julia Roberts wanted to be a vet, but later she decided to study acting like her older brother and sister.

In 1990 Julia became a star almost overnight for her part in *Pretty Woman*. Between 1993 and 1997 she made a range of different movies. Then in 1997 she returned to romantic comedy with *My Best Friend's Wedding*. In 1999 another romantic film, *Notting Hill*, was very popular.

Julia was now one of the top stars in Hollywood. She was paid $20 million – the most ever paid to an actress – to appear in the film *Erin Brockovich*. This dramatic film was a huge success, and won her an Oscar in 2001.

Mary Pickford (1893–1979)

Mary Pickford began working in movies as an extra for D. W. Griffith's Biograph Company and became the first star of the silent screen. From 1913, a succession of sweet and innocent roles, such as *Rebecca of Sunnybrook Farm* (1917) and *Pollyanna* (1920), made her 'America's sweetheart'. In 1919 she formed United Artists with Charlie Chaplin, Douglas Fairbanks, and D. W. Griffith, to ensure film profits went to them rather than the studios.

Shirley Temple (b.1928)

Shirley Temple started acting in short films at the age of four, and won an Oscar when she was five for *Stand up and Cheer* (1934). She became America's favourite child star, usually playing the part of a little orphan who got her way with adults by smiling sweetly and dancing or singing. Unfortunately, she did not succeed in becoming an adult actress and made her last film, *Fort Apache* (1948), at the age of 20.

Brigitte Bardot (b.1934)

French actress Brigitte Bardot began working as a model but was tempted into film acting by a director who saw her picture on the cover of *Elle* magazine. She later married another director, Roger Vadim, and starred in his film *And God Created Woman* (1952). She was known for her good looks, and has achieved perhaps greater success than any other French actress.

Nicole Kidman (b.1967)

As a teenager Nicole Kidman was tall and gawky, but she spent as much time as she could at the St Martin's Youth Theatre in Melbourne, Australia. She made her film appearance at the age of 14. In 1989 she appeared opposite Tom Cruise in *Days of Thunder*. The two married in 1990 but divorced ten years later. In 2001 she proved her versatility when she starred in *Moulin Rouge*, in which she also sang and danced.

Filmmakers

D. W. Griffith

American film pioneer and director
Born 1875   Died 1948 aged 73

David Wark Griffith left school early to work as a lift-boy to help support his family before becoming a touring actor. He tried to write plays and in 1908 he sold some story ideas to early filmmakers and this brought him the chance to direct a movie.

He made over 400 silent films (usually lasting only 12 minutes) in which he and cameraman 'Billy' Blitzer developed the use of many basic cinema techniques that have become standard today: close-ups, long-shots, fades, and cutting

It takes about ten years to master the subtle art of being able to hold one's audience.
D. W. GRIFFITH

between shots. Then came two great epics of the silent cinema. The first was the hugely profitable three-hour *The Birth of a Nation* (1915), which is now considered to be the first feature-length film ever made. This epic was followed by the even more ambitious but financially unsuccessful movie *Intolerance* (1916).

Griffith made more movies, some with sound, but in the 1930s he found it impossible to raise backing for the kind of films he wanted to make.

Cecil B. De Mille

American film director and producer
Born 1881   Died 1959 aged 78

Cecil B. De Mille started his career as an actor, but he soon became a director instead, and founded a film company which later formed part of Paramount Pictures. As a director he started making silent comedies, but he became more famous for *The Ten Commandments*, which he made twice, first as a silent film in 1923 and then again with sound and colour in 1956. This and his other 'epic' films based on stories from the Bible and from history were famous for their huge crowd scenes and their spectacular special effects, like the parting of the Red Sea in *The Ten Commandments*.

⬇ Cecil B. De Mille (right) photographed during the filming of *The Ten Commandments*.

Sergei Eisenstein

Russian film director
Born 1898   Died 1948 aged 50

Sergei Eisenstein's father wanted him to be an architect, but his real love was for the theatre. His chance came when he had to leave his engineering training to serve in the army in the Russian Civil War of 1918. There were theatre groups in the army, and Eisenstein was able to join in as a helper and director.

After the Civil War, and until his death, he directed films. Eisenstein showed his genius for putting together scenes in an interesting and exciting way. He believed that a film director should create something more than just a series of pictures. He called this the art of 'montage', and many directors have been influenced by him.

⬆ A poster for Hitchcock's thriller *The Man Who Knew Too Much* (1956)

Alfred Hitchcock

English film director
Born 1899   Died 1980 aged 81

Alfred Hitchcock was the son of a London poultry dealer. He was good at drawing and got a job writing and designing captions for silent films. He soon worked his way up to become a film director. In 1926 *The Lodger* began his long series of suspense thrillers, in which he makes a very brief appearance each time. His film *Blackmail* (1928) was the first British talking picture. He directed *The Thirty-Nine Steps* (1935) and several other films in England, but then moved to Hollywood and became even more famous as a director of frightening thrillers such as *Rebecca* (1940), *Psycho* (1960), and *The Birds* (1963).

Samuel Goldwyn (1882–1974)

Samuel Goldfish was a Polish orphan who emigrated first to London, then America. There, he and his brother-in-law set up as filmmakers. Taking the name Goldwyn, he became a top producer and an influential star-maker. When his own company became part of M.G.M. (Metro-Goldwyn-Mayer) in 1924 he left to become an independent producer. Films such as *Wuthering Heights* (1939) and *The Little Foxes* (1941) were typical of his use of famous writers and adaptations of their work.

John Ford (1895–1973)

John Ford got his first job in movies as a props man before beginning to direct films. He developed his skills on dozens of short films and westerns. *The Iron Horse* (1924), a silent movie set around the building of the Union-Pacific railway, was his first huge success. Human dramas such as *The Grapes of Wrath* (1940) and *The Quiet Man* (1952) won Oscars. Ford is best remembered, though, for directing classic westerns such as *Stagecoach* (1939).

Frank Capra (1897–1991)

Capra was born in Sicily but moved to America as a child. His first taste of Hollywood came when he was an extra in John Ford's film *The Outcasts of Poker Flat* in 1919. He became hooked on movies but it wasn't until 1926 that he directed his first film, the silent movie *The Strong Man*. Among his most famous films are *It Happened One Night* (1934), *Arsenic and Old Lace* (1944), and *It's a Wonderful Life* (1946).

Luis Buñuel (1900–1983)

Spanish director Buñuel pioneered a type of filmmaking that became known as 'surrealist cinema' because of their disconnected narrative style. His use of unusual imagery, often with a nightmarish quality, in films such as *Robinson Crusoe* and the *Phantom of Liberty*, had a huge influence on later filmmakers.

Walt Disney

American cartoon filmmaker
Born 1901   Died 1966 aged 65

Walter Disney grew up on a farm, and enjoyed sketching the animals. He established his own film company in Hollywood in 1923, creating Mickey Mouse in 1928 and Donald Duck in 1934. These quickly became the world's favourite cartoon characters. Then he made full-length animated films, including *Snow White and the Seven Dwarfs* (1937), *Pinocchio* (1940), and *Bambi* (1942). Sometimes he was criticized for changing famous stories, such as *The Jungle Book*, to suit his cartoons.

His film company was the biggest producer of cartoons, but it also made children's films with real actors, such as *Twenty Thousand Leagues under the Sea* (1954), and films like *Mary Poppins* (1964), which combined cartoon characters and real actors.

In 1954 he opened Disneyland, the huge amusement park in California. He planned the even bigger Disneyworld in Florida, but this did not open until five years after his death.

> **"** *If you can dream it, you can do it. Always remember that this whole thing was started with a dream and a mouse.* **"**
> WALT DISNEY

⬆ Walt Disney's most famous character, Mickey Mouse, at Disneyworld in Florida.

Ingmar Bergman

Swedish film director
Born 1918 Died 2007 aged 89

Ingmar Bergman is Sweden's most famous film director. He worked as a theatre manager before he started in films in the 1940s. He brought a fresh approach to filmmaking and his movies often have a dreamlike quality, using flashbacks and very emotional scenes that were unusual at the time. He has made many art films, the most famous of which include *The Seventh Seal* (1957) and *Through A Glass Darkly* (1961), for which he won an Oscar. He retired from filmmaking in the 1980s, and his last film was *Fanny and Alexander* (1982), which was largely autobiographical.

Federico Fellini

Italian film director
Born 1920 Died 1993 aged 73

Federico Fellini worked as a journalist and scripted a radio serial before director Roberto Rossellini got him into movies as a writer and then director. The Oscar-winning *La Strada* ('The Road', 1954) made him known internationally. *La Dolce Vita* ('The Sweet Life', 1960), a rather humorous look at fashionable society in Rome, was probably his greatest international success. However, it was less typical of his work than his films that mixed dream and reality, exploring personal memories and problems, such as *8½*, about a film director stuck in the middle of making a film and unsure how to go on.

Satyajit Ray

Indian film director
Born 1921 Died 1992 aged 71

With a musician mother, writer father, and writer and painter grandfathers, Satyajit Ray was brought up in artistic circles. He, however, originally planned a career in science but changed his mind while studying with the poet Rabindranath Tagore, who was a friend of the family). Ray then became interested in book illustration instead.

Working on the story of Apu, a Brahmin boy growing up in poverty in a Bengal village in India, made Ray want to make a film of this book. Helping French director Jean Renoir to film *The River* on location in India increased his interest in cinema and he determined that he would break into the movie industry.

Over the next five years, using amateur actors and filming mainly at weekends, he made *Pather Panchali* (completed 1955). The film won a major prize at the Cannes Film Festival and was followed by two other films that continued the story of the hero Apu. These two films were *Unvanquished* (1956) and *World of Apu* (1959). Among the best of his other films are *The Music Room* (1958) and *The Chess Players* (1977).

For his contribution to the film industry, Ray was given an honorary Academy Award just a few weeks before his death in April 1992.

⬆ Satyajit Ray (left) directing one of his films. He liked spontaneity, and preferred to use the first filming of a scene rather than a retake.

» See also Rabindranath Tagore p. 177

> **"** *The director is the only person who knows what the film is about.*
> SATYAJIT RAY **"**

Jean-Luc Godard

French film director
Born 1930

French filmmaker Jean-Luc Godard has become one of the most famous European directors of his generation. He began to be interested in film while studying at the Sorbonne in Paris, and while there he was involved with the group that later characterized New Wave cinema.

Godard began his career as a film critic, establishing the magazine *Cahiers du cinéma* in 1951. It was not long before he was trying his hand at directing.

His first feature film was *Breathless*, released in 1960. This movie was typically New Wave in style – with the characters offering 'asides' and using real situations rather than sets.

During the making of his next film, *Le Petit Soldat*, Godard met the Danish actress Anna Karina, whom he later married. She starred in several of his other films until their divorce in 1967, including *Vivre sa Vie*, *Bande à parte*, and *Piertot le fou*.

Most of Godard's films are very political in content – some people have even said that they are revolutionary. Godard uses film to comment on political events such as wars or colonialism. Several of his films also show the influence of Karl Marx and his Socialist teaching – highlighting elements such as the class struggle. He continues to make films into the twenty-first century, most recently with *Vrai faux passeport* (2006).

❯❯ See also Karl Marx p. 80

Francis Ford Coppola

American film director
Born 1939

Francis Ford Coppola studied film at college and afterwards he began writing movie scripts. It wasn't long before he had won his first Oscar, for screenwriting the film *Patton*. But Coppola really wanted to be a director, so he started his own production company and in 1972 he released his most famous film, *The Godfather*. This is now considered to be one of the greatest films of all time, along with its sequel – *The Godfather Part II*.

Throughout the 1970s Coppola was much in demand as a director, and he secured his reputation at the time with *Apocalypse Now* (1979), a dramatic and horrifying movie about the Vietnam War. The film went hugely over budget and experienced many problems in production, but is still considered a classic today.

After this Coppola's career seemed to decline, and he made several films that were not so successful. By the end of the 1980s, his production company was bankrupt. He made a comeback in 1992 with *Bram Stoker's Dracula*, which was a box-office smash and started him on the road to recovery.

⬆ The Godfather of filmmaking – Francis Ford Coppola.

Martin Scorsese

American film director
Born 1942

Martin Scorsese's first major success was *Mean Streets* (1973), which made Robert De Niro's name. De Niro also starred in *Taxi Driver* (1976). Scorsese then began working on an ambitious biography of the boxer Jake LaMotta, *Raging Bull*. This movie, filmed in black and white, earned De Niro an Oscar.

The Last Temptation of Christ had to be postponed because of lack of money, so the director turned his hand to more commercial projects. The biggest box-office smash of this period was *The Color of Money* (1986), which gave Scorsese enough money to film *The Last Temptation of Christ*.

He moved to more traditional films throughout the 1990s, but he returned to his gang roots with *The Departed* in 2006, for which Scorsese earned an Oscar.

⬆ Fassbinder on the set of *Despair*.

Rainer Werner Fassbinder

German film director and writer
Born 1946 Died 1982 aged 37

Rainer Werner Fassbinder was born in Bad, a town in Bavaria. His father was a doctor and his mother was a translator. Later, his mother starred in several of Fassbinder's films.

He studied drama in Munich and directed his first play in 1968.

The following year he made a film called *Love is Colder Than Death*, but this was not well-received. However, his next movie, *Katzelmacher* won several awards and Fassbinder never looked back. He was remarkably prolific, making 41 films in less than 15 years. His last film was *Querelle*, which was released the year that he died of an overdose, at the age of only 37.

Orson Welles (1915–1985)

Orson Welles became famous in 1938 for presenting a radio play about invaders from Mars as if it were a real newsflash. People listening to *The War of the Worlds* were terrified and thousands of them fled in panic. A few years later he made *Citizen Kane* (1941), in which he also starred. The new techniques he used for combining sound and pictures in this and other films, including *The Magnificent Ambersons* (1942) and *Touch of Evil* (1958), inspired many other film directors.

Stanley Kubrick (1928–1999)

Kubrick made his first film in 1951, when he was 23. Although it was only 13 minutes long, it launched his career. He went on to both write and direct some of the best-known films of the 1960s and 1970s, including *2001: A Space Odyssey* (1968) and *A Clockwork Orange* (1971). His last movie was *Eyes Wide Shut*, starring Tom Cruise and Nicole Kidman, completed just before his death.

Ridley Scott (b.1937)

British filmmaker Ridley Scott is famous for making films such as *Alien* (1979) and in particular *Blade Runner* (1982). This was not a great hit when it was first released, but is now considered a classic of modern cinema. After a few flops in the late 1980s and early 1990s, he was back on form with *Gladiator* (2000), for which he received an Oscar nomination.

Quentin Tarantino (b.1963)

American director Quentin Tarantino burst on to the movie scene with *Reservoir Dogs* in 1992, which became an instant classic and resulted in a new generation of fast-paced, explicitly violent films. He followed up his success with *Pulp Fiction* (1994), which helped revive the career of actor John Travolta. In recent years Tarantino has become less popular, but films like *Kill Bill* (2003 and 2004) and *Hostel* (2006) were still box-office hits.

Steven Spielberg

American film director, writer,
and producer
Born 1947

As a boy, Steven Spielberg began using his father's cine-camera to film toy trains. At school he made several amateur science-fiction films. His big impact on the cinema came in 1975 with the tense thriller *Jaws*, which quickly made more money than any other film. After making *Close Encounters of the Third Kind* in 1977, he broke box-office records again with the success of *Raiders of the Lost Ark* (1981) and *E.T.* (1982), which made more than 700 million US dollars. His film *Jurassic Park* (1993), with its amazing dinosaur special effects, again broke all box-office records. In 1994 Spielberg was awarded his first Oscar for Best Director for his ground-breaking film *Schindler's List*. This black and white movie about the Holocaust also won six other Oscars, including one for Best Film.

⬇ Steven Spielberg comes face to face with the star of one of his most famous films, *E.T.: The Extra-Terrestrial*.

Pedro Almodóvar

Spanish film director and writer
Born 1951

Pedro Almodóvar is the best-known Spanish filmmaker of his generation. His movies are characterized by often confusing narratives and complex emotions in his characters. His films have been described as shocking, but they are also very influential.

Almodóvar's parents hoped he would be a priest but young Pedro had other ideas, and by the age of 12 he had become obsessed with films. He moved to Madrid in 1969 to pursue a career in the film industry. His first feature film, *Pepi, Luci, Bom…* was made in 1980 to mixed reviews. Many people thought he was too 'modern', but by the time he made *Women on the Verge of a Nervous Breakdown* in 1988, he was being hailed as a filmmaker of originality and genius, a reputation he still has today.

> ❝ *I don't want to imitate life in movies; I want to represent it. In that representation, you use the colours you feel, and sometimes they are fake.*
> PEDRO ALMODÓVAR ❞

Dancers

Anna Pavlova

Russian-born ballerina
Born 1881   Died 1931 aged 49

Anna Pavlova's unusual talent for dancing was spotted while she was still at school. She was enrolled at the St Petersburg Imperial Ballet School and in 1906 the Imperial Russian Ballet gave her the title of prima ballerina. A year later she danced *The Dying Swan*, a ballet that had been specially created for her by the choreographer Michel Fokine.

By 1913 Pavlova had decided to leave Russia to set up her own company. Her aim was to bring ballet not only to the great European and American cities, but also to places such as India, Africa, and South America, where this form of dancing had hardly ever been seen before.

Over a period of 20 years she covered thousands of miles and gave nearly 5000 performances, amazing audiences with her lightness and grace. From 1912 she was based in London, where she proved to be an inspiration to a younger generation of dancers both in England and abroad.

> « *Although one may fail to find happiness in theatrical life, one never wishes to give it up after having once tasted its fruits.* »
> ANNA PAVLOVA

Vaslav Nijinsky

Russian ballet-dancer
Born 1890   Died 1950 aged 60

Vaslav Nijinsky's parents were dancers, and both he and his sister followed in their footsteps. When he was ten he was enrolled in the Imperial Ballet School in St Petersburg, Russia, where his natural talent was soon built upon.

By the time he was 20 Nijinsky was touring the world. The great ballet producer, Diaghilev, made him the star of many of his ballets. Nijinsky was always looking for new techniques and styles, and he often offended classical ballet fans by his interpretations. Much of what he did, though, was later recognized and used in modern ballet.

Nijinsky's later life was touched by tragedy. By the time he was in his thirties he was showing signs of mental illness that developed into schizophrenia. This became progressively worse and he spent much time in hospital. He died, after much sadness and suffering, in London in 1950. He was reburied in Paris in 1953.

◎ Nijinsky in a scene from the ballet *Scheherazade*.

Gene Kelly

American dancer and actor
Born 1912   Died 1996 aged 83

Gene Kelly will always be remembered for his singing and dancing in the musical film *Singin' in the Rain* (1952). He was a dance teacher before finding stage work on Broadway, where he was spotted by Richard Rodgers. He eventually made the move to Hollywood and starred in musicals such as *An American in Paris* and *Brigadoon*. He also designed stage sets and choreographed many musicals. By the 1960s, though, musicals had become less popular, and Kelly began to appear in television shows and directed some films, including *Hello Dolly!*

Business Leaders

John D. Rockefeller

American industrialist and multimillionaire
Born 1839   Died 1937 aged 97

John Davison Rockefeller was a businessman when the first oil well was drilled in America in 1859. Four years later he started an oil refinery in Ohio. By 1870 his company, the Standard Oil Company, began to buy up many other oil companies and this marked the beginning of the Rockefeller empire.

By 1882 Standard Oil had 95 per cent of all the refining business in America. This monopoly made him into a multi-millionaire. Once he had made his fortune, Rockefeller began to look for good and useful ways to spend his money. In 1891 he paid for the University of Chicago to be established, and he later set up the Rockefeller Institute for Medical Research (which later became Rockefeller University) in New York City.

In 1913, after retiring from the oil business, he began the Rockefeller Foundation to finance charitable activities.

> 〝 I believe in the dignity of labor, whether with head or hand; that the world owes no man a living but that it owes every man an opportunity to make a living 〞
> JOHN D. ROCKEFELLER

Henry Ford

American manufacturer of early cars
Born 1863   Died 1947 aged 83

Henry Ford was born on his family's farm in Michigan, America, but he did not like farming. At 15 he became an apprentice in a machine shop, and in 1893 he built his first car. He drove it for about 1500 kilometres, then sold it and built two bigger cars. Then, in 1903, he started the Ford Motor Company.

Using light, strong steel, he built cheap cars for everyone to buy. In 1908, he built the first Ford 'Model T', the 'Tin Lizzie', which sold for $825. He was soon selling a hundred cars a day. By 1927, 15 million Model Ts had been made, and the Ford Motor Company was worth 700 million dollars.

The cars were made on an assembly line: as they slowly moved the 300 metres through the factory, workers completed simple single tasks on them. It was boring work, but Ford paid the highest wages in the industry.

Early Fords were simple, cheap, and reliable: 'Anyone can drive a Ford' was one slogan. But keeping things simple sometimes meant less choice. 'You can have any colour you like,' said Henry Ford of his Tin Lizzie, 'so long as it's black.'

⬆ Henry Ford, with his famous Model T, first built in 1908.

J. Paul Getty

American multi-millionaire oilman
Born 1892   Died 1976 aged 83

Jean Paul Getty went to university in southern California and in Oxford before joining his father's oil company. By the age of 24 he was a millionaire, and in 1930, when his father died, he took over the company. Before long he had taken over other companies to form a business empire of more than 100 companies, headed by his own Getty Oil Company.

Outside of business his main interest was in art, and he used his considerable fortune to buy many paintings and sculptures. In 1953 he founded the J. Paul Getty Museum, in Malibu, California, to house his art collection.

Bill Gates

American founder of Microsoft and major figure in the computer world
Born 1955

Bill Gates began writing computer programs at 13. He went to Harvard University, and while he was there he developed BASIC, a simple and easy-to-use computer programming language. He believed that personal computers (PCs) would eventually spread to every home and office. So in 1975 Gates and his school friend Paul Allen founded the company Microsoft to develop software (computer programs) for PCs.

Microsoft expanded, and in 1981 produced MS-DOS, the operating system used on most PCs. In 1983 they created Windows, a program in which the user points at icons (small pictures) with a hand-held pointer (a mouse) and clicks on them to open files and programs.

By 1993 Microsoft had become the world's largest computer-industry company, and Gates was very rich: by mid-1997 his personal fortune was estimated at $42 billion, making him the richest person in the world. In recent years, Microsoft has been accused of trying to monopolise the industry, particularly Internet access.

➡ Billionaire Microsoft founder Bill Gates.

Mayer Amschel Rothschild
(1744–1812)

German Mayer Amschel Rothschild built up his own banking business and, with his sons, he started branches across Europe. Anselm worked with him in Frankfurt. Nathan started the London branch in 1804. Jakob set up the Paris branch in 1811. After their father's death, Salomon Mayer and Karl Mayer opened branches in Vienna and Naples. The family fortune was made during the wars against Napoleon I, when they lent money to the warring countries.

Cornelius Vanderbilt (1794–1877)

Cornelius Vanderbilt left school at 11 and when he was 16 he borrowed money to buy a ferry boat. It was the first of many business operations that would make him one of the richest men in the world. By 1846 he was a millionaire. At the age of 70, he started to buy railway companies, and made even more money. By the time he died, he had amassed a fortune of 100 million dollars.

Andrew Carnegie (1835–1919)

American businessman Carnegie started working in a cotton factory. He worked very long hours, but read as much as he could. He started a company in 1863 to make iron railway bridges instead of wooden ones. Ten years later his company began to produce steel too. He was very generous with his money: before he died, he had paid for 2811 free public libraries around the world, and he also established pension funds.

Richard Branson (b.1950)

In 1969 Richard Branson started up Virgin, a successful record mail-order company. Soon afterwards he founded Virgin Records. The company expanded into publishing, recording, and selling other products, and changed its name to the Virgin Group. Branson has continued to extend the Virgin brand into new areas, most notably Virgin Airways, Virgin Railways, Virgin Radio, and Virgin Cola.

Movers and Shakers

William Wilberforce

English leader of the campaign to end slavery in the British Empire
Born 1759   Died 1833 aged 73

William Wilberforce was member of parliament for Hull from the age of 21. His life's work began when he met John Newton, the captain of a slave ship, who had realized how wrong it was to buy and sell human beings as slaves. From 1785, Wilberforce campaigned to stop the slave trade. Finally, in 1807, parliament passed a law to abolish it. But employers in the West Indies still wanted slaves, and the trade continued secretly. So Wilberforce and his supporters decided there must be a law stopping people from owning slaves at all.

After another long campaign, a law to abolish slavery in the British Empire eventually went through parliament in 1833. By this time, however, Wilberforce's health was failing and he died shortly afterwards.

Sojourner Truth

American anti-slavery campaigner
Born c.1797   Died 1883 aged about 86

Sojourner Truth was born into slavery and was originally called Isabella. She was abused as a young woman and between 1810 and 1827 she had at least five children. Then in 1827 she was freed under a New York law that banned slavery. One of her first acts as a free woman was to fight a court battle for the return of her youngest son, who had been sold illegally as a slave in the South.

She came to believe that God wanted her to preach His message of love, so in 1843 she changed her name to Sojourner ('traveller') Truth and became an evangelist. She began to travel through the states of the North, where she often attracted very large crowds. As well as preaching Christianity she also spoke against slavery and, from the 1850s, in favour of votes for women.

Sojourner Truth's message to her audiences was that as Christians they should oppose slavery.

William Caxton (c.1422–1491)

Caxton learned how to use the printing press recently introduced by Gutenberg in Germany, then set up his own press in Bruges, Belgium. Here he printed his English edition of The History of Troy, completing it in 1473. In 1476, he set up the first printing press in England, at Westminster. During his lifetime, Caxton printed about 110 books. He also published Chaucer's Canterbury Tales, making it available to many new readers.

Sequoya (1760–1843)

Sequoya was probably the son of a British trader but he was brought up by his Cherokee mother. He felt it was important that the Cherokee people had their own writing system to keep them independent of white Americans. Adapting letters from English, Greek, and Hebrew, he came up with an alphabet of 86 symbols. He taught it to young people and it was soon in use in schools, books, and newspapers.

Elizabeth Fry (1780–1845)

Elizabeth Fry was an English prison reformer. She believed that prisoners should be helped to become better citizens. At that time prisons were often violent places and full of disease, but Fry insisted on visiting them. She ensured that women prisoners were always looked after by women staff. She also made prisons start educating or training some of their prisoners, so they could get jobs when they were released.

Louis Braille

French inventor of a reading system for blind people
Born 1809   Died 1852 aged 43

Braille is a system of raised dots on paper that can be read by touch. It was invented by Louis Braille when he was only 15.

Born near Paris, Braille was blinded by an infection after an accident when he was three.

He went to a special school where he excelled in music, becoming an organist and cellist. He later became a teacher at the school.

Louis Braille spent most of his life improving and refining his reading system. It uses six dots in 63 combinations to provide letters, punctuation marks, numbers, and musical notation. Blind people can 'read' the dots by running their fingers lightly across the page.

Florence Nightingale

English founder of modern nursing
Born 1820   Died 1910 aged 90

Florence Nightingale was born into a wealthy family, and received a good education. However, when she grew up she decided she wanted to be a nurse. This caused bitter arguments with her family, who thought that nursing was not a job for respectable women. It was not until 1851 that Nightingale got her own way and started work in a small London hospital. She was so successful that the secretary of state for war asked her to go to the Crimean War to take charge of the nursing of wounded British soldiers.

She set sail in 1854 with 38 nurses. Within a month they had 1000 men to look after. Nightingale worked 20 hours a day to improve the nursing of ordinary soldiers. Every night she visited the wards, and the soldiers loved her as 'the lady with the lamp'. Her story was published in newspapers back home and she

⬆ Florence Nightingale, the 'lady with the lamp', pictured doing her nightly rounds during the Crimean War.

became a national heroine. The public donated £45,000 for her to spend as she saw fit. In 1860 she spent it on the development of the Nightingale training school for nurses at St Thomas's Hospital, London. In 1907 she became the first woman ever to be awarded the Order of Merit.

» See also Mary Seacole p. 229

Thomas Barnardo

British founder of Dr Barnardo's children's homes
Born 1845   Died 1905 aged 60

Thomas Barnardo was a small, sickly child with poor eyesight, but despite this he was always clever and high-spirited. At 21 he moved to London to study medicine, but he abandoned his studies to preach and teach among the poor families of the East End. Appalled by the plight of the homeless children he saw in that area, Barnardo began to raise money to provide homes for them.

Barnardo had lots of energy, remarkable powers of organization, and a flair for fund-raising. In his lifetime nearly 60,000 needy and disabled children were sheltered and schooled in the homes that Dr Barnardo had established. He strongly believed that no child should be denied help, whatever their circumstances. His influence led to the state taking greater responsibility for protecting children against neglect and abuse.

> *If I were called away tomorrow and if the whole work … were to collapse … I believe enough good has been done and such an abundant harvest has already been reaped, as would well repay … all expenditure of money, time and effort which have been devoted to it.*
> THOMAS BARNARDO

Booker T. Washington

Founder of Tuskegee Institute, a famous college for black Americans
Born 1856   Died 1915 aged 59

Booker Taliaferro Washington was nine years old when slavery was abolished. When he was 16 he travelled 800 kilometres to a school for black teachers. Later, he started a college for black students in Alabama. The students themselves built most of it and Washington persuaded some rich white Americans to give donations.

In a speech in 1895, he said that blacks and whites could be separate like fingers, but that they could work together like a hand. At that time Washington thought black people needed education and jobs more than civil rights.

Sigmund Freud

Austrian psychologist
Born 1856   Died 1939 aged 83

Sigmund Freud worked with patients who were very depressed or who often had behavioural problems. At the time the treatment for mental illness was lots of rest in the hope that things would improve. Freud decided instead to talk to such people at great length. He believed strange behaviour was often linked to past worries, which often reappeared in dreams and nightmares. Although patients could not at first remember what had made them so unhappy, Freud found that over time these memories returned. After talking to Freud openly, many patients felt much better.

Emmeline and Christabel Pankhurst

Leaders of the suffragette campaign to win votes for women in Britain
Emmeline Pankhurst Born 1858
Died 1928 aged 69
Christabel Pankhurst Born 1880
Died 1958 aged 77

Emmeline Goulden married a lawyer, Richard Pankhurst, who believed that women should have the same rights as men. In 1903,

> We are here to claim our rights as women, not only to be free, but to fight for our freedom. That is our right as well as our duty.
> CHRISTABEL PANKHURST

after her husband had died, she and her forceful eldest daughter Christabel founded the Women's Social and Political Union, the 'suffragettes'. They and their supporters interrupted political meetings, smashed shop windows, and did all they could to win women the right to vote. When they were arrested they went on hunger strike. Christabel escaped to Paris in 1912 to continue the campaign. They became quite ruthless, and even broke with Emmeline's younger daughter, Sylvia, because she worked independently from them with poor women in London's East End.

Eventually, in 1918, women over the age of 30 in Britain were given the vote and in 1928, all women in Britain were given the same voting rights as men.

Emmeline and Christabel Pankhurst posing in prison uniform to rouse sympathy for the suffragette campaign.

Carl Jung

Swiss psychologist
Born 1875   Died 1961 aged 85

Carl Jung was originally a follower of Freud, but Jung believed that we are all born with certain problems relating to what sort of people we are. Some people, for example, will always feel better in company; Jung called these 'extroverts'. Others are happier on their own; Jung called these people 'introverts'.

Jung discovered that his patients' dreams could sometimes give them a good idea about where they were going wrong in their lives. For example, if someone always dreamt about wild animals, Jung might suggest this was because they were refusing to face up to angry feelings. He would suggest that they turn this energy into something creative. This interest led Jung to study art and myths from all over the world. The strong similarities he found within them proved to him that all human beings are much the same.

⊙ Jung eventually broke from Freud's ideas.

Mary Seacole (1805–1881)

Mary Seacole's mother was black and her father was a Scottish officer with the British army in Jamaica. In 1854 Seacole went to England to join the nurses whom Florence Nightingale had taken to the Crimea. She was turned down because she was black, so she went out to the Crimea at her own expense and opened a store and eating-place near the front lines. Seacole showed great bravery, going among the men with medicine and supplies of food.

Robert Baden-Powell (1857–1941)

Baden-Powell served with the British army during the Boer War. He trained some black African soldiers to scout out enemy country. He taught them to notice details in the land, organizing them into small groups so that they could act more quickly. When he returned to Britain he was surprised to learn that his *Aids to Scouting* was being taught in schools. He rewrote it as a book for boys and in 1908 founded the Boy Scout Movement.

Albert Schweitzer (1875–1965)

Schweitzer was a man of strong convictions and was passionate in his belief that all life was precious. Because of this he went to Lambarene in West Africa to work as a mission doctor. He stayed there for the rest of his life. In 1963 the hospital at Lambarene treated 500 patients, although its methods were getting out of date. Schweitzer received the Nobel Peace Prize in 1952 for 'efforts on behalf of the Brotherhood of Nations'.

Mother Teresa (1910–1997)

In 1928 Mother Teresa was sent to India to teach at a convent in Calcutta. In 1948 she left and moved into the slums of Calcutta, where she gathered destitute children and sheltered them. She opened a Home for the Dying in Calcutta, as well as a leper colony. After that, she opened over 60 schools, orphanages, and homes for the dying worldwide. In 1979 she received the Nobel Peace Prize.

Marcus Garvey

Jamaican campaigner for the rights of
black people
Born 1887   Died 1940 aged 52

In 1914 Garvey started the
Universal Negro Improvement
Association (UNIA) in Jamaica.
He said the black peoples' struggle
for fair treatment was like the
African countries' fight against
European rule. In 1917 he started
branches of the UNIA in America.
Garvey's movement soon had
branches all over the world. Then
the UNIA was banned in African
countries and Garvey was accused
of fraud and deported from
America to Jamaica. He died
in povert. However, his ideas
inspired many others to work to
win equality for black people.

Christiaan Barnard

South African surgeon who pioneered
heart transplants
Born 1922   Died 2001 aged 78

Christiaan Barnard became a
surgeon at the Groote Schuur
Hospital in South Africa. During
a time in America he learnt a lot
about heart surgery. He returned
to Groote Schuur to concentrate
on open-heart surgery, designing
an artificial heart-valve. He began
doing heart transplants on dogs.
Then he and his colleagues
performed the world's first
transplant on a human patient,
Louis Washkansky, with the heart
of a car-accident victim. Although
Washkansky died some days later,
Barnard's work proved that, given
the right conditions, heart-
transplant operations could work.

Malcolm X

American civil rights leader
Born 1925   Died 1965 aged 39

As a boy, Malcolm Little saw his
home burned down by the Ku
Klux Klan (a group dedicated to
terrorizing black people). He later
moved to Boston, where he was
imprisoned for seven years for
burglary. Here he became a
follower of Elijah Muhammad,
founder of the Nation of Islam.
Working for the Nation of Islam,
Malcolm toured and lectured,
campaigning for black Americans
to seek self-government, not
equality with whites. He told them
that they had to be prepared to
use violence as a means of self-
defence. It was then that he
changed his name to Malcolm X.

After quarrelling with Elijah
Muhammad, Malcolm X left the
Nation of Islam and formed the
Muslim Mosque, Inc. In 1964 he
formed the Organization of Afro-
American Unity to promote links
between black people in Africa
and America. Hostility continued
between his followers and the
Nation of Islam and he was shot
and killed at a rally in New York
City. His autobiography remains a
bestseller and a film about his life
was released in 1993.

⬆ Malcolm X at a Black Muslim rally in Washington DC in 1961.

Steve Biko

South African civil rights leader
Born 1946   Died 1977 aged 30

Stephen Biko went to the University of Natal in South Africa in 1966 to study medicine. He soon became involved in student politics and in 1968 he helped to found the South African Students' Organization. His main concern was for his own black people who suffered oppression under the apartheid system, which separated blacks from whites and deprived black people of their basic rights.

In 1972 Biko gave up his medical studies to help form the Black People's Convention, which worked to raise black people's awareness of oppression and to give them a sense of pride and hope for the future. His activities brought him into conflict with the government and he was often arrested and prevented from speaking in public.

Then in 1977, after being arrested once again, he was so badly beaten in the police cells that he died before he could be brought to trial. Since his death he has become a symbol of the anti-apartheid movement.

» See also Nelson Mandela p. 53

> « *The basic tenet of black consciousness is that the black man must reject all value systems that seek to make him a foreigner in the country of his birth and reduce his basic human dignity.*
> STEVE BIKO »

Martin Luther King Jr

American civil rights leader
Born 1929   Died 1968 aged 39

At the age of 15 Martin Luther King Jr went to college on a special programme for gifted students. After gaining his degree in divinity in 1948, he trained to be a Baptist minister. He became a pastor in Montgomery, Alabama, and joined the struggle for black peoples' rights straight away. He led a boycott of the buses in Montgomery because they had separate seats for blacks and whites. Eventually the bus company allowed all passengers to sit anywhere they chose.

This victory convinced King that the best way for black people to win their rights was to break laws in a non-violent way. In Atlanta and Birmingham, he led 'sit-ins' by blacks in 'whites only' eating places. In August 1963,

⬆ Martin Luther King waves to the crowd during the civil rights march in 1963.

200,000 people joined his march on Washington. At the end of this march, he gave his famous 'I have a dream' speech. Here is an extract:

'I have a dream that one day on the red hills of Georgia the sons of former slaves and the sons of former slave-owners will be able to sit down together at the table of brotherhood. I have a dream that my four little children will one day live in a nation where they will not be judged by the colour of their skin but by the content of their character.'

The next year the Civil Rights Bill was made law and King was given the Nobel Peace Prize. In 1968 he was killed in Memphis, Tennessee. Only the night before his death, King said: 'I may not get to the promised land with you, but I want you to know tonight that we as a people will.'

Heroes
Davy Crockett

North American folk hero
Born 1786   Died 1836 aged 49

Davy Crockett was famous as a bear hunter and for braving the unknown forests in what is now the USA. In 1827 he was elected to Congress, where he defended the land rights of poor farmers in western Tennessee. When he was not re-elected in 1835, he set out for Texas, which was fighting for independence from Mexico. He died in the Battle of the Alamo against the Mexicans.

Buffalo Bill

Scout for the US Cavalry, actor, and Wild West showman
Born 1846   Died 1917 aged 70

Like many other people in the 'Wild West', William Cody (Buffalo Bill's real name) had little schooling and could just about write his name. By the age of 11 he was working to support his family. Later he fought in the American Civil War. After that he made his living supplying buffalo (bison) meat to railway workers. Cody's skill in shooting buffalo gave him his nickname.

During the 1870s, Cody was a scout with the cavalry who were fighting the Native Americans. His hair-raising adventures made him famous, and he appeared on the stage in plays about himself. Cody became best known for his Wild West Show, an exhibition of horsemanship and mock battles which toured all over the world.

> *From what I've seen, the Indian is a free-born American who'll fight for his folks, for his land and for his living ... just like any other American.*
> BUFFALO BILL

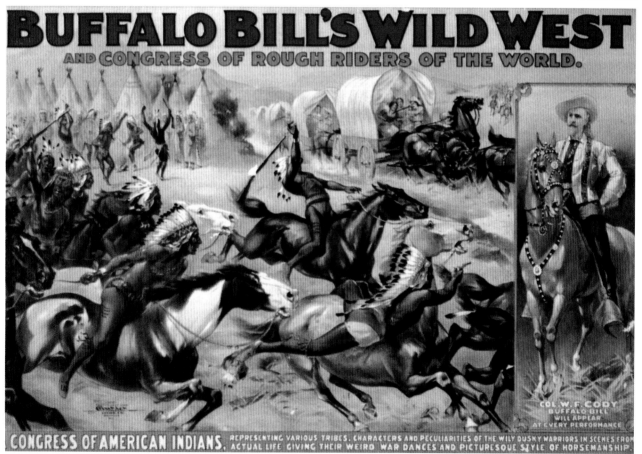

⬆ A poster from 1899 advertising one of Buffalo Bill's popular Wild West shows.

José Rizal

Filipino nationalist
Born 1861   Died 1896 aged 35

José Rizal is known as the father of Filipino independence. The son of a wealthy landowner, Rizal proved himself to be a brilliant medical student in Spain and Germany. While abroad he became leader of a group of students who wanted reforms in the Philippines, which were then a Spanish colony. Rizal wrote two novels, which called for an end to the wealth and power of Spanish friars in his country. He also wanted equal rights for all Filipinos and Spaniards although he did not call for complete independence from Spain. Returning home, he founded a school and hospital, but was falsely accused of plotting revolution and was executed. This convinced Filipinos that Spanish rule must come to an end.

Pancho Villa

Mexican bandit and freedom fighter
Born 1877   Died 1923 aged 46

Imagine a gang of Mexican bandits galloping across a dusty plain – guns slung across their backs, bullets in cross-belts on their chests, sombreros hanging behind by their straps. That was Pancho Villa and his band.

Even Villa's early life is like a film script. It is said that as a young man he killed his boss's son because he assaulted his sister, and had to escape into the mountains.

Revolutions and governments came and went in Mexico at the turn of the century. Villa sometimes sided with the revolutionaries and sometimes fell out with them. Miraculously he stayed alive, even when he killed a number of Americans and President Wilson sent an army after him.

Eventually he made peace with the Mexican government, and settled down as a farmer. A few years later, though, he was killed by one of his old enemies.

➥ Pancho Villa fought for freedom for Mexico.

Daniel Boone (1734–1820)

Daniel Boone hunted with the Native Americans as a child, and grew up as skilled as they were in tracking. On his first attempt to lead settlers to the West, Boone's 16-year-old son was killed by Native Americans. Two years later he completed the journey and founded Fort Boonesborough in Kentucky. For 20 years he led the defence of this settlement against attack. Later he took his family further west to Missouri.

Paul Revere (1735–1818)

American Paul Revere led the so-called 'Boston Tea Party' to protest against British taxation in his country. On 16 April 1775 he received a warning that the British troops were approaching to capture a munitions store and two patriots who were hiding at Lexington. Paul Revere rode through the night to warn the people. At Lexington the British soldiers were made to retreat by a larger force. This was the beginning of the American Revolution.

Edith Cavell (1865–1915)

After working as a governess in Belgium, British Edith Cavell became matron of Belgium's first training college for nurses. When Germany invaded Belgium, Cavell joined a group of people who helped British and French soldiers escape to The Netherlands. Hundreds of soldiers passed through the cellars of her clinic to safety. Cavell was caught and shot by the Germans on 12 October 1915. She met her death calmly and bravely.

T. E. Lawrence (1888–1935)

In 1914 Lawrence went to Cairo as a British intelligence officer to help Arab troops free their country from Turkish rule. Lawrence led dashing camel-back raids to dynamite railway lines. After the Turks were defeated, Lawrence became a hero, but he retired to write *The Seven Pillars of Wisdom*, which describes his experiences. He was disappointed when Britain and France did not give the Arabs complete independence.

Villains

Jesse James

American outlaw
Born 1847   Died 1882 aged 34

At the age of 15, Jesse James joined a group of southern guerrillas and fought against the Unionists in the American Civil War. When the war ended in 1865, Jesse and his brother Frank formed a gang of outlaws. Over the next ten years they carried out many daring robberies and hold-ups. Then, in 1876, one bank robbery went wrong. Most of the gang were killed or captured, but

> *My life was threatened daily, and I was forced to go heavily armed. The whole country was then full of militia, robbing, plundering and killing.*
> JESSE JAMES

Jesse and Frank escaped and formed a new gang. There was now a price on their heads, and in 1882 a gang member shot Jesse and claimed the reward.

Legend has turned Jesse James into a hero, but he was really the leader of a ruthless gang who murdered at least ten people.

Ned Kelly

Australian outlaw
Born 1855   Died 1880 aged 25

From the age of 15 Kelly was constantly in trouble with the law. Between 1878 and 1880 he operated in the Kelly Gang with his brother and two others. They were famous for holding up and killing three policemen in 1878. Many were outraged by their crimes, but to others Ned Kelly became a hero. He claimed to be fighting for justice for the poor against the rich and powerful.

The final shoot-out came after an attempted train ambush. Kelly tried to escape in a suit of armour, but was shot in the legs. He was tried for murder and hanged.

Billy the Kid

American outlaw in the Wild West
Born 1859   Died 1881 aged 21

By the age of 12, William Bonney had knifed a man for insulting his mother. In 1877 he became involved in a war between two cattle-ranching families. As the leader of one of the gangs, he was involved in several gun battles. He returned to cattle thieving and murdering after the war. A sheriff called Pat Garrett was determined to catch Bonney, now known as Billy the Kid. He was captured in 1881 and sentenced to hang, but he managed to escape. Two months later, Garrett cornered him and shot him dead.

Although films show him as a popular hero, Bonney was a vicious murderer and a thief.

⬆ Brad Pitt in the 2007 film *The Assassination of Jesse James by the Coward Robert Ford.*

Rasputin

Favourite of the Russian royal family
Born 1871   Died 1916 aged around 45

Rasputin was the son of Russian peasants. He presented himself as a holy man who could heal people. In 1905 in St Petersburg – the capital of Russia at the time – he met the Russian empress (tsarina), Alexandra, and the emperor (tsar), Nicholas II. Their son, Alexei, suffered from haemophilia. This meant that if he cut himself, the bleeding would not stop. Because Rasputin was able to make Alexei feel calm, he became popular with Alexandra.

In 1914 Russia went to war with Germany. The following year, the tsar left the court and took command of the Russian army. While he was away, Alexandra, under Rasputin's influence, dismissed government ministers, and replaced many of them with incompetent men. Rasputin seemed to have a strange power over the tsarina, and he and Alexandra were largely responsible for the tsar's failure to respond to the ever rising tide of discontent amongst the Russian people, which eventually led to the Russian Revolution (1917).

A group of noblemen tried to kill Rasputin, to remove his evil influence. They poisoned him, shot him, and when none of this worked, they threw him in the River Neva, where he drowned.

》 See also Nicholas II p. 25

The famous Russian priest Rasputin.

Tomás de Torquemada

(1420–1498)

When Isabella became Queen of Castile, she feared the different religious groups because she was a Catholic, and so she established an Inquisition – a system of law courts that would examine people suspected of not being true Christians. In 1483 Isabella placed Torquemada in charge of the Inquisition. Its trials were often conducted in secret, under torture. Before Torquemada's death the Inquisition executed over 2000 people.

Guy Fawkes (1570–1606)

In 1604, a small group of Catholics plotted to kill King James I. They invited Guy Fawkes to join them because he was good with explosives. They hired a cellar under the House of Lords and filled it with gunpowder, planning to blow it up on 5 November 1605. Guy Fawkes agreed to light the fuse, but the plot was discovered, and on 4 November he was arrested. He confessed, and was tried and executed.

Al Capone (c.1899–1947)

In 1920 the sale of alcoholic drinks was banned in America. This ban lasted for 13 years and many criminals, including Capone, made fortunes selling alcoholic drinks illegally. Capone operated in Chicago, becoming rich and influential through crime. He was very brutal, and was involved in the St Valentine's Day massacre. He was not arrested because he bribed many policemen and other officials. Eventually, in 1932, Capone went to prison for not paying taxes.

Bonnie and Clyde

Bonnie Parker (1910–1934) and Clyde Barrow (1909–1934) were two of the most notorious outlaws of the 1930s. They and their gang went on a crime spree that lasted nearly two years, in which they robbed banks and petrol stations. They were finally caught in a police ambush in 1934. As they tried to run away they were both shot and killed.

Ball Sports Stars

W. G. Grace

English cricket hero
Born 1848 Died 1915 aged 67

William Gilbert Grace was born near Bristol, and was taught to play cricket, along with his two brothers, by his mother. Mrs Grace must have been a very good coach, because all three Grace brothers ended up playing first-class cricket for Gloucestershire.

'W. G.', as he was known, made his debut at the age of 16. Although he later qualified as a doctor, he carried on playing cricket until the age of 60. He completely changed the way cricket was played and was so popular with spectators that notices were sometimes displayed outside grounds, saying: 'Admission sixpence; if Dr Grace plays, one shilling.' During his career, which lasted nearly 45 years, Grace scored 54,896 runs (including 126 centuries), took 2876 wickets, and held 877 catches.

➲ This illustration of cricketer W. G. Grace, England's best all-rounder in his day, is from a 1896 calendar.

Babe Ruth

American baseball player
Born 1895 Died 1948 aged 53

George Herman Ruth went to a school for poor children in Baltimore, which is where he began his baseball career as a pitcher with the Baltimore Orioles. Then, known to all the fans as 'Babe Ruth', he became a member of the Boston Red Sox and hit 29 home runs in 1919.

The next year, playing for the New York Yankees, he hit 54 home runs and became so popular that by 1925 he was earning more money than the president of the United States.

In 1927 he raised his record to 60 home runs in a season, and by the time he retired in 1935 he had scored a career total of 714.

Babe Ruth changed the game of baseball, making it outstandingly popular, as huge crowds gathered to watch him play. He is considered by many to be the greatest baseball player of all time.

⏩ See also Joe DiMaggio p. 236

Donald Bradman

Australian cricketer
Born 1908 Died 2001 aged 92

In his career Don Bradman scored 28,067 runs at an average of 95 runs per innings. His highest-ever score was 452 not out, for New South Wales against Queensland, when he was 21. In his last Test innings as captain of Australia, he was bowled out for 0. Had it not been for that, he would have retired in 1948 with a Test average of over 100 runs per innings.

Joe DiMaggio (1914–1999)

Joe DiMaggio played baseball for the New York Yankees from 1936 to 1951. He was a superb batter and was twice the top scorer for his team. In 1941, he set a new baseball record by making successful hits at least once in each of 56 consecutive games. He was also an excellent outfielder. Even after he retired he remained in the public eye by marrying film star Marilyn Monroe in 1954. The marriage lasted only nine months.

Ferenc Puskás (1926–2006)

Ferenc Puskás was one of the best football players to come out of Hungary in the 1950s. He played for Hungarian team Honvéd and was part of the national team that became known as the Mighty Magyars. He joined Real Madrid in 1956, and his powerful left foot led the Spanish team to several victories. Puskás retired in 1966 and became a manager. In 2003 he was named Best Hungarian Player of the Last 50 Years.

Wilt Chamberlain (1936–1999)

Wilt Chamberlain was nicknamed Wilt the Stilt because he was so tall – a towering 2.2 metres. He had a natural athletic ability that helped him become one of the greatest basketball players in history. He joined the National Basketball Association (NBA) in 1960 and played there for 13 years. In that time he was awarded the Most Valuable Player award four times and won two NBA titles, in 1967 and 1972.

Stanley Matthews

English football player
Born 1915   Died 2000 aged 85

As a boy, Stanley Matthews kicked a small rubber ball around everywhere he went. Practising like this earned him the name 'the Wizard of the Dribble' because of his skilful ball control.

Matthews played his first football league match in 1931 and his first for England in 1934. He won an FA Cup winners' medal while playing for Blackpool Football Club in 1953. He helped to set up three goals in this amazing match after Blackpool were losing 3–1 to Bolton with only minutes to go. This extraordinary game is now known as the 'Matthews final'. Matthews was still playing first division football when he retired at the age of 50.

In 1956 Stanley Matthews became the first European Footballer of the Year.

Jack Nicklaus

American champion golfer
Born 1940

Although he only started to play the game at the age of ten, Jack Nicklaus showed his golfing potential by playing a round of only 69 shots over a 6.49-kilometre course when he was 13. While still at Ohio State University, he became US amateur champion. Then, when he turned professional in 1961, he began an outstanding run of tournament successes by winning the US Open championship in 1962.

Since then the 'Golden Bear', as he is known to his fans, has won more major tournaments than anyone else in the history of the game. His successes include four US Opens and five US Masters championships.

⬆ Jack Nicklaus – the Golden Bear.

Garry Sobers

West Indian cricketer
Born 1936

As a boy in Barbados, Garfield Sobers was good at all sports, but eventually he decided to devote himself to cricket. He made his Test debut when he was 17. He was an excellent batsman, scoring a Test match record at the time of 365 not out for the West Indies against Pakistan in 1958. He held this record until 1994 when Brian Lara scored 375 runs for the West Indies against England. This was not his only record. He was the first player to hit six sixes in an over – an achievement he reached in county cricket 1968.

Sobers could also bowl left-handed in two different styles: fast-medium and slow spin, which made him a fearful opponent on the cricket pitch.

When he retired in 1974, his Test match record was 8032 runs, 235 wickets, and 109 catches, making him one of the best all-round cricketers in the world.

Rod Laver (b.1938)

A left-handed player, Rod Laver won the Australian Amateur championship in 1960. Two years later he did the 'Grand Slam', winning the Australian, French, US, and Wimbledon championships in the same year. He turned professional, and was barred from the championships until they became 'open championships' (for both amateur and professional players) in the late 1960s. In 1969 Laver won the Grand Slam once again.

Margaret Court (b.1942)

Margaret Court won 64 Grand Slam tennis titles between 1960 and 1973, more than any other woman. Court was the first Australian woman to win Wimbledon (1963), and the second to take all four Grand Slam championships (1970). She captured the Australian title a record 11 times and has won a record 13 titles at the French championships. She was also three-times winner of the Italian, German, and South African championships.

Billie Jean King (b.1943)

American tennis player Billie Jean King won 20 Wimbledon titles in her career – six of them the singles title – as well as five US Open doubles and four US open singles. She was a strong campaigner for equal rights in sports, and made a name for herself in 1973 due to the 'Battle of the Sexes', a tennis match she played against men's Wimbledon champion Bobby Riggs. Billie Jean won the match.

Björn Borg (b.1956)

Swedish tennis player Björn Borg became famous in the 1970s and 1980s for his rivalry with American John McEnroe, and the games they played were some of the most exciting ever seen. Borg won five consecutive Wimbledon titles and six French Open titles. He retired after losing to McEnroe in the 1981 Wimbledon final, but staged a comeback in 1991. He retired properly in 1993.

Pelé

Brazilian football player
Born 1940

Edson Arantes do Nascimento was given the nickname 'Pelé' by the friends he played football with as a boy. He showed so much promise for his first club, Noroeste, that he was signed by the top club Santos and was picked to play for Brazil when he was only 16. A year later, in 1958, he scored two goals to help Brazil win the World Cup final.

In a career that lasted until 1977, Pelé showed that he was the complete footballer, combining speed and ball-control with fierce and accurate shooting. Before leaving Santos to play for the New York Cosmos in 1971, he had scored 1216 goals in 1254 games. He played 110 games for Brazil, winning World Cup winners' medals in 1958 and 1970.

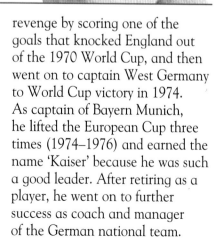

Pelé, who wore the number 10 team shirt, is thought by many to be the greatest football player of all time.

Franz Beckenbauer

German footballer and manager
Born 1945

Franz Beckenbauer played his first game for Bayern Munich at the age of 18, and after just 25 games he was picked for West Germany. In 1966 he was in the team that lost the World Cup Final to England. Beckenbauer gained his revenge by scoring one of the goals that knocked England out of the 1970 World Cup, and then went on to captain West Germany to World Cup victory in 1974. As captain of Bayern Munich, he lifted the European Cup three times (1974–1976) and earned the name 'Kaiser' because he was such a good leader. After retiring as a player, he went on to further success as coach and manager of the German national team.

Johann Cruyff

Dutch football player and manager
Born 1947

Johann Cruyff was arguably the best Dutch player of the 1970s. He was one of the team that perfected the style that became known as Total Football because every player could move in and out of different positions, giving the team a great advantage over its opponents.

Cruyff grew up in Amsterdam and dreamed of playing for the city's team, Ajax. He had achieved this aim by the time he was 16 and he later helped the club to win many trophies. He was named Footballer of the Year three times in the 1970s and was generally regarded as one of the greats in a golden era of football.

After he retired as a player, Cruyff became a manager of his beloved Ajax and later for Barcelona, where he had also played during his career.

Imran Khan

Pakistani cricket captain
Born 1952

Imran Khan perfected his cricket at school in Lahore, Pakistan, and in Worcester, England, before going to Oxford University where he captained the cricket team in 1974. He then took up county cricket, playing for Worcestershire and for Sussex.

He made his test debut for Pakistan in 1971 and became captain in 1982. He has played for his country 75 times and is only the third player to score over 3000 test runs and take 300 test wickets. In 1983 he became the second player to score a century and take ten wickets in a Test match. In first-class cricket he has scored over 16,000 runs and taken over 1200 wickets.

Javed Miandad and Imran Khan were the only players to appear in all of the first five World Cup tournaments. Khan has also taken a record 34 wickets in World Cup matches.

➋ Imran Khan captained Pakistan to victory in the World Cup in 1992.

➋ Martina Navratilova is still considered the first lady of tennis, having set new standards for female players throughout the 1980s.

Martina Navratilova

Czech-born American tennis champion
Born 1956

Martina Navratilova was born in Czechoslovakia, but moved to America in 1975 when she started to become a successful tennis player. In 1981 she became a US citizen and the following year she was the first woman professional tennis player to earn more than one million dollars in a season.

Her favourite championship has always been Wimbledon, where she has won nine singles finals (1978–1979, 1982–1987, and 1990), beating the record set by fellow American, Helen Wills Moody. She was the most outstanding woman tennis player of the 1980s.

Diego Maradona

Argentinean footballer
Born 1960

Diego Maradona was voted South American Footballer of the Year in 1979 and 1980. After leading Argentina's youth team to World Cup success in 1979, he joined the full national squad in their unsuccessful attempt to keep the World Cup in 1982.

Michael Jordan

American basketball player
Born 1963

Michael Jordan was a leading college basketball player at the University of North Carolina. He began an outstanding career with the Chicago Bulls, becoming the NBA's Most Valuable Player in 1988. By 1992 he had achieved a record average of 32.3 points in 589 games for the Bulls. Jordan competed in the 1992 Barcelona Olympics with the 'Dream Team', which consisted of top millionaire professional players instead of the usual college amateurs. The team easily won the Olympic gold medal. He finally retired in 2003.

In 1986, as Argentina's captain, he lifted up the World Cup after brilliant performances throughout the tournament. He led Argentina once again in the 1990 World Cup final, although they were beaten 1–0 by West Germany.

Shane Warne

Australian cricketer
Born 1969

Australian Shane Warne began his cricket career in 1991, playing for Victoria. He was noticed by the national selection committee and joined the Australian second team for a tour in Zimbabwe. He soon joined the first team and although his early performances were not great, he quickly found his stride and his leg-spin technique made him one of the most valued players on the Australian team.

He was later made captain, and helped Australia secure the Ashes in the 2006–07 series. He retired from international cricket in January 2007.

> Be patient... Don't worry if blokes are whacking you out of the park because you still have the opportunity to get him out next ball.
> SHANE WARNE

Michael Jordan retired from basketball in 1998, but came back and joined the Washington Wizards for the 2002 and 2003 seasons.

Magic Johnson (b.1959)

Earvin Johnson earned the nickname 'Magic' when he was 15, after scoring 36 points in a single basketball game. He went on to join to Los Angeles Lakers, where he led one of the greatest teams of all time. He also helped the US team to an Olympic gold medal in 1992, although he had retired the previous year. After this he made a surprise return to the NBA in 1996 and made the Basketball Hall of Fame in 2002.

Zinedine Zidane (b.1972)

French footballer Zinedine Zidane started his professional career playing for Cannes and Bordeux, before a move to Italy and Marcello Lippi's Juventus team. In 2001 he transferred to Real Madrid. Zizou, as he is nicknamed, first played for his national team in 1994, and he is best-remembered for leading France to victory in the 1998 World Cup, when he was captain. Zidane retired in 2006 and is active in charity work.

Ronaldo (b.1976)

Brazilian footballer Ronaldo has enjoyed huge success. He has won World Player of the Year three times – a record that only Zinedine Zidane has matched. His career has seen him move from teams in Brazil to Holland and Spain. In 2007 he transferred to Milan. It was on the international stage, however, that Ronaldo proved his worth, helping Brazil to a 2002 World Cup win as the highest goalscorer of the competition.

Steffi Graf

German tennis player
Born 1969

Steffi Graf became a professional tennis player at 13, and within three years had become one of the top ten tennis players in the world. From August 1987 to March 1991 she reigned as the top female player, winning a record number of international tennis tournaments.

In 1988 Graf completed an unequalled 'Golden Grand Slam', winning the four most important individual tournaments (the US Open, French Open, Wimbledon, and the Australian Open), plus the Olympic gold medal. She helped Germany win the Federation Cup, one of the three major team tournaments. She has earned her place in history as one of the world's greatest sportswomen.

Pete Sampras

American tennis champion
Born 1971

As a child, Pete Sampras found an old tennis racquet and started hitting a ball against the garage door. He was encouraged by his parents and turned professional when he was 16. Two years later he was one of the world's top ten players. That year he won the US Open, the first of his Grand Slam titles. He was the youngest ever winner in the men's singles.

In 1993 Pete became No. 1 in the world and won Wimbledon for the first time. He went on to win the men's singles title there a record seven times. His total of 14 Grand Slam titles is also a record.

Eldrick 'Tiger' Woods

American golfing star
Born 1975

Tiger Woods has been swinging a golf club almost since he could walk. By the age of three he was playing on a nine-hole course, with a cut-down golf club.

As an amateur golfer, Tiger won six US Amateur titles. However, in 1996 he turned professional. He won six of the

Roger Federer

Swiss tennis champion
Born 1981

Roger Federer is the best tennis player of his generation. He started playing when he was just six, and went on to win the World Junior Tennis Championship in 1998. After that he climbed quickly up the world rankings.

⬆ Tiger Woods was the youngest person ever to win a Grand Slam.

25 events he entered in his first season.

The next year, aged only 21, Tiger won the US Masters, one of the four top golfing events.

In 2000 Tiger won three of the four Grand Slam events and became golf's highest money earner. In 2001, he won the US Masters and became the first golfer in history to hold all four golfing Grand Slams at once.

He really came to international attention in 2001, when he beat champion Pete Sampras in the Wimbledon quarter-finals. Federer has since broken record after record. He was the first player to win three Grand Slam singles titles in a year three times. He won Wimbledon in 2007 for a fifth time, which meant that he had equalled Björn Borg's record.

Combat Sports Stars

Joe Louis

American world-champion boxer
Born 1914   Died 1981 aged 67

Joseph Louis Barrow became a professional boxer in 1934 and world heavyweight champion in 1937. He was the first black man to be allowed to fight in the world championship for 22 years.

Nicknamed the 'Brown Bomber', Joe Louis successfully defended his title a record 25 times over a period of nearly 12 years. Out of 66 professional fights, he won 63; 49 were by knockouts.

Rocky Marciano

American world-champion boxer
Born 1923   Died 1969 aged 45

Rocky Marciano was born in Massachusetts, USA. His uncle taught him to box when he was young, and he boxed for the army during World War II. In 1946 he won the armed forces amateur tournament. He turned professional the following year and the victories started rolling in.

Marciano was ranked as a heavyweight, although he was much lighter than many of his opponents. However, his tough, determined style resulted in 49 wins out of 49 matches – 43 of them by knockout.

He won the world havyweight championship in September 1952, knocking out the reigning champion Jersey Joe Walcott in the thirteenth round.

Marciano successfully defended his title against Walcott the following year – dropping his opponent in the very first round. He continued his successful defence for another three years, before retiring, unbeaten, in 1956. Marciano died in a plane crash in 1969.

> « Why waltz with a guy for ten rounds if you can knock him out in one? »
> ROCKY MARCIANO

↑ Rocky Marciano knocks out Jersey Joe Walcott in 1952 to take the world heavyweight title.

Muhammad Ali

American world-champion boxer
Born 1942

After winning the amateur 'Golden Gloves' championship in 1959 and 1960, Cassius Clay from Louisville, Kentucky, became Olympic heavyweight champion in 1960.

He became known for his claim to be 'the greatest', and although many people thought this was arrogant, Ali soon proved it to be true. He turned professional after the Olympic success, and within four years he was champion of the world.

Clay converted to the Islamic faith in 1964, and changed his name to Muhammad Ali. Because of his beliefs, he refused to be called up into the American army to fight in the Vietnam War. His refusal to serve his country resulted in the world title being taken away from him, and he was banned from boxing from 1967 to 1970.

He returned to the ring in the 1970s and, although he lost his title twice, he won in 1974 – in the

⬆ Muhammad Ali won a total of 56 boxing contents; 37 of these ended in knockouts.

famous Rumble in the Jungle match against George Foreman – and in 1978 against Leon Spinks, thus becoming the first heavyweight boxer to win the world championship three times.

❝ I'm so fast that last night I turned off the light switch in my hotel room and was in bed before the room was dark. ❞
MUHAMMAD ALI

Athletes and Gymnasts

Jesse Owens

American champion athlete
Born 1913   Died 1980 aged 67

Jesse Owens from Alabama was 22 when he took part in an athletics meeting in Michigan. Within 45 minutes he had equalled the world record for the 100 yards, and broken the records for the 220 yards, the 220 yards hurdles, and the long jump. His long-jump world record lasted for 25 years.

The next year, 1936, was Olympic year. Adolf Hitler wanted the Berlin Games to show the world that what he called 'the Aryan race' of white Europeans was superior to any other. After Jesse Owens had demolished that myth by winning four gold medals, Hitler refused even to shake hands with the black American athlete.

Roger Bannister

English athlete who became the first person to run the four-minute mile
Born 1929

Roger Bannister started running while he was at university in Oxford. He was chosen for the 1948 Olympics but he felt he was not ready. Four years later he ran the 1500 metres at the Helsinki Olympics, but was disappointed to come fourth. Determined to do better, Bannister trained harder, and he made history on 6 May 1954 during a track meeting at Oxford, when he ran a mile in 3 minutes 57.9 seconds. The record was broken just 46 days later.

Carl Lewis

American athlete
Born 1961

Carl Lewis comes from a sporting family. His father is a sports teacher, his mother and sister are international athletes, and his brother is a soccer player. Lewis's own career is one of the most successful ever in athletics history. Not only has he had the longest run of long-jump victories ever, but he has also been the world's best sprinter.

In 1983 he had three wins at the world championships. Then, at the 1984 Olympics, he equalled Jesse Owens's record of four gold medals, triumphing in the 100 metres, 200 metres, long jump, and 4 x 100 metres relay. He retained his gold medals for 100 metres and long jump at the 1988 Olympics.

Olympic gold medal winner Carl Lewis was unbeaten in the long jump for 65 competitions in a row.

Scientists have proven that it's impossible to long-jump 30 feet, but I don't listen to that kind of talk. Thoughts like that have a way of sinking into your feet.
CARL LEWIS

Nadia Comaneci

Romanian champion gymnast
Born 1961

Nadia Comaneci burst on to the gymnastics scene at the European championships of 1975 when, at the age of 13, she won four of the five gold medals. The following year she became the first gymnast ever to be awarded the perfect score (10·0) for her performance on the asymmetric bars. By the end of the competition, she had won gold medals for the asymmetric bars and the balance beam, and was the overall Olympic champion, all at the age of 14. In 1989 she left Romania and settled in America.

Michael Johnson

American athlete
Born 1967

Michael Johnson became well-known for his upright running style on tracks around the world. Although unusual, this technique worked well for him, and for several years he shattered one record after another.

Johnson won five Olympic gold medals – two for the 400 metres, two for the 4 x 400 metre relay and one for the 200 metres. The world records for all these athletics events remain unbroken. He also won nine world championship golds. He retired from athletics in 2001, going out on a blaze of glory after seizing two of his gold medals at the 2000 Olympics in Sydney.

⬆ Michael Johnson at the Sydney Olympic Games in 2000.

Fanny Blankers-Koen (1918–2004)

Fanny Blankers-Koen was a Dutch champion athlete. She first made her mark at the 1936 Olympics, but then had to wait 12 years, as the Olympics were not held during World War II, before she could prove herself again. She held six world records at the time, and she managed to defend four of them at the London Olympics. She was the first woman to win four Olympic golds.

Irena Szewinska (b.1946)

Szewinska won silver medals in the long jump and 200 metres, and gold in the 4 x 100 metres relay at the 1964 Olympics. The following year she broke the world record for the 200 metres. She carried on breaking this record regularly into the 1970s, before winning a third Olympic gold medal in the 400 metres at Montreal in 1976. By the time she retired she had ten European championship medals, seven Olympic medals, and four World Cup medals.

Daley Thompson (b.1958)

After showing promise as a junior decathlete, Thompson became Commonwealth champion in 1978. He later won two Olympic gold medals (1980 and 1984), two European championships (1982 and 1986), and one world championship (1983). During this time he set four world record scores. He was the first athlete to hold the World, Olympic, European, and Commonwealth titles all at the same time.

Sergey Bubka (b.1963)

When he was 19 Sergey Bubka became pole-vaulting world champion at the 1983 Helsinki championships. He could not attend the 1984 Los Angeles Olympic Games because of the Soviet Union's boycott. But he seized gold at the Seoul Olympics in 1988 with a vault of 5.90 metres. His fans expected him to defend his title easily in 1992 , but he failed to qualify for the final. He has set the world record for the pole-vault over 30 times.

Speed Sports Stars

Juan Fangio

Argentinean world-champion motor racing driver
Born 1911   Died 1995 aged 81

Juan Fangio has been called the greatest racing driver of all time. He has won a record-breaking five world championships. Before Fangio retired in 1958, he had won 24 Grand Prix races for manufacturers such as Mercedes-Benz and Ferrari. His greatest race was the 1957 German Grand Prix, which he won after a pit stop had left him 48.5 seconds behind. He broke the lap record several times to overtake his main rivals.

Alain Prost

French champion motor-racing driver
Born 1955

Although Alain Prost was very talented at football, he chose to be a racing driver instead. In 1980 he drove in his first Formula One Grand Prix. He has since driven for the McLaren, Ferrari, and Williams manufacturing teams.

Prost roared home first in more than 50 Grand Prix races. He also scored the most points in Grand Prix racing – over 700 – and won the world championship four times. The last time was in 1993, the year he retired.

Prost is also well known for the studious way he plans and tackles each race. This is why he has the nickname 'The Professor'.

Michael Schumacher

German champion motor-racing driver
Born 1969

Michael Schumacher became addicted to speed sports when he was four years old, at the wheel of a home-made engine-powered go-kart. By 1984 he was making a name for himself on the German junior karting circuit.

He had his first Formula One race in 1991. Although he did not finish the race, hs talent was spotted by the Benetton team, and he won a year later. After a move to Ferrari he never looked back, and became the greatest Formula One driver in the history of the sport – winning the championship seven times, with 91 wins in total and starting from pole position 68 times. He retired after the Brazilian Grand Prix in 2006.

⬆ Statistically, Michael Schumacher is the greatest racing driver of all time.

Lance Armstrong

American cyclist
Born 1971

Lance Armstrong is one of the greatest cyclists and most-respected sportsmen of recent times. He was born in Texas, USA, and enjoyed sports as a child. He began to take part in triathlons – running, swimming, and cycling – but later focused just on the cycling. In 1991 he won the US National Amateur Championships and then turned professional. Lots of trophies followed and by 1996 he was the world's number-one cyclist.

In October of that year, however, Armstrong was diagnosed with cancer that had spread to different parts of his body, including his lungs and his brain. Although his chances of survival were not good, he was determined to fight – and amazingly he made a complete recovery.

Getting back on a bike was another matter, and he made a shaky start when he pulled out of the 1998 Paris–Nice race. Slowly, though, he regained his confidence and his ability, and in 1999 he proved his great strength of will by winning the Tour de France. He didn't stop there, either – he won the next six consecutive Tours de France, until finally retiring in 2005.

🅝 Lance Armstrong has received sporting honours from all over the world in testimony to his talent and willpower.

> *I figure the faster I pedal, the faster I can retire.*
> LANCE ARMSTRONG

Bill Shoemaker (1931–2003)

Bill Shoemaker was the world's most successful jockey. When he retired in 1989, he had achieved 8833 wins from 40,350 mounts. He was born weighing just 1.35 kg. His grandmother saved his life by putting him in a shoebox inside an open oven door for his first 24 hours. He began working with horses as a teenager and became a jockey in 1949. He was America's champion ten times and leading money winner ten times.

Eddy Merckx (b.1945)

At the age of 14, Belgian Eddy Merckx discovered cycling and was soon world amateur champion when he was only 18. The following year he became a professional. Between 1966 and 1978 he triumphed five times in the Giro d'Italia (Tour of Italy) as well as winning the Tour de France five times. However, he was always the first to admit that he owed much of his success to the loyal team of riders who supported him.

Ayrton Senna (1960–1994)

Brazilian Ayrton Senna started racing go-karts when he was eight, and later moved to Formula Three racecars, where he won the British Championship in 1983 and 1985. Three years later he won the first of his three Formula One championships – the last in 1991. Acknowledged as one of the greatest racing drivers of the era, Senna was killed during the 1994 Grand Prix at San Marino.

Index

A

B

Isambard Kingdom Brunel

James Cook

Joe DiMaggio

Galileo
Galilei

Karl
Marx

Eva Péron

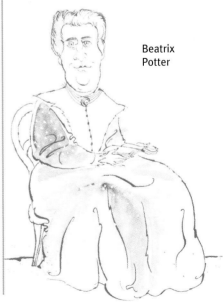

Beatrix Potter

Joseph Stalin

Mark
Twain

Oscar
Wilde